The Journey of Child Development

The Journey of Child Development

Selected Papers of
Joseph D. Noshpitz

Edited by Bruce Sklarew & Myra Sklarew

Routledge
Taylor & Francis Group
New York   London

Routledge
Taylor & Francis Group
270 Madison Avenue
New York, NY 10016

Routledge
Taylor & Francis Group
27 Church Road
Hove, East Sussex BN3 2FA

Printed in the United States of America on acid-free paper
10 9 8 7 6 5 4 3 2 1

International Standard Book Number: 978-0-415-87664-3 (Hardback)

Library of Congress Cataloging-in-Publication Data

Noshpitz, Joseph D., 1922-
    The journey of child development : selected papers of Joseph D. Noshpitz /
edited by Bruce Sklarew, Myra Sklarew.
        p. cm.
    Includes bibliographical references and index.
    ISBN 978-0-415-87664-3 (hardcover) -- ISBN 978-0-203-85685-7 (e book)
    1. Child development. 2. Noshpitz, Joseph D., 1922- I. Sklarew, Bruce. II.
Sklarew, Myra. III. Title.

HQ771.N67 2010
305.231--dc22   2010014940

Visit the Taylor & Francis Web site at
http://www.taylorandfrancis.com

and the Routledge Web site at
http://www.routledgementalhealth.com

Contents

Editors' preface

Bruce Sklarew and Myra Sklarew

When Joe Noshpitz celebrated his 70th birthday, we attempted to characterize his life: his beloved fossils, his passion for science fiction, the human history he fashioned one Passover, his love of Shakespeare, his learned rabbinical sermons, his study of tomboys and Teenage Mutant Ninja Turtles, his examination of the trajectory of the lives of self-destructive youngsters. His writing style combined the "necessary mixture of scientific rigor and literary felicity." His was a lifetime spent in the treatment and study of the child, serving as consummate teacher, editor, scholar, and consultant. He viewed development as the basic science of child mental health, and developmental considerations guided him to an understanding of child and adolescent behavior. He ventured that "*all* stories are examples of personality development, for all stories are ultimately accounts of a moment in someone's life when something happened that mattered. Something changed, and therefore the person (persons) grew differently.... Development is a complex phenomenon that involves melding the genetic foundation with the environment to produce mature growth.... We are enormously plastic, endlessly adaptive creatures and have molded ourselves to fit and survive under the most unlikely conditions. How we do this, with what strengths, and with what limitations, we are only now beginning to understand."

On that occasion he spoke of how "the wind and grit of the years is like a great erosive force that wears away the dross of pique and anger, of hurt feelings and proud sensitivity, to leave me with a mellowed sense of my fellow man. I have reached many times for the stars and found them endlessly elusive, and of necessity I have begun to learn to enjoy the view without having to take it home. I cannot say that I am quite that relaxed by the picture painted by my larger culture, especially in regard to the way it rears its children." Here Joseph sees hope, in the sense that we have many of the tools to know *how* to rear a child. For to be better than we are, we must raise children who are better, "who have firmer consciences, better and firmer defenses and values." He said then that schools must participate, government programs "will pick up the melody.... Families will do better."

Of the abiding unity of his marriage to Charlotte Sorkine Noshpitz, he spoke in this way: "In a room full of quite exceptional people, Charlotte is one of the few who is a genuine hero. She saved hundreds of lives as a [teen-aged] underground fighter in France during World War II [for which she was awarded the *Croix de Guerre*], and the measure of her merit is in a category far away from that which most of us will ever know. Our relationship is like two stars caught up in a binary system in eternal dynamic flux follow-ing complex courses one about the other, now occluding and eclipsing each other, now joining in a formidable display of mutually enhancing bright-ness, caught up in an eternal dance of endlessly changing but ever-linking interplay." Of their beloved son Claude, Joe spoke of him as "the cup into which so many of our hopes and dreams for the future are poured."

He told of being comforted by having taught such men as Robert King and Carl Feinstein and such women as Susan Loughman, each a teacher and healer; and of his work with colleagues like Irving Berlin, Justin Call, Richard Cohen, Saul Harrison, Lawrence Stone, Stanley Greenspan, Paul Adams, Paulina Kernberg, Jules Bemporad, Efrain Bleiberg, Joseph Coyle, and Norman Alessi; and of long friendships with Bernie and Johanna Salwen, Jack and Helen Davis.

Joe's range of exploration was wide. Whether it was Pyramus and Thisbie talking through a chink in the wall in *A Midsummer's Night's Dream*, or characters out of Babylonian history, the Talmud or writings of Nabokov or Avicenna the medieval physician, none escaped his curious attention. When he officiated at our son Eric's bar mitzvah and discussed the power of friendship as exemplified by the biblical Jonathan and David, he provided a lasting life lesson. Whether like Dante, with one foot in the Middle Ages and one in the Renaissance and with the curiosity that drove him, or by his informed and kindly support during our darkest and most difficult days, he never shied from the painful but was a presence to be counted upon. According to legend, Adam was created from a bit of dust taken from the four corners of the Earth mingled with a few drops of water from each of the Earth's oceans. Why, asks a biblical commentator, was Adam created a single individual? To teach us, goes the answer, that whoever destroys one human soul is regarded as if he had destroyed the entire world, and that he who sustains one human soul is regarded as if he had saved the entire world. Joe, like the singular Adam, was one who helped to sustain the world through his thought and action.

To reflect on the complexity of this man, we offer a window into his origins and a selection of memories. Joe's father was a rabbi from Mogilev Podolsky, Ukraine, who after immigrating to the United States co-owned a business that made canvas linings for men's suits. In the course of Joe's father's search for the 5-year-old Joe, who had wandered off one day in the Bronx, his father suffered a heart attack. Joe then shared a room with his father, his two older sisters, with their mother. Joe's father became a book dealer at home. His books were later accepted by the Library of Congress and the University of Maryland archives. He died of a subsequent heart attack when Joe was nearly 11 and preparing for his bar mitzvah—it was a singular loss at a crucial time in Joe's life. We could wonder how these events influenced Joe as an extraordinary and caring mentor and editor, who rewrote many manuscripts in his editorship of the encyclopedic five-volume *Basic Handbook of Child Psychiatry* (Volumes 1–4, 1979; Volume 5, 1987) and two-volume *Handbook of Child and Adolescent Psychiatry* Volumes 6–7, 1998) and other publications but left behind 800 unpublished pages of his work when he died suddenly in 1997. He apparently identified with his rabbi/teacher father as editor and teacher. Joe may have linked his exploration into new territory at age 5, as he went alone into the street, to his father's debilitating heart attack, thereby inhibiting his venturing out to publish his most original work. One such project that fairly asks for further discovery is an extensive tomboy study exploring preadolescent gender issues, including interviews with more than 30 women who had been tomboys as youngsters as well as those who had been hyperfeminine. Carl Feinstein, in his Introduction, discusses other factors that contributed to Joe's difficulty with publishing.

Perhaps Joe's own words on the subject may add some insight as well. Over the years, he would send us preliminary copies of work in progress, adding "to the Everest of documents" we were called upon "to peruse," as Joe put it. It was always a great pleasure, always edifying. One August, in addition to the work he sent, he addressed the issue of not publishing through a poem he had written around the time of his 70th birthday, "which in some measure explains the problem I have in taking the initiative to get my work published." From "Seventy at Last," Joe writes:

> To say I cannot build again the images
> That once could rouse my opalescent dreams
> And drive the fabrication of new schemes
> To herd the specters back into their cages
> And free the burdened child of haunting ills
> Become the mage that the torn spirit stills
> To say I cannot do that would be false.
> This is the time for overleaping stalls
> For writing new graffiti on old walls
> For prancing heavily in some version of a waltz
> And putting lips to shofar sending forth
> A clarion call to every concept worth
> A moment's tense reflection as I muse,
> Creating models that come relatively close.
> Too much is happening; I've no time to lose.
> I don't expect to publish what I find

But I can teach it and thus leave behind
A legacy of understanding and of use
That will enable someone to do better
And find the idiom, the true pacesetter
And write the theme, accurate to the letter
Of what the remote editor in my sky
Demands, which I could never satisfy.

Joe attended college and medical school at the University of Louisville in 1945 and entered the military shortly thereafter, serving in Japan during the immediate aftermath of the atomic bombing of Hiroshima and Nagasaki. One of the key factors in his lifelong study of the child may have originated in his medical work and observations of those who had suffered from the effects of nuclear radiation, particularly children, according to Eloise Steiner. After his military duty, Joe did graduate work in philosophy at Columbia University. He trained in adult and child psychiatry at the Menninger Foundation in Topeka, Kansas, and then served as chief of the Children's Section at Topeka State Hospital. From 1956 to 1960, he worked in association with Fritz Redl, author of *Children Who Hate*, with delinquent children at an in-patient setting at the National Institute of Mental Health. He then began a long career at Children's Hospital National Medical Center in Washington, D.C. During 1975–1976 he originated child psychiatry training programs in Israel. Joe completed adult and child psychoanalytic training at the Baltimore–D.C. Psychoanalytic Institute. For many years Joe taught child development at Howard University School of Medicine. He served as president of the American Academy of Child and Adolescent Psychiatry and of the American Association for Children's Residential Centers. He coedited (with R. Dean Coddington) *Stressors and the Adjustment Disorders* (1990). In describing his difficulty in corralling 52 authors for 37 chapters in this work, Joe commented, "It is said of Beethoven that he would write impossible parts for the French horn and then find impossible horn players to perform them!" In 1991, Joe cowrote (with Robert King) the two-volume *Pathways of Growth: Essentials of Child Psychiatry*. In 1964, his book, *Understanding Ourselves: The Challenge of the Human Mind*, was published by Coward-McCann, Inc. Joe Noshpitz's curriculum vitae as well as a number of unpublished papers can be accessed on the Web at http://www.JosephNoshpitz.com. These include "Some Notes on an Aspect of Identity Formation in Latency," "Magical Thinking," "Discussion of Freud's *Beyond the Pleasure Principle*," "*Love's Labor Lost: A Study in Puberty*," "The Dybbuch (Film)," "Ashkenazi Society," "Yiddish," "Hassidism," and "Kabbalah."

Fred Solomon relates that "in the best interest of the child," Joe could be not only assertive but also authoritative. When working with recalcitrant and delinquent preteens, he assumed the authority of a probation officer, telling the boys that if they were not able to participate in the treatment program they would be sent back to the institution from which they had come. In custody cases, many of which were high profile, Joe would ask the parents to sign a document agreeing to his decision after full evaluation to avoid courtroom battles.

Joe was a superb *raconteur*: he told of a voracious, huge, starved lion that was about to be let out of its cage to devour a Roman slave in the Coliseum. At the last second the slave whispered to the lion, which stopped in its tracks. The emperor called the slave to his box and asked, "What did you say to stop the lion?" The slave answered, "After dinner come the speeches." What a reminder of the power of words, which he sought to reawaken and nourish in all his young patients.

Bruce Sklarew met Joe, then a child psychiatry consultant at the National Institute of Mental Health, in 1961, during observation of a 2 1/2-year-old girl with leukemia who had stopped talking until Joe through play enabled the child to begin to speak. In supervision, particularly with obsessional or schizoid patients, Joe emphasized the importance of eliciting and exploring the patient's fantasies.

When conducting our family Seder, as Joe did for over 30 years, he talked about aspects of the Exodus, sometimes relating it to a contemporary event. One year we noticed that he was checking his notes before the Seder. He proceeded to provide a discourse on human history from its origins to the Exodus from Egypt, thus placing the Exodus in a developmental perspective parallel to his orientation to the theory and clinical practice of child development—an example of his ability to conceptualize in unexpected ways.

When questioned during a *voir dire* about serving on a jury, Joe earnestly said that he had spent his entire life trying to understand human behavior and not to judge it. The prosecuting attorney immediately removed Joe from consideration for jury duty.

In a case conference about a pregnant 15-year-old mother, Joe discussed a powerful motive for pregnancy in teenage girls, that of having a loving relationship with her own baby. Often subjected to maternal deprivation or absence and then raised by relatives, the adolescent identifies with her child when the child is adored by multiple relatives; this provides a transient compensation for the maternal deprivation. However, with a rambunctious toddler, the relatives may become punitive, often hitting the child—no longer adored. The adolescent may then seek another child to repeat the process through identifying with that child or subsequent children.

In the chapters that follow, readers will gain some sense of Joe's ranging intellect and manifold passions through the extraordinary diversity of subject matter and depth of the work, particularly in the area of child development. In his chapter on music, he steps into what can only be called, as in jazz, an improvisational riff on rhythm. "In a very real sense, all mentation, indeed, all psychic experience, is in fact biological." In this work the chasm between mind and body is diminished. René Descartes might take issue with him or, at best, might stir up an interesting conversation. "We are after all biological entities, and our thinking and feeling are no less biological than is our digestion. But we tend to think in dualistic terms about body and mind, so that assertions of this sort are more natural to us than to consider the product of psychological work as biological. Hence the word must be used here in quite a different sense." At the core of life processes, he tells us, are rhythm, meter, temporal regularity. "The jellyfish pulses, the swimming eel undulates, the cilia of the paramecium swing in synchrony, the heart beats, the digestive system exhibits peristalsis, the reproductive system ovulates and menstruates, short rhythms and long ones." Joe goes on to relate this inner rhythmic system to our conscious response to rhythm and to the emerging autonomy of the infant as it gains mastery through repetition or cadence.

Better then to read these chapters for yourselves and the excellent chapter introductions by experts in various fields who were asked initially to think of them as a form of dialogue between the introducer and Joe, as a way to relate his writing to current thinking in the field, to offer a critique of the work and, where appropriate, to provide a neuro-developmental perspective. The journey from "Ethics in Child Development" to "Idealization and Psychopathology," from "Infantile Narcissism" to "Tomboy Studies," from "Music and Visual Art" to "Dance," from "Trauma and Self-Destructiveness" to a "Pathway to Prevention" will not disappoint any reader who chooses to travel alongside Joseph Noshpitz. Through these pages, he will serve as a guide, companion, and mentor to a new generation of child therapists and child analysts.

Acknowledgments

It is difficult to know where to start as we thank those who have joined us in this effort. But perhaps the first ones to thank are Charlotte Noshpitz and Claude Noshpitz. Charlotte encouraged us all the way through our work, allowed us to check with her about the veracity of certain information, and made available to us boxes of Joe's papers. Claude searched through Joe's computer files to rescue materials. We thank you both for permitting us to commence this exploration. We acknowledge with enormous gratitude Paul Stepansky who, of a great mountain of pages, organized what we believe is a coherent book, selecting chapters to be included and finding an order for them. We are grateful to Dr. Robert Wallerstein, who carefully read the entire manuscript—and more than once—in writing his excellent Afterword that includes both personal reminiscences and an overall view of the entire work. Our thanks to Carl Feinstein and Marilyn Benoit for their Introductions to the book that provide context for the work, its relevance to the present thinking in the various fields, and memories that are moving and significant. We note with gratitude our gifted chapter introducers who stepped away from their multiple obligations to consider the work of their mentor, teacher, friend and to do so by bringing current knowledge to bear on Joe's writings and thought. We name them here: Lawrence Stone, Linda Mayes, Carl Feinstein, Gilbert Rose, Theodore Shapiro, Esther Rashkin, Efrain Bleiberg, John McDermott, James Lock, Adrienne Harris, Susan Coates, Alan Apter, Yari Gvion, and Bernard Spilka. We thank Fred Solomon, Robert King, Larry Vitulano, Jack Davis, Joe's sister, Rose Bennett, and niece Eloise Steiner for reading portions of the work and for providing additional information. Our thanks to Frances Eddy for help with typing and to Margo Meyers for her wisdom in assisting in a variety of ways and for her continued support for the project. Let us say thanks to Kristopher Spring, our remarkable associate editor. Never, in all our years of publishing, have we worked with anyone of his caliber and patience and his skill and wisdom in seeing this project through to completion. We thank Paul Stepansky once again for taking us along this route and into the skillful hands of Kristopher Spring.

Contributors

Alan Apter, MD, is professor of psychiatry at the Sackler School of Medicine at the University of Tel Aviv, where he served as chair of the department. He is also the director of the Feinberg Child Study Center at Schneider's Children's Medical Center of Israel, fellow of numerous professional societies and organizations, and has published more than 300 articles and chapters as well as two books.

Marilyn Benoit, MD, is a past president (2001–2003) of the American Academy of Child and Adolescent Psychiatry, has served on the faculties of Howard and George Washington Universities, and is a clinical associate professor of psychiatry at Georgetown University Medical Center, from which she received the Vicennial Silver Medal of Honor for 20 years of distinguished service. She is a nationally known advocate for children and an international lecturer on children's and adolescents' mental health issues. She maintains a private practice in Washington, D.C.

Efrain Bleiberg, MD, is a training and supervising analyst at the Houston–Galveston Institute for Psychoanalysis, director of the Division of Child and Adolescent Psychiatry at Baylor College of Medicine, and vice chair of the Menninger Department of Psychiatry and Behavioral Sciences.

Susan Coates, PhD, is a clinical professor of psychology in the psychiatry department at the College of Physicians and Surgeons of Columbia University as well as a member of the teaching faculty of the Columbia Center for Psychoanalytic Training and Research, where she was also a founding director of the Parent Infant Program. She has a long-standing interest in intergenerational transfer of trauma and in the interface of gender, trauma, and attachment. She is the coeditor of *September 11: Trauma and Human Bonds* (Analytic Press, 2003) with colleagues Dan Schechter and Jane Rosenthal.

Carl Feinstein, MD, is professor in the Department of Psychiatry and Behavioral Sciences and chief of the Division of Child and Adolescent Psychiatry at the Stanford University School of Medicine. He is also the endowed director of psychiatry at the Lucile Packard Children's Hospital. He is trained as a psychoanalyst, but has devoted his academic career to the diagnosis and treatment of children with developmental disabilities. Dr. Feinstein has published extensively on the development of children with cognitive delays, sensory handicaps, language deficits, autism (social deficits), and gene or chromosome abnormalities, while remaining active as a psychotherapist and practicing child and adolescent psychiatrist throughout his career.

Yari Gvion, PhD candidate, is a supervising clinical psychologist who has worked for many years in a psychiatric hospital and in a private clinic with children and adolescents and who has taught in the Clinical Division of the Psychology Departments at Bar-Ilan University and Tel Aviv University.

Adrienne Harris, PhD, is clinical associate professor at the New York University Postdoctoral Program in Psychotherapy and Psychoanalysis. She is the author of *Gender as Soft Assembly* (Analytic Press, 2005) and coeditor (with Steven Botticelli) of *First Do No Harm* (Routledge, 2010) as well as associate editor of *Psychoanalytic Dialogues* and *Studies in Gender and Sexuality.*

James Lock, MD, PhD, is professor of child psychiatry and pediatrics in the Department of Psychiatry and Behavioral Sciences at Stanford University School of Medicine, where he also serves as director of the Eating Disorder Program for Children and Adolescents. He has published more than 200 articles, abstracts, books, and book chapters and is active in research with four projects funded by the National Institutes of Health (NIH) related to eating disorder treatment in children and adolescents. His recent research focuses on integrating treatment research with neuroscience in eating disorders, including examining neurocognitive processes and their functional and neuroanatomical correlates, and his most current research focuses on interventions for anorexia nervosa and bulimia nervosa in younger patients.

Linda Mayes, MD, is the Arnold Gesell Professor of Child Psychiatry, Psychology, and Psychiatry in the Yale Child Study Center and special advisor to the dean in the Yale School of Medicine. She is also chair of the directorial team of the Anna Freud Centre and a member of the faculty of the Western New England Institute for Psychoanalysis. She is a child and adult analyst and coordinates a developmental electrophysiology laboratory for studies of stress and emotional regulation in childhood.

John McDermott, MD, is professor emeritus at the University of Hawaii School of Medicine, where he served as professor and chair of the Department of Psychiatry for 27 years. A fellow of numerous professional societies and organizations, he is editor emeritus of the *Journal of the American Academy of Child and Adolescent Psychiatry* and has published more than 150 articles and chapters and 11 books.

Esther Rashkin, PhD, LCSW, is professor of French and comparative literary and cultural studies and adjunct professor of modern dance at the University of Utah. She has published extensively on the intersections between psychoanalysis and literature, film, popular culture, history, and ideology, including her books, *Family Secrets and the Psychoanalysis of Narrative* (Princeton University Press, 1992) and *Unspeakable Secrets and the Psychoanalysis of Culture* (State University of New York Press, 2008), which won the 2009 Gradiva Award. A former fellow of the American Psychoanalytic Association, she maintains a private practice in Salt Lake City, Utah.

Gilbert Rose, MD, is a former faculty member of the Yale Medical School and the Western New England Psychoanalytic Institute. He is the author of many articles and four books, including *The Power of Form: A Psychoanalytic Approach to Aesthetic Form (International Universities Press,* 1980/1992) and *Between Couch and Piano: Psychoanalysis, Music, Art, Neuroscience* (Routledge, 2004). He is a life member of the American Psychoanalytic Association and a member of the Gardiner Program in Psychoanalysis and the Humanities at Yale University. He has been in private practice since 1955.

Theodore Shapiro, MD, is professor emeritus of psychiatry at Weill Cornell University Medical College and director of child and adolescent psychiatry at the New York University School of Medicine and the Payne Whitney Clinic.

Bruce Sklarew, MD (editor), psychiatrist and psychoanalyst, coedited *Analysts in the Trenches: Streets, Schools, War Zones* (Analytic Press, 2004); *The Last Emperor: Multiple Takes* (Wayne State University Press, 1998); and *Bernardo Bertolucci: Interviews* (University of Mississippi Press, 2000). He is cofounder of *Projections: A Journal for Movies and Mind* and associate editor of the *Journal for Applied Psychoanalytic Studies.* He is associate clinical professor of psychiatry at Howard University School of Medicine and was a faculty member at the Baltimore–Washington Institute for Psychoanalysis. He is the chair of the Forum for Movies and Mind and the film programmer for meetings of the American Psychoanalytic Association. He was the principal investigator of the School-Based Mourning Project in Washington, D.C., and the initiator for Recover, an acute bereavement service at the D.C. Morgue.

Myra Sklarew, MA (editor), former president of the artist community Yaddo and professor emerita of literature at American University, is the author of three chapter books and seven collections of poetry, including *Lithuania: New & Selected Poems* and *Harmless*. Other publications include short fiction, *Like a Field Riddled by Ants*; essays, *Over the Rooftops of Time*; and a forthcoming work, *Holocaust and the Construction of Memory*. Her poetry has been recorded for the Contemporary Poet's Archives of the Library of Congress. She studied biology at Tufts University, bacterial genetics and viruses at Cold Spring Harbor Biological Laboratory, and worked at Yale University School of Medicine studying frontal lobe function and delayed response memory of Rhesus monkeys. She attended the writing seminars at the Johns Hopkins University.

Bernard Spilka, PhD, is professor emeritus of psychology at the University of Denver, where he taught for 40 years. He is past president of the Colorado and Rocky Mountain Psychological Associations, the Psychology of Religion Division of the American Psychiatric Association, and vice president of the Society for the Scientific Study of Religion. He has published more than 200 papers and chapters, eight books, one monograph, and two major federal reports.

Lawrence Stone, MD, is clinical professor of psychiatry at the University of Texas Health Science Center and was president of the American Academy of Child and Adolescent Psychiatry from 1995 to 1997. He maintains a private practice of child, adolescent, and adult psychiatry in San Antonio, Texas.

Robert S. Wallerstein, MD, is former chair and professor emeritus in the Department of Psychiatry at the University of San Francisco School of Medicine and is professor emeritus and supervising analyst at the San Francisco Center of Psychoanalysis. In addition, he has been president of the American Psychoanalytic Association (1971–1972) and the International Psychoanalytical Association (1985–1989).

Introduction: Joseph Noshpitz (1922–1997)

Marilyn Benoit

I met Dr. Noshpitz (as the residents all called him) 35 years ago. To us fledgling child psychiatrists-to-be, he was a giant in the field, larger than life, and someone who awed us with his formulations of the complex cases we presented to him. He discovered motivations, insights, instinctual drives, defense mechanisms in places we had not yet explored or understood in the human psyche. It was a genuine treat to sit back and listen. What an inspiration he was. I longed to grow up professionally to be like him. Now, 35 years later, I have experienced the marvelous transformation from being Dr. Noshpitz's student to sharing a journey with him in the halls of academia and as president of the American Academy of Child and Adolescent Psychiatry. I can say that I became only more awestruck over the years, and I eventually concluded that, for me, it would never be possible to be like him. He will forever remain appropriately idealized. I say that quite comfortably because the more I knew Joe, as I came to address him in my professional adulthood, I discovered in him a bottomless pit of knowledge, interests, and wisdom that I have known in no one else. In reviewing his rather profound and detailed writings on idealization in this publication, I could not help but think how much he provided a positive idealizing object for so many people who enjoyed what was a rarified intellectual orbit around him.

As Joe and I would chat about the state of child rearing, we always believed that our discipline of child psychiatry and the study of child development had informed us a great deal about what children need. We believed that good child-rearing practices could indeed be taught and should be widely disseminated. We agonized about the failure of government to take on a more active role in fostering good child development practices, but, as Joe has written in his paper "Ethics and Child Development," included in this publication, the tension between family rights and government intrusion is one with which we must contend in a democracy. Joe wrote that "the ethical imperative is plain. Every child should not be merely allowed, but actively helped and encouraged to realize the full extent of his or her inherent capacities...." He endorsed universal child care and after-school enrichment programs for all children. He envisioned a societal culture that passionately nurtured the well-being of children from prenatal life to high school. He wrote about the concept of having "child-rearing centers," even conceptualizing details of the curricula including specific cognitive and social-emotional interventions. He gave special attention in his writings to at-risk children and was visionary in how he would include the judicious use of computers in the classroom. Joe would be embarrassed that in 2011 the United States of America has yet to endorse the United Nations Rights of the Child. But those political setbacks did not prevent us from fantasizing about building our own Child Development Institute where we would offer a rigorous didactic and comprehensive practicum, leading to certificates of training to all those wishing to pursue a career in working with children, be they social workers, nurses, foster and adoptive parents, nursery and elementary school teachers, and child-care workers in hospitals and residential facilities. We thought that we could raise funds from private citizens rather than seek any governmental funding to avoid the intrusion of bureaucracy. Though Joe died before any such plan could even reach the gestation period, I still harbor the fantasy of, and should it ever come to pass would be delighted about, cutting the ribbon to open the Joseph Noshpitz Child Development Institute. The in-depth study and understanding of child development were truly Joe's forte. His treatise on *Teenage Mutant Ninja Turtles* is rich with an analysis of psychosexual stages of development and brilliant interpretations. What a treat to read—not in a hurry, but slowly and deliberately, as one would enjoy an exquisite meal.

Joseph Noshpitz's professional biography will be fully reported throughout this book, as the editors and several contributors will address many of his contributions to the field of psychoanalysis and child and adolescent psychiatry. Joe was a scholar who crossed the boundaries of different areas of knowledge, using information from science, history, mythology, anthropology, psychology, philosophy, religion, literature, music, and pop culture. He was no dilettante. His knowledge covered breadth as well as depth. He was masterful at combining, reconstructing, and weaving ideas from the varied fields, and, in so doing, he created new palettes, new patchwork quilts of knowledge with amazing new insights. Myra Sklarew, coeditor of this publication, recalled one of the notable Seders conducted by Joe for more than 30 years. She stated that "Joe's words that day were an exploration of the essence of the Jewish religion." He spoke about there being a "curious abstraction" in the relationship of Jews to their God, a relationship unencumbered by intervening figures to be found in certain other religions. With God being such an abstraction, and hence less available for identification, Joe believed that Jews clung more to their autonomy, sometimes at great cost to themselves. Could Joe's insight about the Jewish relationship to God be a core issue in the trajectory of child development in Jewish children? My own sense is that Joe struggled with conflicts about God in his life, and this surfaces in his writings not only about religion but also on loss, separation, and trauma and possible influences on development. His own loss at age 10 1/2 of his father, who had been a rabbi in Mogilev, Russia, must have played a part in his deliberations about the role of religion in containing man's rage over his inevitable disillusionment with the all-powerful God, as discussed in "The Ethics of Rage." Myra commented that "Joe taught us about the journey, about adventure and curiosity, and about learning. He taught us about autonomy and individual responsibility. He taught us all to ask questions and to listen carefully for the answers." Her recollection of her relationship with Joe prompted her to recall and quote the poet Cavafy addressing Odysseus:

> When you set out for Ithaka
> Ask that your way be long,
> Full of adventure, full of instruction...
> Do not hurry your journey.
> Ithaka gave you the splendid journey.
> Without her you would not have set out.

Another person who shared Joe's life journey was Jack Davis, founder of the Grove School, a residential facility for troubled youth in Connecticut where Joe served as chair of the board. These two men shared a 50-year friendship. They would speak weekly, and Joe and his wife Charlotte would spend Thanksgiving and other holidays with the Davis family. Jack described Joe as being passionate about all aspects of life, including his love of food, especially bagels and lox. During the Thanksgiving holidays, "he would construct a sandwich in engineering fashion.... Everyone looking on in amazement, and he managed to devour this, then had another two with finesse and smiles ... almost like a ballet!" Jack describes Joe's dilemma when visiting Joe prior to his heart surgery. Joe needed to choose a heart valve made from either tissue or plastic. Joe's father had been a rabbi, and Joe was conflicted about choosing a porcine valve for religious reasons. It was when the doctor said, "Joe, it is not edible," that Joe decided to accept the pig valve. Other than that difficult decision, Jack thought that Joe was a good decision maker who did not ruminate and agonize about decisions he needed to make for the Grove School. Joe identified the need for the seven-volume *Handbook of Child and Adolescent Psychiatry*, but financing it was a problem. "Joe did not understand money ... so that's where I came in," said Jack. As so very many of us, Jack was an ardent admirer of Joe. "I admired everything about Joe. There was a magic in being together." Jack and Myra, as others, commented on Joe's willingness to share himself with others: his true generosity of spirit. He shared his wisdom, his collections of shells, rocks, fossils, coins, his medals, and as Jack said, "the pleasures and the pain." Joe allowed his friends to have genuinely intimate relationships with him. The intensity of those relationships comes through so palpably when friends speak about him. He changed their lives, as indeed they changed his.

One of Joe's idiosyncrasies was that he always wrote with a pencil. Jack shared a poignant story about sending pencils to Joe when Joe founded child psychiatry fellowship programs and clinics in Israel. Jack would send hundreds of pencils to Joe, but Customs made it difficult for Joe to retrieve them. Jack got an 11-page letter, in pencil, from Joe complaining about the hassles he endured. Jack was proud to have been the person who gave a gift of a computer to Joe, who then transitioned from pencil writing to word processing on the computer and, in Jack's words, "became enamored of it." Those of us who knew Joe well were not at all surprised that when he died he was at his computer.

We all knew that Joe loved to write and that he was a gifted writer and editor. He committed his thoughts to paper with diligence and elegance. Carl Feinstein referred to him as a "stylistic czar." Virginia Anthony, executive director of the American Academy of Child and Adolescent Psychiatry (AACAP), where Joe served as president from 1973 to 1975, stated that Joe influenced her own writing, "finding him every day in what I write." She referred to his "flourishes that often conveyed so much." Virginia thought that in his work as president of the AACAP Joe Noshpitz was transformational. She described him as "changing the face of the academy through sheer force as if a giant were lifting up the earth." He extended his reach globally, establishing a child psychiatry training program in Israel. As far back as 1973 his presidential address was on the issue of national health insurance. Now, three decades later, despite the passage of a health reform bill in 2010, national universal health insurance is completely off the table for consideration. At the AACAP Joe was associate editor of the journal, and in that capacity he was responsible for the "turn-down letters." Virginia believes that even when rejecting a paper, the authors must have felt privileged to receive one of Joe's letters, "which were several pages long, always encouraging and advancing scholarship."

As stated earlier, Joe was generous of spirit. It was that generosity that made him invite the young Efrain Bleiberg to participate in a panel on narcissism after reading his paper on that topic. Efrain said, "I was honored to be invited by this revered man who had preceded me at Menninger." They continued to offer that panel at the American Academy of Child and Adolescent Psychiatry annual meeting over the next 10 years. As chair of the panel, Efrain noted that Joe Noshpitz was sensitive to everyone's narcissism. He kept the panelists on track with an attitude of "*Nu kinderlach*" ("Come on, kids"), getting them to address the issue of kids' emotional pain rather than get stuck on their own narcissistic issues. Joe was described by Efrain as being "rabbinical." He served as a mentor, being attentive, scholarly, and focused on kids' feelings. He was "old-fashioned, in a very Jewish way: meticulous, compulsive." Efrain spoke about Joe's excitement about the beginning studies of genes and the role of the environment in gene expression. As then residency director at Menniger, Efrain took great pleasure in honoring Joe Noshpitz with the distinguished Arthur Marshall Award at the Menninger clinic, where Joe gave the commencement speech.

Marianne Katz, a social worker whom Joe supervised at Children's Hospital in Washington, D.C., described him as "wise, very thorough, very humanistic." A subject in Joe's tomboy study, she learned that tomboyishness was a variant of normal development. As so many others who experienced Joe, she too felt embraced by Joe's warmth of spirit. Simple gestures on his part made her feel special. She felt that he wanted people to be good and sensitive to others. She delighted in his "breadth of knowledge, his areas of knowledge, and his understanding of human beings. I was just in awe." She believes that Joe most influenced her with his advice that in making diagnoses one did not have to rush to a decision. I believe that we should send that message to the insurance companies in this day of single-session diagnostics.

Charlotte Noshpitz and Joe Noshpitz were married for 47 years and have one son and two grandsons. Charlotte states, "It was an interesting life." She felt fortunate that Joe chose to take her along on his trips rather than accept honoraria; together they traveled throughout the world. On each trip Joe would go fossil hunting. Though he worked hard, Charlotte said, "It was very easy to live with him." Because she lost her mother and brother in the Holocaust, she spoke of missing her adolescence. Quite poignantly, Charlotte stated, "I did not know how to be the daughter of someone." Joe lost his own father at age 10 1/2. Perhaps their shared Eastern European backgrounds and adolescent losses created a common bond. They met at the Menninger Clinic when she came from France to do a 9-month internship as an art therapist. It was not at all surprising to me when she responded to my question as to what was the "glue" in their relationship: "We discussed ideas." She had asked Joe to promise her that they would not have a television in their home, and he abided by that promise until their son was 13 years old. Like others, Charlotte said she loved the "goodness in Joe and the feeling he had for others. With him one does not feel alone." There was a very maternal manner about Joe. "Like the Torah, which means 'teaching,' he embraces you and teaches you everything." Charlotte believes that Joe's legacy is that he taught by example, by being authentic.

I spent a very special evening with Joe one warm summer evening when he joined my husband and me for dinner. His wife, Charlotte, was on one of her regular trips to France, her homeland. Joe and my husband shared a breadth of knowledge and enjoyed chatting for most of the evening. After dinner, I shared with Joe the book that inspired me to become a physician. Not many people know this about me. The book was my father's and was called *The Household Physician*. This was a very comprehensive medical book written for missionaries who ventured into parts of the world where no medical care was available. It was beautifully illustrated with overlapping color plates representing every organ and covered all diseases and their remedies (mainly homeopathic) known to man at that time. I loved reading that book, for hours at a time. I became extremely curious about the inner workings of the body, and this sparked my unwavering interest in medicine. My husband, Geoffrey Brown, had the good fortune of finding a copy for me in a secondhand bookstore in Oxford, England, where it had been published. Joe was intrigued by the book and spent much time leafing through it and commenting on the information it contained. It was one of those intimate moments that endeared him to me. As with Marianne, he made me, too, feel special.

Carl Feinstein

I first met Joe Noshpitz in the early 1970s, when I was a Ginsburg Fellow in the Group for the Advancement of Psychiatry, Committee on Adolescence, where Joe was a member. Within a few years, he became a primary mentor in my earliest training and faculty years in child and adolescent psychiatry at Hillcrest Children's Center and Children's Hospital National Medical Center at George Washington University in Washington, D.C. As with many other young child psychiatrists, he profoundly influenced my entire intellectual and ethical development in my chosen field of study with his extraordinary, generously shared gifts as a thinker.

I entered child and adolescent psychiatry with a primary curiosity to learn how people came to be the way they are; that is, I always saw psychological development as the key to psychological understanding. Joe was the perfect mentor for this endeavor. He was first and foremost a developmental thinker. For him, child development began in infancy. The roots of socialization, compassion and empathy, love and hate for self and others, the interplay between life-affirming and destructive inner impulses, the formation of gender identity and all other forms of identification, the foundations of morality, the underpinnings of all forms of communication, and both receptivity and expressivity in the arts all began their unfolding in interaction with the primary caretakers in the first weeks, months, and years of life.

Joe exerted his powerful educational influence on his friends, colleagues, and students in many ways. While drawing upon his formidable intellect, wide-ranging scholarship, quickness to recognize the importance of new research findings, and ability to integrate information from many fields of knowledge, his greatest resource derived from his poetic gifts as a lecturer. Poetry, to be meaningful rather than dry or academic, must be an expression of deep and personal experience and must be expressed without reservation. While Joe's level of scholarship was remarkably high, whenever he addressed a topic in child development, he communicated the results with a level of conviction that seemed to flow directly from the experience of the child transmitted unfiltered through Joe's own consciousness to his audience. Joe was remarkably in touch with the subjective psychological world of the infant. In this sense, to me and to many of my fellow students he seemed more an oracle of child development rather than a presenter of intriguing hypothetical deductions, partially substantiated by experimental studies.

Many readers of the essays in this book, particularly younger readers and those who never heard Joe speak, will ask, "Why is that so many of these pearls have never been published before?" Other readers may scratch their heads and wonder why several of these essays address in what must now appear as prescient depth such topics as the remarkable elaboration of infant

social development and early identifications in the first year of life. These topics, despite the rich literature in related disciplines, are just beginning to be
noticed by mainstream child and adolescent psychiatry. Why didn't Joe publish more? Why did these compelling narratives, so full of insight, seem to
disappear beneath the waves, only to surface an entire professional generation
later?

My own answers to these questions are complex, and perhaps contro-
versial. Probably first and foremost among them is that Joe's ideas were
temporally out of sync with the major intellectual movements in both psychoanalysis and in child and adolescent psychiatry. As a psychoanalyst,
Joe's emphasis on the first 3 years of life (especially the first, preverbal year)
as the foundation of psychological development, put him mildly but uncom-
fortably at odds with the then dominant psychoanalytic establishment's
preference for the structural theory of psychoanalysis, which emphasized
the role of oedipal conflict and verbally articulated memories from somewhat later in childhood. Here, I believe history will judge that Joe was correct and ahead of his time.

Although not an experimentalist himself, Joe was very quick out of the
gates to respond to the pioneering research in infant development being carried out by Daniel Stern and by numerous university-based child development
laboratories. Joe taught his students in the 1970s and 1980s concepts such as
intersubjectivity, theory of mind and mentalization, social referencing, plus
the many proofs of infant cognitive abilities that are just recently, well into the
twenty-first century, beginning to have traction in psychoanalytic circles.

Ironically, however, it was not this mild discordance with his contemporary psychoanalytic colleagues that limited Joe's influence in his field.
Far more important was that the dominant trend in child and adolescent
psychiatry, beginning in 1970s and continuing almost to the present, was
to turn away from the study of the developmental origins of psychopathology altogether and to embrace a more static and descriptive classification
of child psychiatric disorders based on their putative similarity to adult disorders. This new orientation is embodied in the *Diagnostic and Statistical
Manual of Mental Disorders,* third edition (*DSM-III*) and *Diagnostic and
Statistical Manual of Mental Disorders,* fourth edition (*DSM-IV*) and is
virtually memorized by every student of child psychiatry.

Thus, at the same time Joe was describing the interactions between negative
identifications in the first year of life and later traumatic exposures as causative
of self-destructive behavior in adolescence, crowds of trainees were increasingly
attending lectures where the young leaders in the field were insisting that developmental theories were irrelevant and that the skills child psychiatrists needed
to acquire involved the translation of adult diagnostic criteria into the mildly
modified versions required to make the exact same diagnoses in children.

An entire generation of child psychiatrists, many of whom are now
in the prime of their careers, have less understanding of the importance

of development in the first 3 years of life for later mental health or psychopathology than those fortunate few of us, who learned it from Joe, before this approach was submerged in a tidal wave of a developmental Kraepelinianism. It is only in the past few years, depleted by the absurdity of making four or five separate *DSM* diagnoses (none of which adequately capture the nature of the problem the child is experiencing) is child psychiatry beginning to return to its roots in developmental psychopathology.

It became common among those who knew and learned from Joe, especially during this psychiatric epoch from which we are just beginning to emerge, to refer to him as from "an age when giants walked the Earth." Joe seems, from this perspective, as a lonely hero from the Greek Pantheon, now faded away, or as an Old Testament prophet, or like Roland, alone in the age of Charlemagne, sounding his horn but unable to hold back the invading hordes. While we cherish this mythic image of Joe, it does not fully explain why Joe did not publish most of his writings, including the essays in this book.

Casting Joe as a brilliant but archaic Old Testament prophet whose voice was drowned out in a more modern age is also wrong in an important way. Joe was a keen student both of developmental neuroscience and the latest research in evolutionary psychology. Reverberations of his long-standing interest in evolutionary psychology appear in his essays on the arts, found in this volume, and these stand up very well to the most current research advances in this field 25 years after he wrote them. Less obvious in these published essays is his deep interest in the earliest stages of brain development, including intrauterine development. However, I report here that Joe would frequently come into my office to show me the latest papers in developmental neuroscience. In addition, Joe was an avid reader of the entire scientific literature in infant development, often involving meticulous and ingenious experimental design to identify physiologic or behavioral indications of cognitive skills from well before volitional communication appeared.

Joe's position between developmental neuroscience and clinical child psychiatry was solely that of a translator and teacher of developmental neuroscience to clinicians and not that of a creator of new neuroscience. One minor reason Joe did not publish his writings was because there were very few formats in the child and adolescent psychiatric journals for a scholar and theorist such as he to bridge the gap between the burgeoning field of developmental neuroscience and the declining interest (from that period) in developmental psychopathology in the psychiatric literature. Needless to say, Joe was not the kind of man who would bend his publications in a direction away from his own fully formed interests simply to suit an audience that he must have believed had lost its way.

Perhaps a more important reason Joe did not publish his writings had to do with his personality and character. Joe was an essayist who needed to be accepted on his own terms. He was fully aware of and confident in his intellectual gifts and relished his role as a trusted and charismatic teacher. While he was a consummate editor of textbooks, who in his role of editor insisted on the highest standards of annotation and documentation of sources and references, I suspect that he was impatient of subjecting himself to those very same editorial standards. Joe knew what he knew and believed what he thought. He deliberately preferred to write in a more authoritative and poetic style and cared to cite the intellectual influence of others on his own writing only when it was clear to him that he had learned from them.

I doubt that Joe had any interest in citing other authors, simply to bolster his argument by documenting that others had written related ideas, when he did not feel indebted to them for advancing his thinking or supplying him with needed information. Yet citing others to bolster the credibility of one's own ideas as well as to forestall the inevitable sniping from published scholars who would otherwise be piqued at being overlooked by another scholar's literature review is the very political stuff of conventional academia. It is the game that all academics, except perhaps those of the most exalted rank and fame, must play if they wish to publish and advance their careers. Joe would not play this game.

We still must ask ourselves, "Why not?" since in Joe's case it meant that he failed to reach the full audience to which he was entitled. I often ask myself this question. It would be far easier and less frustrating for me, in my work as a teacher of child psychiatry, if I could show my bright but demanding students that some of my most important convictions about child development and psychopathology have a long-published lineage and, in fact, that I learned them from Joseph Noshpitz and if I could cite his publications and those of more current writers who cited him in their own research and writing. I would even wish to cite him in my own publications. But there we are. Joe did not wish to subject himself to the homogenizing strictures of academia, and it is only now, many years after his death, that many will have this opportunity to learn from him.

Chapter 1

Ethics in child development

INTRODUCTION

Lawrence Stone

In his paper "Ethics in Child Development," Noshpitz examines the intense and dynamic issues associated with parenting, schooling, socialization, and the growth and development of our youth. He offers meaningful elaborations and analysis of many of the central problems and challenges faced by our current and future generations. He emphasizes the importance of the development of common sense, popularly supported, and fundamentally sound regimens and structures developed by the current and future creators and caretakers of the forthcoming generations.

In the past, unfortunately, many of those who care for children have reacted as if they were reading a weather report. You want to believe it, but you wonder about it. You may rely on its details and therefore make some constructive plans for your immediate and future circumstances, or you may doubt its accuracy and therefore make nonprecautionary plans, or you may pay it no attention and make no preparatory responses. Thus, primarily through all of our societal history, we have the age-old hit, miss, or do-nothing responses to the devastating issues and concerns of children's development. "Based on the expectation of a significantly more diverse child population by 2020, and the large number of children living in poverty, greater attention is needed on vulnerable children and their potential for a healthy and productive adulthood" (Cheng & Jenkins, 2009, p. 2491).

Committing to children is a wise investment for the future of the United States in the global community. Much research has documented persistent or increasing child health disparities by population, disease, affluence (Koplewicz, Gurian, & Williams, 2009), violence (Helander, 2008), maternal health (Feldman, Granat, Pariente, Kanety, Kuint, & Gilboa-Schechtman, 2009), geography, and other risk factors, but there is a paucity of research on successful interventions. As seen in this paper, the issues Noshpitz addresses are essentially issues of today and tomorrow.

He presents a review of child development concepts with an analysis of many of the central issues along with a brief examination of common ineffective actions and goals. Noshpitz follows this with his conclusions for reforms, new pathways, and predictable outcomes. He examines the roles of the mother, father, and other family members, neighbors, schools, teachers, and society. They are falling short of the goals of healthy biological, psychological, and social development for children. While spelling out the details, he maintains that we cannot rely on the past for our solutions for tomorrow but rather for guides to avoid development's stagnation and to devise new and creative methodologies for healthy child development. He clearly expresses the preeminent role that "society" must create for the protection and healthy development of our future, namely, our children.

In a personal communication, Emilio Dominguez, a Spanish friend and colleague and expert on the family, wrote in response to Noshpitz's paper:

> The consequences of our failure to meet our collective responsibility to assure our children's complex developmental needs are in the news every day: serious child abuse cases all over the world, child exploitation, children made into soldiers to fight wars, used for sexual objects, and so many other atrocities. And we have the less reported cases of neglect and abuse, all with serious consequences for all children and later for all of society. It is one thing to raise children to be puppets or ideologues; it is another to seek to enhance each child's capacity for altruism, cognitive achievement, emotional maturity, aesthetic self-realization, and warm interpersonal relations.

In a recent article in *Journal of the American Medical Association* (*JAMA;* Mercy & Saul, 2009), many of the points Noshpitz makes about the importance of early interventions in childhood experiences and development are highlighted. Of particular note, this issue of *JAMA* had 11 articles pertaining to some aspect of children's mental health and emotional growth. What a change from earlier times when Noshpitz supported me in a quest to bring "current issues" forward as prime content for a major series of medical textbooks in 1979 and 1987. I personally felt at the time his urging and encouragement to examine, analyze, and elaborate all aspects of life that impacted the mental and emotional growth and development of our children and adolescents. The goal was to bring forward, evaluate, and present the unique emotional and behavioral impacts of new and developing phenomena. Out of this was to come greater awareness, sharper insights, and productive interventions in the quest for diminished mental morbidity and improved emotional growth and stability in our young people.

It is hard to tell whether we are gaining in these areas. We currently see more and more electronic addiction and microinvasions of our human systems and functions, our privacy, our uniqueness, our behavior, and even our ambitions. There is debate and conflict over the values and the boundaries of our individuality. Among all of these dynamic challenges, Dr. Noshpitz, we miss your wisdom and thank you again for this paper and your forever timely forethoughts. My recommendation to a new reader is to read the conclusions first; if you find that you have little disagreement, then read from the beginning to learn more about "how to"; if you found large disagreements, then read from the beginning to learn more about "why to."

To review, synthesize, and comment on but a few parts of the works and information left behind by Joseph D. Noshpitz, MD, is personally challenging and gratifying. What responsibility. What an honor. What a privilege. What a pleasure.

References

Cheng, T. L., & Jenkins, R. R. (2009). Health disparities across the lifespan. *Journal of the American Medical Association, 301*(23), 2491–2492.

Feldman, R., Granat, A., Pariente, C., Kanety, H., Kuint, J., & Gilboa-Schechtman, E. (2009). Maternal depression and anxiety across the postpartum year and infant social engagement, fear regulation, and stress reactivity. *Journal of the American Academy of Child and Adolescent Psychiatry, 48*(9), 919–926.

Helander, E. (2008). *Children and violence: The world of the defenseless.* London: Palgrave MacMillan.

Koplewicz, H., Gurian, A., & Williams, K. (2009). The era of affluence and its discontents. *Journal of the American Academy of Child and Adolescent Psychiatry, 48*(11), 1053–1055.

Mercy, J. A., & Saul, J. (2009). Creating a healthier future through early interventions for children. *Journal of the American Medical Association, 301*(21), 2262–2264.

ETHICS IN CHILD DEVELOPMENT
Joseph D. Noshpitz

Traditionally, child development has been a family matter. Every child grows within a human context; there is always a surrounding milieu of one or more adults whose efforts and activity are essential to the child's survival. The complex interplay between infant and caregiver, their mutual regulation and interaction, and the meaningful consequences of this exchange to both child and milieu have been documented many times. Nor does this interplay stop with infancy. It persists lifelong, with a highly varied evolution of duties, roles, and responsibilities as the years progress.

What ethical principles apply to this universal human pattern? At the outset, it is evident that we are concerned with the interactions between a presumably adult-rearing person and a relatively helpless and dependent individual in need of rearing. The act of rearing an infant implies mandatory access to such biological necessities as caring, nurturing, and protecting. It would be unprincipled to allow a helpless child to go unfed, untended, unprotected from avoidable danger, or deprived of necessary medical care. But these are the easy positions.

In our day, child development has been studied as never before in history. As we have continued to observe babies, a host of needs have come to be identified, needs that are a great deal more subtle and complex than the short list of biologic necessities previously set forth. This added array includes needs for appropriate stimulation, needs for responsive attention, needs for acquiring solace, needs for playful interaction, needs for emotional nurturing, needs for identifying the specifics of temperament, and needs for making the necessary adaptations to that profile.

Once we gain such an improved and more detailed knowledge of children's emotional, cognitive, and interpersonal needs, we come face to face with a number of pivotal ethical dilemmas, namely, how important is it that these needs be met? More to the point, if we perceive that meeting these needs is a valuable good, even a critical necessity, should not these needs be met, consistently and appropriately? If they really should be met, if this is genuinely important, then, in turn, would it not follow that we have to ponder whose responsibility it is that this be done? The easy answer is that it is the family's responsibility—as it always has been. End of discussion. But in an era of rapid advances in knowledge, where the average family might well be unaware of what is known about child development, in an era of radical dissolution of extended families, of both parents working, of frequent and rapid family fragmentation—in short, of major changes in the meaning of the word *family*—is it not reasonable to inquire: In some measure, should this not become society's responsibility? Should not child rearing become a shared responsibility between family and society? For if we do not face this issue, how else can we be sure that all children are getting what we know they must and should have? That, in particular, is the troublesome question challenging so many of our most cherished principles. For there is no obvious way to ensure the appropriateness of child-rearing practices without some form of monitoring of what goes on in each home where a child is being reared. Once we embark on that line of reasoning, however, we encounter another great good whose tenets would be violated by such monitoring.

One of the most precious and valued usufructs of liberty is the freedom to interact with one's family in the privacy of the home without officious governmental scrutiny, surveillance, or interference. This is a cherished and protected principle; it is celebrated in the ancient phrase "a man's home is his castle." It would take an extraordinary state of affairs to breach such a cordon of values. There is, however, much to suggest that such a condition has indeed arrived. Let us consider this in greater detail.

It has long been assumed that a family is the best rearing environment for any given child, that there are both sacred and sentimental reasons for maintaining a bastion of privacy around the rearing of children, and that the biologically derived, intuitive knowledge and life experience of parents (formerly of mothers, more recently of mothers *and* fathers)—hopefully backed by the wisdom of grandparents—is the surest ground for healthy individual development of the child. And even where it is not, even where a family fails at its child-rearing mission, the ideal solution is to provide the child with a temporary (foster) or permanent (adoptive) alternative family, one that will offer the necessary sage and intuitive upbringing.

Jecker (1993) makes the point that there are a number of ethical principles underlying the relationship of society to family. Although she is making these observations in connection with spousal abuse, they can readily apply to our topic as well. These principles hold true both in the late stages of pregnancy and beyond. To begin with, there is a principle akin to that celebrated in the Hippocratic Oath: First do no harm. That seems self-evident and needs no discussion. Then there is society's duty to do those things that support and help enhance the welfare of each family and child. The current concern in America with providing jobs and health care are examples of this principle in action. Finally there is the requirement to allot the goods of that society in a manner that is just.

Jecker (1993) notes that modern ethicists have come to regard the preservation of self-respect within a society as a profoundly important social good (Nozick, 1974; Rawls, 1971; Waltzer, 1983). I would add that fostering individual development is of even greater importance. Such enhancement of growth experiences not only underlies any hope for self-respect (or, as we term it, self-esteem) but also makes possible the maximum realization of the means of maintaining such self-esteem a lifetime through. For it is in furthering of one's capacities for cognitive competence, emotional self-regulation, and interpersonal bonding that skilled and discerning developmental support reaches its apogee. It is in realizing these potentials that good child rearing offers its truest contribution to creating and maintaining self-esteem.

One of the products of our cultural history, however, is that the extension of justice has tended to stop at the family door. As a society, we are loath to view events within the boundary of family life as meriting the same application of justice considerations as is true for extrafamilial events. For example, the history of the "discovery" of child abuse speaks volumes for the difficulty we have in allowing ourselves even to think about so distressing an idea as the misuse of children within that center of social sanctity, the family home. The syndrome of recurrent multiple fractures and subdural hematoma in infancy was an x-ray diagnosis that had been known for years (Caffey, 1946). Roentgenologists diagnosed it all the time. It was not until a courageous pediatrician connected that with the voluminous evidence of child abuse that the true diagnosis began to be made (Kempe, Silverman, Steele, Droegmuller, & Silver, 1962). The 16 years it took between the initial x-ray description and the subsequent behavioral diagnosis is a concrete measure of the profound unwillingness our society experienced toward dealing with the associated ethical issues.

A somewhat similar state of affairs exists in the realm of spouse battering. Thus, Warshaw (1989) examined medical records where women had been treated by doctors and nurses for injuries highly suggestive of abuse and found "nondetection, nonintervention, and nonreceptiveness to be the norm" (in Jecker, 1993, p. 776). In attempting to understand this state of affairs, Kurz and Stark (1988) suggest that they want to help medical staff members feel comfortable about actually asking probing questions about the source of the injuries because they may regard such an inquiry as "an invasion into 'personal affairs'" (in Jecker, p. 777). After all, people are likely to find such an inquiry offensive (Sugg & Inui, 1992). As a result, even so conservative a voice as the American Psychiatric Association (AMA) is beginning to assert that to consider domestic violence as a private matter is "a common misconception that should be abandoned" (Council on Ethical and Judicial Affairs, AMA, 1992).

Translated into our own realm of concern, this illustrates an extreme, although unfortunately by no means uncommon, state of affairs where one ethical principle, the right of a family to the privacy of the home, is confronted with another, the right of a child to grow without maltreatment.

One may well argue, however, that since child abuse is in fact an extreme case, it is not something that should be allowed to set the cultural tone for all child rearing. What happens, however, if we find that children have other needs besides the relatively obvious one of protection from physical harm? What if the researchers in child development determine, for example, that each child requires a minimum of interactive stimulation? Some 50 years ago, Rene Spitz (1945) described hospitalism, the syndrome of the under-stimulated child. In our day, this has translated itself into laws that con-sider "neglect" of a child a grave and actionable offense, one that permits society's representatives to enter a home and, if necessary, remove a child outright. Here the issue not only is one of physical abuse but also involves the psychological harm to the child as well as the physical dangers an unsu-pervised child can encounter, which together arouse society's reaction.

Kaplan (1991) quotes a U.S. Department of Health and Human Services report (1988) as dividing neglect into three categories: physical, educational, and emotional. For the preschooler, physical and psychological neglect are the chief culprits and often go hand in hand. In the wake of such depri-vation, serious damage to the child's developmental processes can ensue. The neglected youngster is often left cognitively handicapped, emotionally stunted or disturbed, and unable to enjoy a full and satisfying interpersonal relationship with anyone. The ethical implications of such a state of affairs seem straightforward enough. Aside from the empirical problems of how much this eventually costs society in terms of compensatory and ameliora-tive efforts (e.g., social services, investigative services, educational services, special education, the many elements of the penal system), there is the mat-ter of how much children suffer as they yearn for care and closeness—and do not obtain them. How much punishment-seeking behavior follows as the only way to get the much-needed attention, how much travail then ensues on the part of both the child and the family (often extending later on to the community), and how much of a burden of self-hatred and self-devastation becomes yoked to the child as a permanent fixture to carry forward into later years? There is much pain in all this.

The ethical imperative is thus very powerful to order society as to prevent such unfortunate sequences from taking place. But each such consideration brings us face to face with the vital issue of the inviolability of the home.

It is well to pause a moment and study this question. There have been a num-ber of instances when the issue was addressed and various solutions found. For example, if a parent refused (e.g., on religious grounds) to allow prescribed medical treatment to be extended to the child, this was deemed legally to be a form of neglect, and the court might well insist on the treatment being given or even go so far as to take such a child out of the parents' hands.

Then there is the matter of adequate supervision. Children who have not yet reached puberty who are left unsupervised may well be considered to be legally neglected and, in some instances, removed from the home. In many jurisdictions, criminal penalties could also be applied to the neglect-ing parents.

Thus, there are a number of situations that, if brought to the attention of the authorities, might lead to society crossing the family threshold and taking some action to correct.

But is this way of doing things appropriate, adequate, or sufficient? There are several considerations that bear on this question. To begin with, the determination as to whether a child is neglected or abused is largely a matter of happenstance. A neighbor phones in (or doesn't), or another member of the family decides (or hesitates) to take action. Sometimes it is a school teacher or counselor who notes bruises on the child's face and body or is the distressed recipient of some account of sexual molestation—and alerts the authorities. In other instances, perhaps in the majority of such cases, if the child says nothing about the abuse, or no one happens to notice anything (or, noticing, prefers not to get involved), then the situation simply goes on. No action is initiated and no relief afforded. In many life histories, flagrant abuse has thus continued for months or years without and intervention on behalf of the child.

Moreover, this deals only with the more overt and manifest forms of destructive parental behavior. What of the more covert patterns, the less massive but nonetheless corrosive forms of psychological abuse and neglect? What of the home where the parent is ignorant, or depressed, alcoholic, or mentally ill? What of a rearing environment where the parent is overwhelmed, facing myriad consuming personal problems, and unable to cope? Or the home where devil worship, superstition, some unusual cult pattern or family tradition results in highly deviant rearing practices (e.g., a child required to participate in ritual scorning of one of its members or ceremonial torture of animals)? What of the home stressed by tyrannical parents who use children as instruments of their power hunger, religious zealots whose child care consists of forcing children to obey the tenets of their particular doctrine, or a severe compulsives whose children must comply with the rigors of their extraordinary rituals? What price all the advances in our knowledge of child development in the face of such caretaking constellations? The key question again and again is: How do we balance the ethical matter of families' right to privacy and their freedom to bring their children up as seems best according to its lights against children's and families' right to mental health-promoting, nonabusive, nonexploitative rearing? And, by implication, how much is the child's healthy development a matter of public and societal concern?

There is a more cogent question still. Does the average family bring its children up in adequate fashion? Here we may seek statistics, but all we are likely to find is opinion. The few figures we do have suggest that nearly 20% of the population shows a sufficiently overt form of symptomatology as to merit psychiatric diagnosis. That implies a huge burden of guilt, anxiety, depression, addiction, and other forms of stressed adjustment—so huge, in fact, that social planners scarcely consider ways and means of coming to grips with the full reality of these figures. But if that many people are troubled enough to show symptoms, how many people are troubled in fact—but not quite enough to spill over into overt expression? How many suffer from subclinical symptoms? It is not unrealistic to assume that for every individual who is diagnosable, there are perhaps two who are pretty uncomfortable but whose symptoms do not reach the level of meeting the necessary criteria. In the face of such considerations we begin to edge over from mere statistical questions to existential questions: What is the true state of the human condition? How much unhappiness and maladjustment is "normal," in the sense of being normative (i.e., typical of the average individual)?

Translated into the concerns that are central to the present thesis, we have to ponder whether a different and more aware, more developmentally oriented kind of child rearing could head off some of this mass unhappiness. By implication, it is all too likely that *most* parents need some measure of help in their child-rearing behavior. With the best will in the world, parents will often have blind spots or overreactions to particular traits their children manifest. Many children will have unique needs that it would take a certain expertise to detect and address. The "fit" between parent and child may be a source of stress to one, or the other, or both. Often this is not apparent to the parent at the time it is happening, yet it may have far-reaching effects in terms of the child's subsequent development.

Hence, the case for some level of expert observation and intervention can be made readily enough. If a significant input of skill and knowledge during the early formative years could be brought to bear on every child-rearing constellation, it could be expected to have a number of desirable outcomes.

1. To begin with, it should raise the general level of happiness within the culture to some degree. Much of the pain incurred during any individual life span arises out of the conflicts and tensions built into personality from the earliest years. If these conflicts could be identified and their intensity eased by proper responsiveness to infants' needs, then they should grow up with less defensiveness, less inner turmoil, greater self-confidence, more trust, and a more comfortable pattern of self-regard and self-esteem in subsequent years.
2. Throughout the lifespan, the quality of interpersonal relations will always reflect the tenor of early interactions with one's caretakers. That is not to say that later events do not affect the character of interpersonal behavior; they can and do. But the early competencies or failures will always persist in some degree and, in many instances, dominate the way individuals orient themselves within their social world. This will be particularly evident in cases where early experience has been extreme in some way, extremely deprived, or extremely secure and rewarding. But even in less dramatic circumstances, the scarlet thread of early relationship experience will weave its way through the subsequent patterning of social behavior. Hence, the skillful identification of sites of early stress in interpersonal interaction, coupled with

appropriate help toward lessening such stress, could have far-reaching consequences.

3. Perhaps the most important outcome of properly structured early patterns has to do with superego formation, the inculcation of appropriate regulatory presences within the personality organization is given far too little address in child developmental literature. Few things are more important than this dimension of child rearing. The tightly packed quality of a high-tech civilization, where everyone depends on the integrity of communication networks, powerful memory storage, instantaneous retrieval capacities, the translation of information and instruction into fabrication processes, and the like, makes for an extraordinarily exposed social arrangement. The recent airing of the prevalence of computer viruses gives some hint as to how vulnerable our systems are. Introducing such a virus into a public information network is like pouring a culture of lethal microorganisms into a community water supply. Stories of a disgruntled employee taking a powerful magnet into a storage space filled with magnetic data tapes and destroying them all within a few minutes add to the sense of the relative ease with which such complex arrangements can be undone. Our very advances as a society have made us increasingly dependent on one another and, in particular, on our general level of conscience. When a city has too many individuals with seriously deficient inner regulatory apparatuses, that community comes to be experienced as unlivable by a large percentage of the population. And all this without even beginning to address another product of our technology, namely, the amount of energy (in the form of explosives and projectiles) a single individual can transport and use in destructive fashion. Today, one person, properly armed, probably has the firepower of a World War II platoon. Ultimately, the major protection a society has against such depredations must be the general level of conscience throughout its people. Anything that affects that even in slight degree is of incalculable influence on the future and success of that society. Hence, over the long term, the inclusion of this criterion as one potential consequence of improved childrearing is of signal importance for the larger social order.

This then is the case, the ethical basis, for inviting the state into the home and, more than that, into that peculiarly personal and heretofore sacrosanct domain, the arena of family–child interactions. For what is being pondered here is an arrangement by means of which every pregnant woman, every family with a newborn, and every constellation where a child is being reared would be reviewed by developmental specialists, both to assess and, where necessary, to take a significant participatory role in that rearing process.

In effect, the state could be asked to assume the role of considering each child development sequence as part of the public responsibility of that community; each pregnancy intended for term would then be regarded as a matter of substantial public significance. The assumption would be that whether that development is fostered or mismanaged has implications for society as well as for that family: the potential the mother–infant dyad (whether embryo, fetus, or newborn) brings with it will add its bit to the corpus of public capacity, or it will detract from and burden the public's ability to pursue the well-being of that collectivity as well as that of each separate member. Everyone counts; the strengths each one brings are part of the communal strength, and the burdens each one carries are weight piled on the public's shoulders. Unhappiness is a contagious disease, and a wise state will take intensive preventive action to inhibit its initiation, minimize its severity, and shorten its duration.

It is important to be clear about what is being suggested here and what is not. This is not a proposal to have the state take over child rearing and to have children brought up in keeping with some government-dictated model. We have seen some of that in fascist and communist societies, and it has often impressed thoughtful people in the West as among the most monstrous and socially disfiguring aspects of such a sociopolitical system. It is one thing to raise children to be puppets and ideologues; it is another to seek to enhance each child's capacity for altruism, cognitive achievement, emotional maturity, aesthetic self-realization, and warm interpersonal relations. In our public education system we have successfully achieved a kind of approach to schooling that is by and large free from the excesses of both fervent patriotism and religious dogma. (We continue to argue about the boundary conditions—and that is probably an expression of cultural health.)

The same principles can govern the address to the earlier levels of development. All approaches and all interventions would have to strike a balance between being culturally sensitive, interpersonally tactful, and fundamentally humane and bringing help where it is needed, dispelling ignorance where it exists, and fostering optimal patterns of growth-promoting behavior. There would also have to be tough-mindedness present: there are people who should not rear children—or should not rear them without someone present in the home to assure the mental and physical well-being of both the rearers and the infant—and it is vital to identify such instances early and act to prevent destructive patterns from emerging. It is the psychological equivalent of adequate immunization.

Clearly, however, as we ponder such an approach, it is evident that there is a price to pay. But it is not an unheard of price; something like this has happened before. Not so many centuries ago, parents considered the education of the child as a primary responsibility of the family. The family determined whether a child should be taught to read, write, and cipher: if the child were taught, it was the family who did the teaching and brought in a tutor, and, in time, it was the family who decided if the child needed more advanced preparation and should go off somewhere to study.

Much later, this gave way to a different style of preparation. Education was taken over by the state. Every child was required to go to school; it became a matter of law. To fail to educate a child was identified as a form of neglect; the state could take a child away from parents who withheld the child from this essential ingredient of care.

This was an enormous transformation, and it meant giving over to the state what was formerly taken for granted as solely the responsibility of the home. After age 5 or 6, the rearing of the child was no longer exclusively the province of the parents; it became a task shared between the public professionals and the private kin.

To be sure, various compromises could be made. Instead of the child being educated in a public school, families could turn to a private school where their own values might be more precisely realized, they could opt for a religious education where the instruction was more in keeping with familial principles and ideals, or they could even educate their children at home if they would accept close surveillance and rigorous safeguards. But this affected only a tiny percentage of the young; the key reality remained that the average child had to be taken to a specialized setting and put in the hands of nonfamily members who had the expertise and institutional backing to accomplish this part of the child's rearing.

Today yet another element has crept in. There is a tendency for out-of-family experience to begin at much younger ages, often from the first year of life on, certainly from well before the child begins formal schooling. The entire process of child rearing is thus tending ever more toward shared home–nonhome participation. The character of such out-of-home experience is, however, at best an uncertain beast. A sizable percentage, probably the majority of such care, is managed through highly informal arrangements, for example, a relative, the teenager of the neighbor who comes into the home or who lives down the block and takes in local children, an impromptu or ad hoc consortium of neighbors who help each other out, an arrangement among parishioners using volunteers in a church basement. This is so pervasive that the current bestselling book series purchased by grade-school girls is *The Baby-sitters Club*. Beyond such impromptu forms of child management, many agencies now provide more structured kinds of care. But these too offer a wide range of quality which the average parent may have great difficulty assessing. The need for including these sites of care into some kind of coherent public system is pressing, has been strongly advocated, and goes largely unaddressed. Moreover, this meets only the outside face of the problem; it does not attempt to come to grips with what is happening in the home.

Empirically, the address to this cluster of intrafamilial issues is not new. In fact, some aspects of such an approach are already written into law. There is a government program in the United States called Early Periodic Screening, Diagnosis and Treatment (EPSDT), which requires that all infant recipients of welfare be evaluated regularly for physical and emotional development and that any deficiencies be remedied when they are discovered. To put it as kindly as possible, this law has not been systematically enforced. It is not quite a dead letter, but, like the roentgenologic findings previously mentioned, its implications have simply been avoided (Children's Defense Fund, 1978). In a number of settings, different patterns are being developed involving home visitation that would begin to fulfill such an ethical mandate (Olds, 1992; Sluckin, 1989). The point is, the empirical realities attending such an approach have already been considered and addressed—at least in part. But in America the address is half-hearted; as a nation we are averse to transgressing the ethic that preserves the family boundary as sacrosanct. Child development knowledge has, however, arrived as such a level that we must consider whether in all conscience we can continue to maintain this stance. Once we have the skills and the knowledge to enhance the rearing of the *average* child, can we justify withholding that input from any child?

Ethically, children deserve the optimum exposure to growth-promoting experience; ethically families should have the maximum benefit of the culture's skill, knowledge, and expertise in this critical realm. This is a matter with profound implications. In a very real sense the future of any people will be a function of the characteriologic integrity of the individuals in the society. It is now all too self-evident that the growth of character—in terms of impulse control as against impulse enactment, self-destructive as against self-enhancing tendencies, prosocial as against antisocial values, capacities for empathy as against selfish or narcissistic orientations, and the fostering as against the stunting of altruistic potentials in personality development—is profoundly affected by early experience. Nor can one resort to genetic rationalization to explain away disturbed behavior. Genetic realities do indeed make for particular styles of adjustment. Nonetheless, despite the importance of the highly varied genetic makeup of our society, fully 50% of the ensuing behavioral emergents will be determined by the character of early interactional experience (Plomin, DeFries, & MacLearn, 1980). Thus, regardless of how good their endowment might be, for most children inadequate rearing practices can go far to blunting or limiting the realization of their inherent potential. Contrarily, despite genetic endowment that might be associated with alcoholism, criminality, or mental illness, adequate child rearing can head off the expression of the inherent tendencies or temper the degree of their expression. The ethical imperative is plain. Every child should be not merely allowed but also actively helped and encouraged to realize the full extent of his or her own inherent capacities, to be as fully human, humane, and accomplished as lies within the limits of that child's genetic promise. Nothing else will do.

There is the other ethical dimension as well. One of the goals of every family, and, indeed, of a worthy society, should be to maximize the capacity for happiness of each member. Translated into action, this means that trust, self-esteem, and sensitivity to and the ability to relate to oneself and others all should be fostered and strengthened by the nature of the child-rearing practices employed. In most instances, however, with the best will in the world, parents are not aware of what this requires or are unable to deliver it even if they know it. The result is that authors like Henry David Thoreau describe the lives of "quiet desperation" that so many people experience, and the Beatles touch a chord when they sing, "All the lonely people/where do they all come from?" The general level of unhappiness in the world, albeit unquantified, is nonetheless all too apparent. The challenging reality is that by now we know enough about the human condition in general, and about child development in particular, that a significant fraction of this more or less universal distress could be prevented.

There is an ethical imperative that grows out of such awareness. To know how to prevent unhappiness and not to act on that knowledge is an act of violation. Responding to our culture's knowledge of child rearing, and bringing it to bear on the working of every family in the land is the bounden responsibility of the entire society. It means, to be sure, a great deal of sacrifice. In particular we are thus called on to sacrifice some of our right to privacy. We would have to allow the wall around family life to be breached by the state. We would have to subject our child-rearing practices to scrutiny, to criticism, to intervention. This is a very dismaying idea. But the alternative, in its perpetuation of unhappiness, in its promise for the erosion of the true basis for society, and its opening of our culture up to the dangers of massive disruption, is even more troublesome.

It should not be beyond the capabilities of an advanced society to devise appropriate means to achieve the goals set forth here. It involves a balance between the two sets of values. Functionally, this means a compromise between privacy on one hand and growth enhancement on the other. Albeit difficult and implying sacrifice, if the ethical implications are truly weighed, we have reached a point in our understanding of development where this can begin to be accomplished.

References

Caffey, J. (1946). Multiple fractures in long bones of children suffering from chronic subdural hematoma. *American Journal of Roentgenology and Radium Therapy*, 56, 163–173.

Children's Defense Fund. (1978). EPSDT in practice: What's happening in the field? *American Journal of Orthopsychiatry*, 48(1), 77–95.

Council on Ethics and Judicial Affairs, American Medical Association (AMA). (1992). Physicians and domestic violence. *Journal of the American Medical Association, 267*, 3190–3193.

Jecker, N. S. (1993). Privacy beliefs and the violent family: Extending the ethical argument for physician involvement. *Journal of the American Medical Association, 269*(6), 776–780.

Kaplan, S. J. (1991). Physical abuse and neglect. In M. Louis (Ed.), *Child and adolescent psychiatry: A comprehensive textbook* (pp. 1010–1019). Baltimore, MD: William and Wilkins.

Kempe, C. H., Silverman, F. N., Steele, B. F., Droegmuller, W., & Silver, H. K. (1962). The battered child syndrome. *Journal of the American Medical Association, 181*, 17–24.

Kurz, D., & Stark, E. (1988). Not-so-benign neglect. In K. Yilo & M. Bograd (Eds.), *Feminist perspectives on wife abuse* (pp. 249–265). Newberry Park, CA: Sage.

Nozick, R. (1974). *Anarchy, state, and utopia.* New York: Basic Books.

Olds, D. L. (1992). Home visitation for pregnant women and parents of young children. *American Journal of Diseases in Children, 146*(6), 704–708.

Plomin, R., DeFries, J. C., & MacLearn, G. E. (1980). *Behavioral genetics: A primer.* San Francisco, CA: Freeman.

Rawls, J. (1971). *A theory of justice.* Cambridge, MA: Harvard University Press.

Sluckin, A. (1989). Looking out for emotional abuse. *Midwife Health Visit Community Nurse, 25*(3), 93–96.

Spitz, R. A. (1945). Hospitalism: An enquiry into the genesis of psychiatric conditions in early childhood. In R. Eissler et al. (Eds.), *The psychoanalytic study of the child* (Vol. 1) (pp. 53–74). New York: International Universities Press.

Sugg, N. H., & Inui, T. (1992). Primary care physicians' response to domestic violence. *Journal of the American Medical Association, 267*, 3157–3160.

U.S. Department of Health and Human Services. (1988). *Study findings: Study of the incidence and prevalence of child abuse and neglect.* Washington, DC: U.S. Department of Health and Human Services.

Waltzer, M. (1983). *Spheres of justice: A defense of pluralism and equality.* New York: Basic Books.

Warshaw, C. (1989). Limitations of the medical model in the care of battered women. *Gender and Society, 3*, 506–517.

Chapter 2

Idealization

INTRODUCTION (TO CHAPTER 2 AND CHAPTER 3)

Linda Mayes

How is it that as humans we reach for an ideal of who we should be and hold others up to our individual, national, or cultural ideals is the subject of Chapters 2 and 3. In asking about the "role of the ideal in everyday life," Noshpitz shows his creative ability to frame a question in a way that facilitates imaginatively playing with the concept. Through this framing, he is able to consider how ideals are a part of learning even as infants strive to walk independently, an adolescent boy asks a girl out on a first date, or an adult goes for his first job interview. In these and countless other real-life examples, he argues that the ideal is always present, sometimes prominently in the foreground as, for example, when the young basketball player practices hours on end to achieve a semblance of perfection like his idol, and sometimes quietly in the background as in the models or standards that are available for imitation (and encouragement). This is a fresh take on the ideal grounded in everyday life, and, as such, it is easy to underestimate the profound implications of Noshpitz's statement that in every act of learning or developmental progress "there is always the inner awareness of what this would look like if perfected, how it could best be done, how it could most closely be made to approach the ideal." He is arguing that having a model, someone to imitate, is a prime motivator of learning and that it is peculiarly human to compare ourselves with such standards as an individual and group motivator for moving forward. From this commonsense approach to the ubiquity of ideals, he makes the theoretical argument that an individual collection of ideals is contained within the mental structure of the superego and that this individual collection, or ego ideal, shapes and regulates personality.

But how do these "ideals" arrive in the course of development? How is it that the infant has an ideal of "perfect crawling" to strive for or that children have a sense that there is an ideal more perfect than they and worth striving or reaching for? Like many theorists focusing on the centrality of early relationships, Noshpitz argues that ideals are an inherent part of the early interactions between parent and child. If all goes well, parents idealize their children, and, vice versa, he argues, children idealize their parents. He is arguing for a fundamental "idealization mechanism" that is a part of human relationships. We might make a parallel link between Noshpitz's theoretical argument here and Donald Winnicott's (1956) primary maternal/parental preoccupation as a necessary precursor state for the infant's individuality to emerge or for Hans Loewald's (1978) point that the infant's instinctual life takes shape in the early mother–infant relationship. Recent formulations by Peter Fonagy and Mary Target point to parents' ability to mentalize their infants' affective states as key to shaping infants' individuals minds. Winnicott, Loewald, Fonagy, and Target, like Noshpitz, are arguing that infants' representations of affective and bodily experiences are "given voice and shape" in how parents' respond to the infant. For example, the infant's hunger and associated discomfort are both labeled by a parent and also linked, if all goes well, to another's concern and wish to alleviate that discomfort (2002).

But Noshpitz carries the theory one step further in arguing that there is an inherent human need to idealize another person and that the infant, in a near automatic way, idealizes (for better or worse) a parent's behaviors toward him and that those behaviors become the infant's internal template of the ideal. So parents who idealize their infant and through their behavior convey to the baby a sense of perfection give the infant an internal template of a personal, positive ideal. Conversely, parents who neglect, ignore, or misinterpret the infant's distress as a burden and attack on them also give the baby an internal ideal template that is in this case of someone not worth caring for or striving to emulate, or as Noshpitz writes, as someone who does not deserve to have anything good happen to him or her. These kinds of negative inner ideals have a pervasive impact on all aspects of development including learning. With this inner template, there is little worth striving for in children's sense of themselves as an unworthy person.

In this novel concept of an idealization imperative as an essential part of human development, Noshpitz gives ideals a psychological liveliness. Using terms such as *glow, imperious, demanding compliance,* and *clustering,* he conveys the dynamic quality of ideals that can be positive and constructive or negative and destructive. The mixture between positive and negative ideals and the relative domination of one or the other leads to what Noshpitz calls those "gusts of great positive or enormous negative effort humans so often display." Indeed, he suggests that our very humanity, even the tragic side of each of our lives, is our "wobbling" between our efforts to live up to our inner ideas to better ourselves and, at the same time, devalue, even destroy, what we have achieved and what is most valuable to us. As Noshpitz also suggests, it may be easier for us to accept positive ideals than negative, destructive ones. But human culture has no shortage of negative ideals in demonic icons in religion and popular culture and an attraction to the grotesque, hideous, and horrifying, representing our own self-destructiveness. We are attracted to tragedy and horror exactly because, on some level, we recognize the potential in ourselves, or as the saying goes, "There but for the grace of God go I."

How negative ideals are a part of all human development and how the balance between negative and positive ideals link to risk for psychopathology are the links between Chapters 2 and 3. In normal development, idealization is always linked to disillusionment—when we fail to live up to our own ideals or when others fail us. And especially in infancy, when idealization is automatic, infants, at the height of their ideal expectations, inevitably experience disappointment, for no parent can be ideal or perfect at every moment. These inevitable moments of disillusionment set the core for the negative ideals that are a part of every individual's cluster of ideals. Thus, how well the balance between the positive and negative ideals is maintained is central to the link to psychopathology. In normal development, the positive ideal cluster outweighs its negative counterpart; that is, self-acceptance is dominant, and even under stress individuals are confident about their own worthiness and sturdiness. The negative ideal, while present, functions as an inner brake. When the balance between positive and negative ideals is more or less equal, individuals are more easily buffeted against disappointment and less vulnerable to stress. And when the negative ideal predominates, individuals "live always in the shadow of self-criticism, self-devaluation, and even self-hatred," leading to a range of defensive and compensatory responses setting the stage for childhood psychopathology, the subject of detailed clinical descriptions in Chapter 3 that draw on both case material and well-known stories and tragic characters such as Dorian Gray.

In considering these two chapters, we need not accept Noshpitz's apology offered in the beginning of Chapter 2 for what he says is a "hypothetical and very tentative formulation." By positing a near automatic human need for idealization, he offers a remarkably fresh contribution. He takes an everyday condition—our need to emulate others and reach for an individual ideal—and weaves an accessible theory of both normative development and psychopathology based in the earliest of relationships.

References

Fonagy, P., Gergely, G., Jurist, E., & Target, M. (2002). *Affect regulation, mentalization, and the development of self*. New York: Other Books.

Loewald, H. W. (1978). Instinct Theory, Object Relations, and Physic-Structure Formation. *J. Amer. Psychoanal. Assn.*, 26:493–506.

Winnicott, D. (1956). *Primary maternal preoccupation, in through paediatrics to psychoanalysis*. London: Hogarth.

IDEALIZATION

Joseph D. Noshpitz

In attempting a scientific proof, we always seek for direct evidence of what is to be demonstrated. As in many detective stories, however, sometimes we have to be content with circumstantial evidence, at least for a while. That is, we find a suggestive train of data bits that can be best explained in a given way. This does not make the case; it merely offers a possible model of what might be true. Still, to have a working model is by no means a trivial accomplishment; one can at least take potshots at and to prove it is false, or, failing that, can pursue studies as though it were true and see if indeed the predictions made on that basis do pan out. Needless to say, all this introduction is to apologize in advance for a hypothetical and very tentative formulation that cannot be demonstrated directly but that might be tested in a variety of ways. Without further ado, then, let me launch into my theme.

A pervasive and indeed ubiquitous aspect of mental functioning is the formulation of ideals. Given the richness and the power of realistic, logical thinking, it is not immediately self-evident why such an idealizing function should be present. After all, in an evolutionary sense, reason should be advantage enough; why should the human being have acquired the capacity and strong tendency to form ideal versions of the element of experience? If a creature is already able not merely to configure reality and to sort out the logical implications of experience but also to conceptualize abstractions, what positive benefit then follows from the capacity to put an ideal spin on the elements of that experience?

The use and presence of idealization is everywhere. Man is an idealizing animal, and the tendency to come up with some glorified or demonized version of reality seems to be as natural as biology. We live in a world shadowed by the presence of ideal configurations that are inherently unattainable but whose positive forms ever beckon to us, ever lure us with their siren song, and ever confront us with our failure to attain to the idealized state toward which we strive. Indeed, upon reflection, it seems that much of the stress and study of our thinking is in terms of how closely do we, and those with whom we become significantly engaged, live up to or depart from a lurking ideal version of what we think our own or the other's behavior should be?

In view of the omnipresence of this factor of our inner lives, it seems appropriate to ponder the origins of this tendency to idealize, to consider its development, and to review its implications for our everyday functioning. In particular, such a study is likely to cast light on those themes that bridge between the aesthetic, the literary, and the religious on one hand and the scientific and the psychological on the other. For the ideal partakes of the qualities of both realms of human endeavor and is indeed the proper subject matter for each. Beyond that, we might seek to determine whether it plays a role in the creation of the mental and emotional disturbances that are so much a part of the human experience.

In its very nature, the ideal is an elusive entity, one that does not lend itself comfortably to formal exegesis and direct observation. Like such concepts as *meaning*, it is as commonplace as it is ineffable. It is a slippery stuff we work with here, the material of inner experience, without ready referents in external, observable forms. To seize such an entity by the foot, to hold it wriggling in our conceptual grasp, to pin it down to the point at which formulations can be made that will be generally recognized as solid and valid data bits—that is a very considerable challenge indeed. Perhaps, then, it were best to begin by attempting to demonstrate something of the role that ideal formulation plays in our mental life and some of its implications for human adjustment. Beyond that, we can seek to find its place in the formulation and maintenance of certain forms of pathology. This, in turn, could well lead us to a definition of sorts, one that probably cannot contain the essence of what we are here discussing but that might indeed sufficiently circumscribe the field so that, trapped within it somewhere, is the idea we are pursuing. Then it becomes a matter of closing in on it, recognizing all the while that as we get nearer and nearer it becomes ever more difficult to state the final outline of what we are after.

The ideal and the everyday

It may well seem exaggerated to speak of the ideal as playing a role in everyday life. We are likely to consider such concerns as more appropriate to the works of artists and philosophers or as part of our experience in houses of prayer. Let me suggest, however, that we are likely to encounter the phenomenon of idealization in far more commonplace aspects of our thinking. Let us take, for example, the matter of how young people acquire the life skills they need to make their way.

To attain a skill is to achieve a measure of mastery, which in turn brings with it an associated feeling of competence. For the young person—both child and adolescent—each such skill acquisition increases the sense of self-respect, self-esteem, and self-confidence.

Every developmental epoch makes its own demands. There is a time when babies learn to express delight through their smile, when they attain the ability to sit up without support, when they achieve the capacity to regulate their state by getting back to sleep if they wake up, and, presently, by sleeping through the night. In time they are crawling and walking and acquiring language and so on and on for one stage-specific attainment after another, often enough with many such efforts proceeding simultaneously side by side, sometimes in parallel and sometimes in mutual interdigitation and reinforcement. Some of the beginning work on coping and separation depends on the ability to crawl and to walk away from the caretaker and presently to communicate at a distance by means of language; this is then further supported by the new achievement of being able to retain the image of the significant other and to call it up as need be for comfort.

Later skills come in due course as development proceeds—but each involves a learning process, and each has to be incorporated into an existing hierarchical organization. For beginning toddlers, the ability to keep their balance when erect is a major issue and central preoccupation; a year or two later, however, walking is taken for granted, and other issues are in the forefront. While going through toilet training, children may have the attendant problems of mastery and control much on their mind; once the necessary work is done, once the necessary rituals, patterns, and practices for socially acceptable elimination are taken for granted, that universe of striving fades into the background to be replaced by newly emerging concerns about phallic yearnings and fears.

It is likely that the kinds of issues faced by the average developing child are in some measure determined by genetics. All normal children must develop the capacity to talk, to walk, to cope with separation, and so on, and their ability to learn these things at all is inherent to the human constitution. On the other hand, the limits of their capacities are also set by their genetic state. No human is likely to be as agile as even a somewhat retarded gibbon. Humans can be gifted in terms of musculature and coordination, and they can learn and practice and work toward ever greater efficiency. But their genetic limitations are such that they will never swarm up a tree with the inherent competence of even a very average monkey. Humans' learning capacities, while wide-ranging, are in the nature of things limited by the nature of their humanity.

These learning capacities are basic to all skill acquisition. Hence, to study the one, we need to focus sharply on the other.

When we do concentrate our gaze in this realm, it becomes apparent that the learning of a skill is a biphasic phenomenon. It involves at once a perceptual/cognitive/motor dimension and a simultaneous act of ideal formation. Both elements are always present, and they continue to be in active interaction, one with the other, thereafter.

When we speak of learning, what we usually think of is the perceptual/cognitive/motor aspect of this activity. It includes observing, modeling one's behavior according to the circumstances (accepting instruction within a formal teaching–learning structure, or catching on to a skill merely by trial and error, or by seeing someone perform it well), getting some understanding and a measure of cognitive grasp on what the skill entails, and engaging in a series of practice efforts in an attempt to perfect it. It is indeed the latter element that tells us about the ideal dimension, which is part of all skill learning. For there is no encounter with a skill, no effort at skill mastery, without a simultaneous notion of what the performance of that behavior pattern would be like if it were done perfectly. This allows practice and improvement to take place—individuals have a sense of a level of competence toward which they strive, an ideal of what the shape of that skill would be if perfectly enacted. Once such an ideal is established, children have an inner model to emulate and an inner spur toward ever greater striving toward the level of attainment they picture within.

This holds true whether the skill involves competence in debating, in opening up a conversation with a boy or a girl at a party, in engaging in a sport, or in defending oneself when insulted. There are a wide variety of abilities in social interactions, in pleasurable diversions, in acquiring or displaying cognitive achievements, in accomplishing motor feats whether on the sport field or on the dance floor, many of which are of considerable importance to youngsters. But along with each area of encounter and engagement, there is always the inner awareness of what this would look like if perfected, how it could best be done, how it could most closely be made to approach the ideal.

If we shift now from the level of observation to the realm of theory, it is likely that, psychodynamically, the ideal formations of which we speak become part of the superego. Within the superego, there exists a vast sea of ideals, all collectively marshaled under the aegis of the ego ideal and all acting together to form one of the superordinate regulating principles of personality.

In this course of child development, I suggest that idealization is one of the earliest mechanisms to appear. As I see it, this tendency to idealize is very much part of the initial caretaker–infant interaction, when, under optimal conditions, a state of mutual idealization seems to prevail. Mother sees baby as utterly delicious, indeed, infinitely precious, and, within a few weeks after birth, baby is greeting mother's advent with that wonderful toothless smile and with every evidence of total adoration. It seems safe to say that for baby, when things go well, mother is not merely a biologically satisfying presence. In my view, there is a profoundly important psychological dimension here—namely, for baby, mother's presence is glorified, transcendental, wreathed with an angelic halo. In brief, she is idealized.

Unfortunately, the process of idealization is not necessarily positive; it can be negative as well. To understand this, we must look more closely at what ideal formation involves.

In brief, the mechanism of ideal formation is an automatic process, an internalization of intense experience regardless of its quality. Thus, when things do not go well for baby, when mother in neglectful, unheeding, or abusive, then the idealization mechanism continues to work as before, only this time with a negative sign. Those painful experiences then become larger than life; indeed, they become intense and malevolent. As is true of the positive idealizations, they too cluster in the child's superego—but not as inner punishers, inner tormentors, inner haters. Just as babies internalize the love of the one set of experiences, they internalize the hatred of the other they do so in total, massive form that dwells thereafter in the very core of their mental life. This will later act to demean, disparage, and frustrate their attempts at positive achievements. The inner voice conveys a consistent message. It says, in effect: "Everything bad that happens, everything that goes wrong, all the trouble in the lives of those close to you, they are all your fault; you are wicked, you have done wrong, and you don't deserve to have anything good happen to you."

It is evident that, once established, such an inner presence becomes a site for endless later difficulty. In particular, again and again it will act to prevent youngsters from mastering what they must.

But life is always more complicated than our models, and it is likely that babies will have both positive and negative experiences, often enough at the hands of the same caretaker. If enough positive·experiences do ensue, it may well be that the amount of inner self-love coming from these internalized affectionate and approving encounters will more than counterbalance the early negative nucleus. If that occurs, youngsters will emerge with the inner world dominated by an essentially positive superego organization and will feel worthwhile, self-confident, and eager to try to strive toward the ideal level as they go about their skill acquisition. If, however, the negative ideals dominate and the prevailing inner voice speaks harshly and critically, subsequent experience will serve only to confirm the initial formation. If children feel unloved and hence unlovable, deficient and hence doomed to deficiency, devalued and hence driven to self-accusation, soiled or evil and accordingly worthy of self-destruction, then they will either turn away from skill acquisition to begin with, or, even if they acquire them, they will find ways of not allowing themselves to use their skills to succeed.

Many youngsters with the inherent talent and intelligence to accumulate many competencies will nonetheless avoid situations offering them pathways toward growth. Within their classrooms, for example, they will create disturbances and distractions and will often get themselves ejected, or they will eject themselves to begin with simply by not attending class or dropping out of school. The inner nucleus that tells them of their badness convinces them that they are hopeless and cannot learn. Often enough the constellation works outside of consciousness—for no reason they can name, they "just" do not feel like going to school.

The same sort of sequence follows in their social lives. They meet a youngster whose look and manner promise a pleasant and positive relationship. Immediately they fall silent and cannot respond, or they act in some way to spoil the possibility of things taking a constructive turn. In brief, their general pattern of self-defeating behavior moves methodically into the realm of both skill acquisition and skill deployment—and they cannot attain what they desire or use what they attain.

Obviously there is nothing simple about such patterning of human behavior. By dint of talent, of unusual genetic endowment, youths may be able to live up to their ideal in one area, be it ballet, basketball, or brainwork of some kind. Where, however, enough negative ideal formation has taken place, there will be other areas, such as those involving social and interpersonal skills (e.g., keeping a friend, interesting a possible sexual partner, or responding to an admirer), where they undo their happiness and achieve that self-defeat which the negative ideal commands.

Indeed, in adult life, it is not rare to learn of great athletes, with most unusual levels of skill acquisition, who get dismissed from playing sports because they gamble, take drugs, attack women, or otherwise block themselves from realizing the fruits of their extraordinary abilities. This is considered remarkable and dramatic when it involves famous figures, who are prominent in the news. It is, alas, commonplace among the less public interactions that occur so frequently in the lives of all too many adolescents.

Sometimes it happens that the balance of positive and negative elements within the inner ideal structure of particular youngsters is almost equal. There are as many inner voices demeaning them and prompting them to destruction as there are positive summons bidding them to attain the highest flights of achievement of which they are capable. Such youngsters are then particularly vulnerable to environmental cues. Under such circumstances, a smile or a word or a phrase or a sneer and a word of blame can tip the balance radically so that on one occasion they perform brilliantly and the next time fail dismally. Ultimately, over time, such uneven and unpredictable performance is likely to turn away potential supporters to cause these youngsters to lose their welcome, and the negative ideal eventually wins out.

The role of trauma

Within this context, the role of trauma becomes very critical. It is often not appreciated that any encounter with trauma can sometimes add an additional increment to the existing negative ideal. Many people exposed to genuinely catastrophic circumstances seem to get over it after a while and to emerge from the experience relatively unscathed. Many others, however (sometimes the figure is given as 15%), do not. They tend, rather, to internalize the trauma, to build it into their lives, and to carry it forward as part of their everyday experience. In effect, they add the cluster of traumatic memories to the aggregate of painful and negatively idealized configurations that are already in place and that make up the negative ideal.

The net effect of the trauma, then, is to add to the negative and to create an additional negative increment that persists. This component of youngsters' superego has not taken over the function of the catastrophic outside force and continues to traumatize them from within. The memories, the dreadful affective components of the experience all recur, all are run through again and again. The youngsters await their reappearance in a state of heightened alertness; any hint of the traumatic event, a particular sound, a suggestive image, a specific odor, can serve to trigger a reliving of the entire experience—with all the accompanying sense of panic and helplessness that such a flood of recall can bring. But worse still, somewhere within, youngsters so often blame themselves, take on the onus of not having done what they could have done, or what they should have done, to avoid, or protect, or otherwise mitigate the destruction. Because of the very nature of the negative ideal, a site for self-blame and self-criticism is already present; the additional trauma adds its voice to the baying pack.

This in turn has enormous impact on the matter of attaining and employing essential life skills. The traumatized child feels too preoccupied to begin with and too unworthy to end with—the development of these skills seem unattainable, or the attainment inappropriate for one such as he or she.

Let us consider, for example, an adolescent learning to dance. Perhaps a family member or a schoolmate is trying to teach him. But dancing involves a certain amount of body closeness, body movement in unison with another person. If the student has brought forward from early childhood some poorly recalled memory of sexual abuse, some sense of violation for which the inner voice whispers that he is to blame, then the minimal arousal of the dance situation is enough to trigger feelings of wrongdoing, of a need for punishment. This begets sufficient discomfort that, in short order, the lesson is broken off and some excuse is found not to go on. Or, if the youngster stays the course, he is awkward, he steps on his partner's feet, he cannot seem to remember the steps or to keep the rhythm or to move as he should. The inner promptings to fail are too powerful; the skill cannot be acquired.

Another instance might arise in the case of a 12-year-old girl who is learning algebra. Let us suppose as well that she is a youngster with good intelligence and a reasonable potential for understanding. But she has come from a home where girls were not valued as highly as boys, and her older brother and new baby brother are the center of the parents' world. From birth on, her needs were always treated as interruptions in and interferences with parental comfort; in a variety of ways she was made to feel unwanted and a burden. She is angry and bitter but most of all feels that it is her fault, she is the one who is lacking and deficient, she is the one who has something wrong with her. She feels driven to fail, both because it is expected of her (and she is in a sense complying) and because it will frustrate and disappoint the parents who value good grades and who will certainly act punitively when she brings home a poor report card. Indeed, the punishment they then visit upon her is not unwelcome; after all, it provides a modicum of relief from the incessant inner yammering of her hostile negative superego.

Among the other messages she hears at home is the information that boys are smart and girls are dumb—and not only dumb, but especially poor at mathematics. How very natural it is, then, for her to be unable to make any sense out of the symbolic forms that algebra requires. Her mind shies away from this attainment of competence. This is smart stuff, and she is dumb. She is not supposed to be able to learn anything like that. To begin with, she cannot open herself up to the very possibility of such mastery. And to end with, she needs the opprobrium that her failure to learn will certainly bring down on her head. The outer rebuke will ease for a time the sting of the inner tirade. All she wants to do is crawl off in a corner and lick her wounds.

It is in this way that the negative ideal makes its forays into the learning life of young people. The acquisition of skills must be understood in its full dimension—it means not only a specific competence to perform a given activity but also a sense of personal growth, a meaningful advance in one's awareness of status, a possibility of attaining special social recognition, an enrichment of identity formation, and all with a corresponding increase of self-esteem.

It means, in brief, living up to the positive inner ideal, which can be achieved only if one can be freed from the mortmain of the negative ideal. The ideal must be pursuable and accepting of a realistic level of attainment; otherwise the individual can never be at a peaceful momentum or balance. More to the point, the factor of ideal formation and the presence of positive and negative ideals is an aspect of living, one that hovers always over the quality of inner life.

Definition

Let us assume then that an idealizing function exists and that it consists of some mechanism in the psychic apparatus, or perhaps a series of processes, that transform experience in a particular fashion. This mechanism takes what people see, do, know, and think and changes it in powerful and unique ways. As we shall see, it always involves a departure from reality; by definition, the ideal is in some other sphere than the real. This transformation involves several elements. It is not easy to specify what the transmutations must be that bring this conversion about, but a partial list of some of the factors is as follows:

1. There is the matter of dimension. In some way, that which is ideal is larger than life, as life is viewed (e.g., the view of an adult is at variance with the views of an infant or child). There is a quality of aggrandizement here, a tendency to puff things out, to make them stretch beyond the dimensions of the conventional. The ideal tends to be big.

2. Ideals possess a less easily defined quality summarized in the word *intense*. Ideals are not quiet things; associated with them they have an extraordinary quantity of what can perhaps best be expressed as energy. To the extent that they make their presence felt, they are not ordinarily trivial or minor elements of experience; they are instead full of life and bulk large on the inner horizon.

3. Ideals are imperious. This is closely allied to the intensity, but it goes beyond it. The ideal implicitly or explicitly requires it being taken into account. The ideal thrusts itself into awareness and demands a certain attention; it will be heard, and, as a rule, it insists on a certain conformity. One may depart from it, but not without knowing that that is happening, not without paying a certain price. There is always a quality of violation in transgressing the demand of the ideal.

4. The ideal speaks directly to the affects. Albeit in some ways a conceptual entity, in others it is far more an emotional message. It is thus not merely imperious in form or intent; it commands powerful troops, sluices large gouts of affect hither and thither within the psychic apparatus, and can have great force in influencing individuals' psychic lives. Another way of saying this is to look upon the ideal organization as a prime regulator of inner experience. It is like an inner agency that sets standards and lays down rules for conformity.

5. Ideals demand compliance. Perhaps this is merely another way of saying that they are imperious; however, the one is a quality that may be perceived and the other a quality that leads to action. Ideals do lead to action; if anything, that is their most significant trait. They are forever grasping at the levers of behavioral control. Thus, many a resolve that has been formed in someone's mind by rational considerations is thrust brusquely aside at the point of behavioral expression, and some heretofore buried ideal now bursts into consciousness and takes over what the person does. For some individuals, their creative work has such a quality; they allow the unseen ideal to take over, and they become the instruments through which it works. The issue of compliance is always associated with the threat of sanctions. The notion of departing from an ideal is always touched with a special kind of dread.

6. Even more difficult to describe, ideals have about them a sort of glow. As was true with imperiousness, this is in one way a part of their intensity, but it goes beyond that in a different way. The ideals are not only larger than life and more intense, but, in a unique way, they are also luminous. They coruscate; they have a preternatural vividness, an inner radiance, an inherent quality that removes them definitively from the realm of the real. We try to find words to capture this quality; for example, we call some things transcendent in an attempt to typify this curious music of the ideal. Ultimately, as with all attempts to depict inner experience, we must fall back on the hope that all

human experience shares much in common and that the reader will thus know what the author is talking about. This is one of the aspects of ideal formation that enhances their ability to command behavior: they seem to come from another realm and thereby must be obeyed.

7. The ideal formations that emerge as a result of everyday mentation tend to cluster together in a mutually interactive way. Some act to reinforce one another; for example, religious ideals, ethical ideals, group values and concepts of justice and fairness may converge in a given psychic organization and form an internally consistent and supportive system that lends quality and coherence to individuals' lives. Alternatively, however, the several subsystems of ideals may diverge widely and even be at war with one another and thus offer rich grist to the pens of both the prose artist and the student of personality dynamics.

Types of ideals

The nature of the word *ideal* tends to suggest that we are considering something noble and positive, something that would improve whatever it influences, that would make for betterment or involve at least aspirations toward the good. But the processes we have described—enlargement, intensification, affective control, imperiousness, commandingness, transcendence, and clustering—are not necessarily inherent only in the good. As we noted earlier, even brief consideration will allow for their characterizing negative and destructive ideals as well. Indeed, it is evident in the lives of many people that they are held in thrall by the reign of a host of hostile and self-destructive inner biddings, that their regulatory system requires them to seek out self-diminishment and failure with the same avidity and urgency that the conventional view attributes to the quest for achievement and self-realization as the product of the workings of the positive ideal. Thus, the message of such a negative ideal would have to be the opposite of what we ordinarily think of as the role of ideals in our lives.

Positive ideals are presumably what urge us toward doing well for ourselves and for our worlds. By the same token, negative ideals would drive us to seek debasement, humiliation, frustration, failure, the blunting of our happiness, and a recurrent pursuit of misfortune.

Since all people are likely to have elements of both kinds present in their regulatory makeup, the alternate domination of the one ideal set or the other would make for those gusts of great positive or enormous negative effort humans so often display. Indeed, when we read a novel where the characters are all good or all bad, we tend to call the protagonists cardboard figures, with only one face to their image. We realize that both regulatory principles are going to be found in any person (except perhaps the saints, who presumably approach the positive ideal but who would undoubtedly be the first to disclaim any such perfection) and to offer a valid image of a human being requires deference to both elements that are inevitably present. It is not as much that we wobble back and forth in the degree to which we live up to or fail to live up to our positive ideals; in fact, we are caught between inner biddings on one hand to achieve what we can and, on the other, to undo our successes, taint out attainments, and destroy what is most valuable in our lives. In rare and extreme cases, this goes as far as to cause us to destroy our very existence. It should not be forgotten that, for every suicide, many suicide attempts do not prove lethal. More than that, for every actual suicide attempt, there are probably hundreds of moments at which suicide is considered. In short, in its most overt form, in many people's lives, the business of self-destructiveness is by no means a rare phenomenon or an occasional variation on the principle theme. It is common, it is often overt, it is even more often subtle, and, as will presently appear, it plays a role in almost all forms of psychopathology.

It therefore behooves us to try to get some sense of how this negative ideal is configured, what is its nature, how does it manifest itself, and what betokens its presence. To begin with, in keeping with the earlier picture, we are dealing with a set of inner regulators that have great emotional power and that seek to assert control over behavior. As an exercise, we can ask ourselves, if we could actually visualize these ideals, both positive and negative, what would they look like? Since we are dealing with inner constructs that obviously have no representational form, this seems like a silly question. However, as we ponder this matter, it becomes evident that such powerful presences in human mentation could not but have pressed so aesthetic and creative a species as our own to attempt some way to say what they experienced in their inner lives. Nor do we have far to seek, for the positive ideal, religious icons of many kinds, images of saints and deities and angels that purport to give face to such idealistic conceptions fill museums and houses of prayer the world over. If we sought merely verbal formulations of their nature, many, many books exist with just such "cardboard" versions of people in an effort to give form to this conception.

On the other hand, images of the demonic in human affairs are by no means in short supply. Whether we look at statues of Kali from the Hindu faith or to representations of Aztec deities of destruction or to our own tradition's grotesques as envisioned by everything from Hieronymus Bosch to the entire industry of horror and slasher movies, there is an ample provision of demons, devils, monsters, fiends, and, in short, the full panoply of spiritual bad guys. The masks of so much primitive art are evident depictions of frightening abstractions that derive from somewhere in human experience. How better to account for such an array of the grotesque and the hideous than to recognize that the monstrous is indeed part of the makeup of the individual psyche and that it resides in the depths of this negative ideal formation with which we are all endowed. This is the begetter of nightmares, of what we call the nightmarish; it is what we encounter when some of these themes come close to the surface. The nightmare gets its emotional power out of its undisguised revelation of our own self-destructiveness; we see or do something to bring ourselves into great danger, to bring ourselves to the point of abject humiliation, shameful exclusion, massive bodily injury, or death. This, in fact, reflects the goal of the negative ideal, to self-diminish, to self-destruct, to self-victimize. It derives from the earliest and most primitive human experiences, and it provides a constant directive toward failure and hopelessness. Much of the drama in human affairs as perceived by our greatest literary artists lies in this inner struggle of humans against their own promptings to self-destruction. They strive for the best but *somehow* contrive to undo the products of their best efforts and to achieve the worst. The greatest tragedies are those deriving from the "heroic flaw," the vulnerable heel of the otherwise perfect Achilles, the element within that undoes all the talents and aspiration and spiritual greatness of the doomed hero. In that sense, many of us are doomed heroes, given to lofty yearnings and seeking to exercise our talents to the fullest, yet, withal, sooner or later doing what eclipses our own brightness and brings about some compromise with what might have been. Indeed, the greatness of many great people lies in that they have overcome the inner urge toward self-destruction more successfully than most. That alone makes them outstanding. We are all like the atom, filled with enormous energy and extraordinary potential yet seldom able to express that with which we are so richly endowed, and, all too often, when we do, we do it in some great explosion of violence that undoes our well-being.

It is apparent that from this standpoint the understanding and clarification of the self-destructive moiety within is a goal of some significance. To begin with, then let us look at how this develops.

Development

One of the most powerful hypotheses that currently energizes many researchers and theorists is John Bowlby's concept of attachment. This, in simplest form, is the tendency for infants to seek proximity with caretakers and for caretakers to be alert and remain close to their young. This formulation describes behavior, not psychological functions. It thus applies to a measurable kind of phenomenon, and it has the heuristic value of requiring no additional assumption, no theoretical or speculative explanations, beyond itself. It can be observed directly, and, in animal experiments, it can be tested and stressed in a variety of ways to determine its various qualities.

All observers of young human infants have been impressed by the intensely social nature of babies and their enormous press to attach to and interact with caretakers. What is more difficult to discern is the image that forms in babies' minds, the kind of picture babies construct of the primary caretaking adults. It is my contention here that from the very outset, babies' behavior is compatible with the assumption that an early form of idealization is present and that babies experience their mother figure as an "ideal other"—larger than life, glowing, omniscient, powerful, commanding, awesome. We cannot at this point discern the details of that image; perhaps it is no more than a concentrated, emotional blur, but, as one observes babies, its quality comes through with considerable force. The eager smile, the rapturous body language all bespeak the intense pleasure of positive engagement. From the outset, babies are drawn to their idealized other as, for the rest of their lives, they will be drawn to what is held to be the ideal. Its joy in closeness is obvious; its relief from distress by the presence, touch, voice, holding of the important other, evident and predictable. For the rest of its life course, this special, intense pleasure is what an encounter with a positive ideal will offer.

This does not gainsay for a moment the existence of a real relationship as well. Between mother and baby, a series of active exchanges, interactions, mutual cueing, and other forms of mutual engagement will be in a state of constant dynamic commerce with the other. Even at this early time, the ideal must confront the real, and the clashes between the two will be critical marking points for the work of development. Both active advance and fixated arrests will flow from these confrontations. Where the caretaker must frustrate and delay gratification or withhold certain items completely (e.g., a baby with milk allergy will have to learn to accept substitutes, a baby growing up in a poverty-stricken setting may not even have enough food all the time), the baby may be offered solace and alternative forms of comfort—and may thus learn to tolerate some measure of failure of the ideal and to master incremental bits of frustration—and in this way be helped to learn self-regulation, trust, and impulse control. Or, a baby who is neglected, or episodically deprived and overgratified, may develop negative ideals, terrifying presences, monstrous versions of a caretaker who brings pain and torment. For such children, the world is a dreadful, pain-filled, unpredictable place, where they are hounded from within as well as deprived from without and in which relationship is to be managed only by magical ritual or by massive emotional protest or by manipulation; only in such a manner can they get minimal solace of urgent needs. In short, they may suffer serious malformations of early character buddings.

The role of disillusionment

The picture so far is of babies trying as best they can to form connections with an idealized caretaker. The idealization is primary: the babies do not choose to do this; they can no more help themselves than they can stop themselves from hearing. They are hungry for social engagement, and, when the interaction is rewarding, the transfiguration of the object into ideal proportions follows automatically. This in turn sets babies up for great yearnings for and expectations of more ecstatic experiences and a proportionally tremendous let-down if the idealized caretaker fails to respond in a good way. Babies need to have these joyous experiences again and again to set up a solid core of positive self-feelings within the regulatory apparatus. By the same token, each time there is a disappointment or a failure in empathic responsiveness, babies are hit hard. It is important to recognize that the sharpest edge is given to these experiences by the frustration of the attempt to maintain the ideal—and the ensuing sequence involves not only the failure to solidify the formation of the positive ideal but also the automatic construction of another increment to add to the negative ideal. It is the fact that babies love so intensely and overvalue so excessively that makes the disappointment in relationship so catastrophic. This, then, is the heart of the traumatic experience; seen from this standpoint, trauma is not so much the flooding of the ego by painful stimuli as it is disillusionment—or the flooding brought on by the dint of disillusionment. (Later on we will hear from victims of terrible natural disasters—hurricanes or earthquakes or tornados—that the truly damaging component of the experience was that they lost their faith in God or that they lost their basic sense of security in the stability of their world.)

In their own primitive way, young babies are perhaps the most extreme of lovers, the most sedulously adoring of devoted followers, and, should bad things happen, the most terrified of victims. By the middle of the first year of life, the intensity of the positive infantile idealization is perhaps at its highest pitch. It is so great that Margaret Mahler was led to believe that the infant literally experiences a sense of fusion with the caretaker. This position has subsequently been challenged by Horner and Stern, but once one considers the nature of the idealizing function, it is evident that any individual—even adults—possessed of such intensely idealized attachment feelings will, at certain moments, experience a sense of merger with the loved one—and will do this side by side with a perfectly clear and realistic awareness of both the self and the other as separate and autonomous.

At this point, children are becoming persons of far greater complexity than before. At 6 months of age, children can retain a sitting position and look out at the work quite differently; they can soon pull themselves up to standing, can manipulate sounds in interesting ways, are beginning to understand the import of many words, and, in interaction with its caretaker, can send many cues that evoke desired responses. Where things have gone well, it is learning about its own competence and developing a nascent self-confidence. And it has frequent thrilling and exciting play interactions with the adored other. Life can be rich, full, stimulating, and instructive. It is, more than anything else, interesting. Over time, however, it is this interest in the world that becomes the serpent in the garden; it is what lures and beckons and begins to lead babies to detach from their caretaker, to invest in the world and, presently, in parts of the self. Babies are entranced by their own capacity to vocalize, by their ability to manipulate objects. They get interested in toys, and some of these draw their affectionate regard. In a few months some element in their treasure house of possessions will become sufficiently idealized that babies will not willingly part with it— and we will call it a transitional object.

Idealization and psychopathology

Once we have encountered the role of disillusionment in infant development, we are able to begin to understand how it contributes to the development of psychopathology. We can consider several different sequences. To begin with, there is the anlagen of normality, where the positive ideal cluster well outweighs its negative counterpart. Where the self-accepting, self-loving, and self-valuing regulatory elements are dominant, individuals feel good about themselves, sense the inner core of self-confidence, and have an organization that makes for resilience in the face of stress. Even in a world that is frustrating, demeaning, and injurious, there is always the inner sense of lovability and worthiness to help tide one over. The negative ideal is there, but it functions as a normal conscience, unusually in abeyance, evoked by temptations that beckon toward transgression, and occasionally punitive in the face of some violation of one's inner code.

Another possible state of affairs is one where the balance is more or less equal between the two regulatory agencies. In such instances, individuals are by no means so comfortable and are far more vulnerable to stress. Indeed, the most striking characteristic of this state of affairs is the responsivity of the person's state to external influences. A word of praise or a critical attack can send the individual into either transports of exuberance or fits of despondency. Even the performance of a learned skill can vary enormously depending on which ideal cluster is in ascendance. For the external event acts as a prompter and reinforcer for the delicately poised inner regulatory system and will tip it one way of the other, depending on the message received. An external attack will provoke an internal assault, whereas an external encomium will arouse the available store of inner self-love. Given a powerful, negative ideal regulator at work, individuals are likely to be moody and very subject to a word of praise here or a critical comment there.

A third possibility will be the heavy weighting of the negative ideal. Here is the true seed-bed for psychopathology. The person lives always in the shadow of self-criticism, self-devaluation, and even self-hatred. His moods tend to be gray, and there are recurrent thoughts of injury or self-loathing. Many defensive patterns will inevitably be invoked. Thus, the individual may resort to dissociation, where a bland, empty, false self to ward off the inner pain. There may be many forms of externalization, such as projection, projective identification, counterphobic efforts, or conversion of the passive into the active, where the inner regulatory self-hatred is denied and instead turned outward and assigned to some external agency. The inner conflict is thus converted to an outer war, and the individual builds his life around the new arena for action—usually achieving the goal of the inner regulator and destroying himself in the process.

Sometimes the defensive behavior takes the form of a reversal of affect, where the self-hatred is converted into a sort of elated self-aggrandizement, a brittle excessive gaiety that is a way of taking flight from the true inner state.

In short, a host of coping and compensatory mechanisms are likely to be invoked by the presence of a dominant negative inner ideal. This is hard to live with as such and would be the basis of much that we call childhood depression. The critical point here is that we are not looking at a state as such; we are encountering a dynamically active product of a particular constellation of childhood experience visited on a vulnerable infant. The additional increments of defensive adaptive constructions that then follow give rise to the various syndromes of childhood disorder. In particular, they make for a condition where the individual is driven in a variety of ways to seek his own downfall, to destroy his own happiness, to undo his own success.

Chapter 3

Idealization and psychopathology
Forms of expression of the negative ideal

Joseph D. Noshpitz

In developing the recognition and description of the idealization function, the resulting superego image that emerged was a relatively simple one: there were a cluster of negative ideals and a cluster of positive ideals, each functions as a regulator, and the ego had to respond to, bear the demands of, and accept the impress of each.

Clinical experience, however, demonstrates that, albeit true in larger outline, this is an all too simple model of how things are actually structured. Thus, certain activations are very specifically context responsive. That is, for a given child, under most circumstances, the inner balance may remain tipped in favor of positive ideal dominance, but, when a particular set of conditions appears, this balance may reverse itself.

To illustrate this, let us consider a 9-year-old boy whose parents have divorced. He lives with his mother and has regular visits with father. In his therapy, it is evident that the youngster admires his father and yearns for his father's approval. However, he also speaks frequently of how frightened he is of his father, how averse he is to sleeping over at his father's house, and how bad his father makes him feel by the harsh critiques directed toward him (if, for example, the 9-year-old does not get the highest mark in class on a test or, if he fails to produce a report card with straight As).

On the other hand, his mother describes the boy as showing very mixed reactions toward her. By and large, he is very attached to her. She gets him many gifts, there are a host of positive activities they engage in together, and they enjoy each other's company. Periodically, however, he turns against her with great violence, both verbal and physical. When he does so, he will use such pseudo-adult terms as "you fucking woman," he will accuse her of being the one to break up the marriage with father, and, at times, he will lose control to the extent of attempting to choke her. Following these outbursts, he will be overcome by remorse, will sob, and will apologize but then will reverse again and justify himself by explaining that it is her fault, that it was she who married his father so that he carries his father's bad genes for rage and violence.

By and large this youngster's language and fund of knowledge suggest high intelligence. He does well in school (although he is at times preoccupied and far away), and his problems seem confined to those intervals when he is home with his mother. His father describes him as a perfectly normal boy, except for his fear of sleeping over (which his father attributes to his mother's malign and unfortunate influence).

In their interactions, his father is said to treat his mother as a nonperson. They have occasional exchanges (confined to such matters as time and place of pickups), in the course of which his father conducts himself in as distant and as curt a manner as possible. At best, he will barely talk to his mother; often he does not respond to her when addressed; he not infrequently hangs up on her in the course of phone conversations; or rolls up the car window should she attempt to address him, and, when he calls for his son or, when the parents chance to meet at school, he is frigid, aloof, and avoids eye contact with her. In the nature of things, there are repeated questions of where and when (When will he pick their son up for a trip? Where they will be going? If father and son are to be away for several days, what hotel or dwelling they will occupy? When will they be back?); under such circumstances, the father is meticulously vague, uninformative, and nonspecific. Much of this is enacted in front of the 9-year-old. On one occasion, after a trip abroad, his father retained the boy's passport. This was during the summer, and the mother also wanted to take their son out of the country. She repeatedly requested the passport and finally stood at the door of the father's residence and insisted that the time constraints were such that she must have it back. The father thereupon became so choleric that the nearby neighbors were alarmed.

The boy's behavior is replete with paradoxes. Although he strives to conceal it, he is an obviously troubled and unhappy child, but, in his therapy, he insists repeatedly that he has no problems, that there have been no attacks on his mother that week, so there is nothing to talk about. (Subsequently, his mother recounts that this is not true.) During his therapy hours, he busies himself by patiently building houses of cards or towers composed of complex stacks of blocks, all of which presently collapse. While this dramatizes the vulnerable and precarious state of his inner control apparatus, it does not address the profoundly self-destructive elements in his makeup. Here, in the critical realm of his psychopathology, he refuses to work. Thus, one set of paradoxes lies in his consistent attempts to evade and to nullify the possible helpful effects of psychotherapy.

Another paradox rests in his approach to his parents. The boy seeks always to placate and to please the father, who is harsh and critical, and, at the same time, he acts repeatedly to provoke and alienate the mother, who cares for him, worries over him, and seeks to promote his healthy development.

The attempt to construct a model of this boy's dynamic inner organization is inherently complex. One needs to posit the presence of a highly charged set of negative idealizations composed in large part of early internalizations. Presumably, these were encountered and incorporated when he was quite a young child, at the time of the acerbic, preseparation exchanges between his father and mother (he was 4 when the father left home). From a very young age, the child lived in a climate of rage, outburst, and confrontation. He had learned to fear his father's wrath and emotional eruptions (which had ultimately led to the parental separation). It would appear that in the child's mind, these events were all connected with himself, with his pre-oedipal and oedipal yearnings, with his inner sense of badness, and with his inability to heal the rift between his parents. This cluster of negative experiences became idealized and stored within his superego as one pole of powerful presence.

The other pole, of course, consisted of his stable and maintained interactions with an unusually caring and supportive mother as well as the moments of gratifying, albeit intermittent, positive experiences he shared with the father.

He came out of it all with an enormous hunger for approval and acceptance by his father and with a sense of intense dependency on his mother. Objectively, he feared his father's wrath; indeed, he sometimes felt a genuine sense of danger when with his father, and he often anticipated punitive, critical responses on his father's part. On some deeper level, it is likely that he was concerned his father might reject and abandon him as he had rejected and departed from his mother. With his mother, he had moments of great tenderness and comfort; when they were together, for the most part he was well behaved and clearly enjoyed their interactions. In much that he said, however, it was clear that he could never quite forgive his mother for failing to protect him from his father (although it is less obvious whether he blamed his mother for not fending off the internal father or the real external person—or both).

As noted, he had other moments when he reproduced the father's attitudes. He was arrogant, demanding, domineering, grandiose, accusatory, grossly insulting, and, occasionally, violent. Sometimes, the complex sequence of inner responses would be all too predictable: if he had just come back from a visit with the father during which he had had to contain his fear and his rage, this would often be a trigger to unleash the force of the negative ideal. During such father–son interactions, the child would be at the mercy not only of his demanding parent without but also of the critical and hostile presence within. He would feel worthless and evil. On his return to his mother's home, he would lash out at her in part, at least, to get her to punish him. He would feel guilty at once for missing his father, for having "caused" his father to leave, and for being the cause of his father's rejection of his mother. He would have to find relief from this guilt. He feared doing any of this punishment seeking with the father—he was much too dangerous—so he would discharge this mass of negative inner tension toward the mother. He was safe with her; she had never left him (except when the father took him away on vacation); she had stated repeatedly that she never would, and no matter what he did, he was sure he could not drive her away. So within that context, his full burden of negative ideal response found expression—and again and again, the mother had a major problem on her hands.

In this clinical vignette, one begins to get a glimpse of how complex is the structuring of the negative ideal. It is evident that ideal structures are organized internally in many different ways and find expression in equally various fashion. They can become a repository for inner hatred and devaluation that remains forever concealed from the world, even from one's intimates. Indeed, if revealed at all, they are likely only to be hinted at by certain odd remarks or unexpected out-of-character responses that the individual evinces and that come to have meaning only in retrospect. It is these accumulations of inner self-hatred that give rise to the unexpected and incomprehensible suicides that periodically impinge on public aware-ness. Or, when stored up in this fashion, they can be endured only if they can find channels for discharge, which are in themselves concealed. Indeed, they may be confined to very limited areas of expression, which are elabo-rately protected. Thus, our young patient, who can tell his father of his ter-ror only via the one overt behavioral oddity of being unable to sleep over, then attempts to discharge the overwhelming inner tensions by provoking and seeking punishment from his mother. It is not altogether surprising that he does so in the one way that to him seems most efficient, by mimick-ing his father (i.e., by doing unto his mother what his internalized negative ideal does unto him). He faces several dreadful challenges. His father left once; he may leave again. In the child's mind, his father left because of him, perhaps because of something he did or failed to do, perhaps because of his mother's preference for him. His unconscious erotic wishes toward his mother are as unthinkable as they are unspeakable. He bears the unbear-able onus of the entire failed marriage and its unhappy sequelae. He at once overcomes the dread of loss of his father by becoming his father (which also justifies his deeply repressed erotic fantasies), and he manages the guilt of it all by driving his mother to set limits and restrictions on his behavior. The attacks on his mother serve at once to express the erotic components of his inner life and to keep them at bay.

This does not begin to exhaust the multiple ways that such inner pres-ences manifest themselves. The warring factions within find expression as compromise behaviors toward the world. It is no surprise that such struc-tural aspects of human unhappiness have been discovered and rediscov-ered many times. Creative artists have sought repeatedly to portray them in various literary forms. Thus, in *Moll Flanders* (Defoe, 1973), an account is given of a certain kind of self-destructiveness. The book is written in the first person by a sort of antiheroine who remarks of a group of men:

...these men were too wicked even for me; there was something horrid and absurd in their way of sinning, for it was all a Force even upon themselves; they did not only act against Conscience, but against Nature; they put a Rape upon their Temper to drown the Reflections which their Circumstances continually gave them; and nothing was more easie than to see how their Sighs would interrupt their Songs, and paleness, and anguish sit upon their Brows, in spight of the forc'd Smiles they put on; nay, sometimes it would break out at their very Mouths, when they had parted with their Monie for a lewd Treat, or a wicked embrace; I have heard them, turning about, fetch a deep Sigh, and cry *what* a *Dog* am *I*! Well *Betty*, my Dear, I'll drink they Health tho', *meaning the honest Wife*, that perhaps had not Half a Crown for herself, and three of four Children: The next Morning they are at their Penitentials again, and perhaps the poor weeping Wife comes over to him, either brings him some Account of what his Creditors are doing, and how she and the children are turned out of Doors, or some other dreadful News; and this adds to his self Reproaches; but when he has Thought and Por'd on it till he is almost Mad, having no Principles to Support him, nothing within him or above him to Comfort him; but finding it all Darkness on every Side, he flyes to the same Relief again, to Drink it away, Debauch it away, and falling into Company of Men in just the same Condition with himself, he repeats the Crime, and thus he goes every Day one Step onward of his way to Destruction.

This paradoxical mixture of self-reproach and self-destructiveness that Defoe describes makes sense if one applies the concept of an internalized negative ideal at war with the positive ideals within. These men are not guilty only when their wives confront them; they are always guilty, always hagridden, always alive to what they know is right, but always at the mercy of the inner demon that drives them so inevitably toward their ruin. With an inner life dominated by such a powerful negative ideal, the very relief they seek compounds the destructiveness of the predetermined outcome—indeed, it is part of the destructive pattern. They know better, but they cannot act better, and the reason for this state of affairs is that the existing inner structures assure that they can seek only self-debasement and injury.

Perhaps the greatest and most notable literary attempt of this kind is to be found in the famous work of Oscar Wilde, *The Picture of Dorian Gray* (1890). To be sure, this is a work of fantasy. Yet its power lies in the extraordinary closeness of the magical elements in the story to the actual state of affairs in the formation of the superego. The antihero of the story is a young man who, at the outset, is altogether charming in appearance but is self-centered, petulant, and demanding in his relationship life. He is seduced into a state of total selfishness by the philosophical meanderings of a cynical aristocrat and begins a career of total venal lechery and debauchery.

He has in his possession a full-length painting of himself, which he hides in a closet where no one but he can see it. As he sinks ever deeper into his life of crime and excess, his physical appearance does not change. Instead, it is the painting that becomes marked and disfigured and transformed. At the end of the story, the painting is that of a monstrous human being with all the vile ugliness of inhuman wickedness and total abandonment to sin etched deeply into its appearance. Dorian Gray is all too aware of what is happening to the painting and grows to loathe it more and more as the story proceeds. At length, he can endure it no longer—he stabs the painting in the heart and falls dead.

In a sense, this is a graphic portrayal of the process by which an internal negative ideal comes to be formed. Each succeeding act of wickedness adds another increment to the image, an image concealed from everyone and known only to the person who harbors it. The acts of wickedness are the violations of the mandates of the positive ideals; from an external point of view, these may be of trivial character, but, as seen by the perpetrator, they are immense transgressions that merit only total condemnation and condign punishment. As they accrue, they come to offer a condition of great danger to the individual. Should they arrive at a sufficient mass, the force of their self-destructive demands becomes critical. As this accrual proceeds, the individual comes under ever increasing pressure to do something—something that will offer relief. Here the sequences that can follow become multipotential. And it is here that our story really begins. For it is in the type and variety of discharge of an inner negative mandate that vital sectors of behavior are given both their color and their form. And the spectrum of possible colors and forms is as various as mankind.

To begin with, the nature of the inner communication from the unconscious negative ideal to the aware self is usually not explosive (in the ordinary sense of that word). Instead, it may be a slow drip of negative feeling that diffuses its coloring throughout everyday experience. Alternatively, it may take form as recurrent waves of negative feeling that surge to the surface at more or less irregular intervals. Again, the negative nucleus may be successfully repressed and lie buried—until some trigger is pulled. Its impact will then be felt, sometimes like a knife thrust of guilty ideation, sometimes like a great avalanche of pain-filled feeling, sometimes like a wild impulse to do something to one's own disadvantage, in any case, something that is released only in response to particular contexts. It were as though specific environmental stimuli could awaken and unleash this inner presence. Sometimes the inner assault is entirely unconscious, although its effects are all too evident. This, for example, can lead to surprising errors, to untoward slips of hand or tongue, or, more seriously, to single-car accidents or other self-destructive events. Indeed, if the intensity of the inner eruption is sufficiently powerful, it can take form as overtly suicidal behavior.

A critical variable that affects the form of its expression is the nature, the array, and the quality of the defense mechanisms and character proclivities that characterize that person's adjustment. These specify whether an individual is an internalizer or an externalizer, whether the effects of the internalized negative message will be experienced as depression or anxiety, whether the inner pain will always be felt in the background or whether it will emerge as a sequence of intrusions into an otherwise comfortable comportment, and so on for many discriminatory variables. Of cardinal importance is the extent and the degree of externalizing tendencies that may be present.

Before we undertake exploring that dimension, however, let us return to the earlier account of the way the negative ideal can make its presence felt. The first image was that of a slow inner seepage of destructive feelings that color everyday life. What this gives rise to is essentially a state of negative mood. For many people, the ability to live with such dangerous inner forces is managed by a pattern of chronic punishment from within. This can include all the panoply of depression: feelings of sadness and unworthiness, a general slowing down of responsiveness to the world, a lack of pleasure in the ordinary sources of human diversion, feelings of being undeserving of praise, of being ugly or hateful or unlovable, all combining to give rise to a more or less stable and persistent inner emotional tone. To be sure, this can in some measure vary in response to circumstances. Yet, in many instances, it tends to be maintained at a given level from which it departs only incrementally.

In terms of the role of the idealizations, the mood with which one lives is the resultant of the vectoral forces generated by the summation of the two ideal clusters. Where negative ideals predominate and produce the more powerful vector, the resultant mood may be colored by a sepia sense of personal badness, a tonic sense of worthlessness, an overhanging feeling of being accused and in the wrong, a threatening sense of foreboding, a press of inner tension that feels like one will explode, or a haunting feeling of imminent danger. Depending on the individual's genetic disposition, this can be sensed as an oppressive heavy sadness or as an awareness of constant, lurking anxiety. The source of these mood states is essentially the same, but the particular subjective quality that emerges as conscious experience is a matter of the underlying biologic/temperamental/personality organization. In one instance, anxiety may predominate, in another feelings of sadness and depression, and in yet another both. Whatever the final form of expression, the dynamo that energizes these feelings is the idealized, hostile, critical, accusatory, inner presence.

Up to this point, our emphasis has been on the workings of the negative ideals. By the same token, should the resultant of which we spoke express the dominance of the positive ideal cluster, this could make for a state of sunny, optimistic, cheerful pleasance, a feeling that God's in his heaven and all's right with the world, a positive state, in short, that may be as tonically persistent as its negative counterpart can be. This would hopefully be the "norm" for people, although for most individuals the shared aggregate of cultural experience suggests that this is only occasionally the way they feel. Obviously little that smacks of hard scientific evidence can be adduced to make the case that this is so or not so. The census bureau does not try to measure the ongoing mood state of the average citizen, nor do the important mental health surveys serve us well in this connection. Indeed, somewhat as is the case with good posture, we recognize it more in its lack than in its presence. Until our child-rearing methods improve, it is not likely that we will be able to protect and cushion our youngsters against the many disillusionments that will mark their development. And the negative ideals will thrive accordingly.

Thus far we have talked of one way that the presence of the negative forces exerts its regulatory sway. It determines the color of consciousness. It specifies what may come to awareness, and it provides the tonic consequence of a destructive ideal organization, the establishment of mood. As noted, however, there are a host of alternative routes for such ideals (and the stream of emotions they generate) to find expression. Thus, this state of affairs may give rise to a number of character structures that include chronic forms of self-defeating, self-damaging behavior. Another channel for such expression is through explosive outbursts in the course of which much work by the positive elements of personality is undone, and individuals offset their own talents and relationship achievements by the episodic eruption of socially unacceptable behavior. For some individuals, yet another variant takes form as a pattern of risk-taking behavior. In these instances, the afflicted persons are driven again and again to expose themselves to the possibility of disaster, often with the feeling that this is the height of pleasure, the greatest possible thrill. In effect, they seek to find a compromise out in the world for the hazardous and uncertain situation within. One of the commonest varieties of this pattern is that of the gambler.

But this is only one of the expressions of the mechanism of projective externalization we spoke of earlier. This mechanism is a fundamental building block for much that is great and much that is disastrous in human affairs. The tendency and capacity to externalize one's inner life, to experience and to reenact in the outside world the full panoply of inner creations, yearnings, and conflicts, make at once for enormous symbolic and esthetic achievement and for the possibility of deadly serious self-destructive behavior. In general, the reason for such externalization is in the service of seeking relief. The regulatory agencies give rise to a sense of tension; something wells up from the unconscious and presses on the inner surface barrier of consciousness. An attempt may be made to press it back down, to make it unconscious once again, and most such efforts are probably successful. Given a state of affairs where the effort to repress is insufficient, where it fails, then some alternative means of management is necessary, and one such means is to take the inner drama (the strife between regulatory voice and reality preference) and to turn it out on one's world. In particular, the most pressing and disturbing affects are likely to be so outwardly emplaced. The gambler, for example, has a mixture of both positive and negative inner messages. The positive ideals tell him he is loved and admired and worthy and that he will achieve whatever he strives for. The negative ideals say that he is evil and should be destroyed. He manages to repress some of the hostile inner voice and allows himself to be carried along by the current of the positive message. He is full of confidence, he has his transitional object (rabbit's foot? lucky coin? some other object connected with the source of the positive ideal?) in his pocket and cannot lose; he is certain that he will achieve, he will triumph, he will attain what he seeks. But he is also committed to self-destruction. He is inwardly driven by his need to fail, to be punished, to be the worthless person the inner presence names him to be. His compromise is to externalize the whole drama. He thrusts himself into harm's way again and again, speaking only of the big win that he is sure will come and ever and again so ordering his life that he loses and loses and loses.

Such a risk-taking lifestyle is not uncommon and, in most instances, results in the mandated failure. Sometimes there are startling successes achieved along the way, and in an occasional case, the very fact of the success validates the positive ideal and enhances it to the point where it comes to prevail. But much the commoner outcome is that the involved individual acts as the slot machine *ingénue*—one hits a minor jackpot early in the evening, and before the night is over, it has all been put back into the machine along with some additional, and much needed, personal assets. It is not by chance that one of the common demeaning terms of our time is to be a "loser." Implicitly, it recognizes a pattern of commitment to failure.

Unlike mood, many of the characteriologic conditions that make for self-destructiveness, albeit stable, do not involve evident affective coloring. The individual may be cheery and positive, upbeat in his approach to life, certainly not evidently troubled. It is only when one studies the history of that person's experience that the red thread of chronic self-destructiveness becomes evident. One or more bad marriages, psychosomatic difficulties, accidents, legal problems, and inability to maintain consistent employment all may be present at different times and in different degrees. In contrast to this, on the other hand, there is a great deal of clinical experience that involves acute episodic outbursts of a destructive kind. Typically, these take form as clonic expressions of affect, emotional eruptions rather than tonic states. Indeed, the child described in the opening example illustrated this—in giving an account of his troubles, little was said about the youngster's everyday mood and much about his explosive outbursts toward his mother. To understand these situations, however, we must redirect our attention to the complex matter of how and where the vulnerabilities are structured and what are the kinds of triggers, internal and external, that unleash negative feelings within.

In fact, it is quite difficult to conduct such an exploration. By and large, we cannot get the data directly. Some of the victims of this condition are all too aware of the negative ideals within and tend to cover up their presence and to keep a veil of obscurity around them. Indeed, as our first approach, we must turn to the theme of concealment. As was true with Dorian Gray, subjectively, the presence of such a negative inner nucleus is often experienced as a taint, a great fault, an inner deformity, something that must at all costs be hidden from the world. Thus, during the latency years especially, such youngsters may early learn to dissimulate, to put on an air of compliance and debonair "ordinariness," while inside they are tormented, subjected to recurrent bursts of self-abuse and inner condemnation, and all too aware of what they regard as a loathsome ugliness within, which they strive by every means at their command to conceal from their social world. Not that this state is hermetically sealed from view. Occasional references they make about being bad, or ugly, or friendless speak volumes for the actual state of affairs. The rather morbid fascination with monsters that preoccupies many children tells something of their inner milieu along with the associated self-feeling. The negative ideal is personified as the monster on the outside. When they see it enacting its fiendish behavior, it stirs up within them a froth of terrifying fantasy. Then, as the alien, demon, zombie, vampire, or werewolf (as the case may be) is eventually conquered or exorcised, it may give significant relief to the inner conflict—for the moment. But only for the moment; such youngsters want to go back and see this show again and again. Often enough, however, whatever relief ensues is far outweighed by the recurrent intrusions of frightening fantasy unleashed by the story. When this happens, the scenes in the movie will have acted like a premature interpretation—they confronted the children with too much, too fast. The visual enactment broke past the repressive barrier and brought the demon within too close to the surface of consciousness. The power of the inner model to exercise its authority is then evidenced by the many days it may take before these children can again endure being alone or being in the dark—that is, for the inner disturbance to be contained, the repressive barrier restructured, and the fears thus generated to die away.

It is important to note again that this inner demonic presence can often be sequestered. Thus, the degree and severity of this internal stress is ordinarily held in repression and may become evident only at certain moments of vulnerability. A common site for such experiences is at bedtime, when children cannot allow the adult to leave them until they are fast asleep. What are they afraid of? The inner negative ideal is often projected onto a cultural myth, like the bogey man. Sometimes a current event is blamed— the news that day carried a story of a kidnapping. Or a more generic theme may appear: "A bad man will come and kill me in my sleep." In the preschool years, such childhood difficulties are quite common. As a rule, parents take them for granted—it is the way children are—parents soothe them, calm their fears, reassure them, read to them, sing to them, or just stay there until their children are asleep. Little thought is given to what must be present inside their minds to have given rise to such concerns. The fact that there is an inner generator of such disturbing preoccupations generally receives no thought at all. When such behavior persists into the grade school years, however, it becomes far more problematic. The parents know something is wrong. They may not do much about it, but they know that their child has a problem.

Less frequent, perhaps, but far more striking, is the state of affairs where children do not allow themselves to *have* access to any conscious awareness of the inner terror. All they know is a sort of inner unease, a sense of not feeling good inside, As a result, and for no reason they can name, they displays a pattern of provocative, punishment-seeking behavior. This keeps the youngsters in a state of constant confrontation with the outside world—they are all too likely to be recurrently admonished and punished (by, e.g., time-out, loss of dessert or privileges, deprivation of gifts or allowance, spanking). The reasons for seeking the punishment are multiple. For one thing, these children may need to atone for their bad wishes or evil thoughts. But far more likely is the grim recognition that a vital balance must be maintained. There is the constant pressing menace of the tormenting inner ideal. The youngsters may submit to it quietly and just suffer. Or they may seek to offset it by finding some source of external punishment, some authority figure or more powerful peer whom one can antagonize. Then, as long as the punishment is being administered, as long as the suffering occurs on the outside, these children are less troubled by the feelings within. In short, they have to satisfy this inner voice, and it can be done by absorbing the pain internally and feeling terrible about themselves or by getting someone else to make them suffer—which allows for a host of coping devices: a sense of injustice, a pattern of denying everything, lying, evading, indulging in elaborate dreams of getting even, and even acts of retaliation.

Obviously, as is true with all human problems, with this condition too there are degrees of disturbance. The children's misbehavior can be of minor degree, annoying but not really troublesome, and evoking scolding or correctional management methods. Or, as in the case cited, there may be episodic explosions of wildly inappropriate behavior that are literally dangerous to everyone involved. When things get to that pass, the social implications are of a different order of magnitude and can create immense turbulence. The obverse side of such behavior implies either that the primary inner demons are of extraordinary proportions in their cruelty and intensity, that the apparatus for repressive containment is particularly deficient, that the external circumstances surrounding the children are filled with tension and amount to a state of chronic trauma, or any combination of these.

ORGANIZATION OF THE NEGATIVE IDEAL

A host of specific contexts likely bring the effects of the inner conflict into overt expression. Obviously these will vary with each individual's temperamental allotment of traits and vulnerabilities and with all the rich multipotentiality of human contexts. One way to try to understand them is by designing a model for how the ideal structures are organized. To the extent that the model is valid, it will reflect the sites of vulnerability and, implicitly, the contexts that are most likely to evoke active responses by an aroused ideal. In effect, we need to seek the "sore points," the places where given individuals are likely to be overly sensitive and hyperreactive to environmental cues. Evidently, in each instance, these will be unique—an individual spectrum of strengths and vulnerabilities that will be characteristic for that personality. The differing lines on this spectrum will each represent some internalized element of those persons' prior experience—something that happened that was of great significance and that was accordingly incorporated into the system of ideals. In the nature of things, some of the experiences will be of immense positive value and will leave traces that will function to encourage, to reassure, to strengthen, to forgive, to make these individuals feel loved from within, and, ultimately, to provide wellsprings of positive feeling that can be drawn on to offset some of the shattering vicissitudes that life can visit even on young children.

The congeries of idealized images of an all-loving, all-embracing mother figure are the product of a series of such internalizations. These begin to accumulate long before they can be registered as recallable images—instead, they form an emotional infrastructure, a bedrock of felt self-confidence, self-assurance, and self-acceptance that becomes the foundation for later interpersonal structurings.

Parallel with the positive experiences, children are amassing the products of negative emotional events, moments of unrelieved pain, of unsolaced fear, of the agonies of abandonment, of all the biological discomforts life can visit on the young, and of all the psychological challenges youngsters are growing ever more able to comprehend. These too are taken in and form their own tapestry of the hateful and the demonic, a series of felt patterns whose imageless voices bay and snarl and threaten ever to assault and flail away from within—or that may indeed give rise to fell images of unmitigated cruelty that pursue children as their prey.

Given these clusters, how then to structure a model that will allow us to understand something of the complex forces that determine behavior—both inner behavior and outer behavior—since both must be comprehended within a single model if it is to be a valid representation of human functioning? A point of departure might well be the notion of identity. Identity has been defined in many ways (e.g., Erik Erikson). One way to describe it is as a collection of discrete aspects of self connected to a common core. Indeed, the image that may best be employed is that of a spiral staircase, where the treads all float freely except where they attach to the central pillar around which they wind as they ascend. Each tread stands unique, separate from the others, with its own substance, color, and qualities and with its own special mission. Yet all have in common their adherence to the pillar that gives to each its fundamental support.

For our purposes, each tread represents one component of what we commonly call identity. For this is a multifaceted entity made up of numerous interlocking components. Thus, one such element is family, another is gender, yet another religion, then race, then ethnicity, and there follow in turn a sense of region, nationality, professional or vocational inclusion group, class belongingness, and so on and on for many more. More to the point, each of these treads describes a certain reality but has, in addition, its own ideal coloring. Thus, one's family is certainly a real presence embodied in the psyche both as a set of well-recognized images, each with its own qualities, and as a kind of ideal presence that has its own peculiar status and mandates. The Jones family includes mother, father, siblings, aunts, uncles, and cousins. But the Jones family also has a certain history, certain traditions, and its own set of principles and values. These function as ideals and may be highly valued in a· fashion that influences both inner directives and the form of social behavior ("We Joneses never engage in violent behavior," or "We Joneses never forgive an insult, and we always give as good as we get"), or, inversely, the valence may be entirely negative ("No Jones ever finished school," or "We Joneses are no good, never have been, never will be"). In any case, the accompanying feelings of belonging, attachment, affiliation, and identification make the family name curiously coextensive with the self. When the family name is insulted, the child is insulted. How he or she handles the insult has many determinants; among them will be the kinds of family ideals that have been inculcated.

Thus, being a Jones can be a rewarding, sustaining element in a child's makeup, it can carry a dire message of inevitable disaster, or it can also be some complex amalgam of the two. If it should turn out that self-hatred as a Jones is already a formidable presence, then the youngster will have a built-in brittleness to his inner structure that will render him especially vulnerable to taunts about his origins. His peers are not likely to overlook this, and the child will encounter jeering and depreciating comments from without, which will kindle the depreciating inner voice and augment the self-devaluation. Depending on his temperament, this can lead to his being overcome with humiliation and grief and subsequently withdrawing. Or, under other conditions, it may give rise to an intense need to fight against this debasing destructive inner message. If he can, he will simply push this out of his mind. Where such an effort at suppression fails to quench the intolerable pain within, it may be followed by projection—one frees oneself of the inner distress by externalizing it—the outer assailant is perceived as voicing the assault that was originated by the inner accuser. Looking at it this way, the child may then feel altogether justified in flinging himself violently against the external attacker.

Obviously, there are all kinds of permutations and combinations that can emerge. The degree and kind of sensitivity about one's family, the specific character of the external onslaught, the presence of positive inner feelings about family that might act as cushions and shields in the face of the inner hostility—and thus ward off the effects of the outer attack—the temperamental proclivity to project against internalized criticism: all those and many other factors serve as shaping tools that give form to behavior. The child insulted by a peer and who experiences an intense sense of injury may pretend indifference in the presence of a teacher or other adult, only to slink away later to cry in private. Or he might simmer quietly all through the rest of the school day and wait after school to "get" his assailants. Indeed, he may recognize the insult as accurate but declare nonetheless that it is unforgivable.

Where a propensity for psychosis is present and the child's tendency to distort reality is marked, the projection may include not only the inner rage about his family but the externalization of his inner dialogue. The victim of the taunting turns on his peer, who is then accused of saying things he did not say, things that in fact were present only in the mind of the victimized child and that are now asserted to have come from without. Both the accusation and its distortions—"I never called you that," "Yes you did"— are greeted with mounting confusion and resentment by the surrounding peers, and the Jones child soon earns such sobriquets as "crazy." When, in addition, denial is resorted to as a primary defense, then the afflicted child will both insist that he did not act in the provocative manner that in fact led to the whole eruption and that his peer did or said things that never happened. Highly stressful sequences follow, and, where there is much of this, the child's academic record presently includes multiple school placements.

So far we have dealt with only one tread on our spiral staircase (the family and its meanings), and it is evident that a single spiral does not account for what happens. In fact, a more accurate model would consist of two such spirals winding around one another: one the array of positive ideals mounting up and spiraling around the central sustaining pillar of the core identity, and the other the negative ideals, rising in parallel. To further illustrate this, let us move to another tread on our spiral, say, that of religion. Thus, a Jewish child growing up in a multiethnic neighborhood will have two simultaneous messages about his Judaism. On the one hand, there are the ancient wisdom, the tenets of the religion as lived taught and practiced, the sense of being one of a special, "chosen" people, the remarkable history (including bitter accounts of martyrdom and victimization), the immense cultural contributions, the richness of ritual, language and practice, and the deep sense of group belongingness that are part of his Judaism. On the other, there are the scorn, the insulting nicknames, the derision, the exclusion, the assertions that he is a Christ-killer, plus the accusations of being a member of a greedy, clannish, exploitative people, who have no sense of honor and are driven only by gain. He encounters situations where the very word *Jew* is an epithet. Moreover, he may have been made to feel alien to and excluded from the dominant, cultural practices of his largely Christian environment. Like the complex set of attachments to and devaluations of his father that we saw in our initial patient, for the Jewish boy we speak of here, his relation to his Judaism will be a multifaceted complex of reactions, with both positive and negative ideals working simultaneously to make him at once proud of and troubled by his religious/ethnic background. In practice, much of this might lie dormant within him and never find full awareness until he faces some of the accusations or the challenges described.

A similar state of affairs can occur with any tread of the spiral stair. If an American boy, born and reared in the United States, were to meet a French child of the same age, they might get into quite a discussion as to the pros and cons of being American as against being European—and our youngster would discover another tread on his spiral stair that heretofore he had taken for granted or, at any rate, never thought much about. Once it has been assaulted, he will discover his nationality as he never has before—and he will find that it is a key element in his identity. In particular, he might become aware that several of his positive ideals about being an American stand face to face with some dubious feelings that this idea evokes in others. On one hand, he knows himself to be a member of the richest and most powerful nation on Earth, one that has literally saved the world again and again, a site of exceptional human freedom, and an inspiration to other peoples. On the other, there may be vague echoes of Viet Nam, or a sense of racist issues as an ongoing sore place in the country's history, or a shadowy feeling about guns and killing, or a focus may fall on things that have entered his awareness about America not educating its children in the best way or caring for its poor and homeless—and so on and on.

All of which his French peer may be dilating on with some glee, while the American youth squirms.

Thus, up and down the staircase of identity elements there are the associated idealizations, both positive and negative, and their consequences. The shaping of behavior is thus a complex matter with numerous subvectoral forces at work. Together, these drive the individual at once to reach upward toward the attainment of the goals held out by the positive ideals and to be crushed by the hopelessness and devaluation insisted upon by the negative ideals.

It is this state of uneasy equilibrium that makes the individual so very responsive to context. The environment suggests and proposes and stimulates and frightens—it offers models, it offers derision and exclusion, and it offers temptations. It is from the interactive flow among the meanings of all these contextual presences on one hand and the internal equilibrium among the various ideal states on the other that behavioral decisions emerge. There is an ongoing process of summing up the total forces at work in each quarter that determines which ideal set will be dominant under which conditions.

It is important to emphasize that the process of summation is not concerned merely with a static internal array of idealizations. It is rather a constantly shifting set of dynamic forces, ever responding and adapting to external configurations, exquisitely sensitive both to current environmental stimuli and to anticipated events that are imagined and reacted to in advance (very much a matter of context)—so that there is an endless sequencing and adding up of inputs from without and messages from within to determine both state and behavior. (One can conceive of this in vectorial terms, with the resultant of the forces at work taking form as behavior.)

More than that, the total array of internal idealizations can transiently give way—or, sometimes, undergo permanent transformation—in the face of highly charged emotional events or novel traumatic experiences. When this occurs, we call it a conversion, an abrupt change in values and lifestyle, which might turn an honest banker into a fugitive thief or transform a narcissistic drunkard into a saintly philanthropist. It were as though there were some inner upending of the value set so that what was once recessive becomes dominant, and what was dominant is now submerged. This commonly follows a highly emotional experience. It can be part of a religious revival, it can be an encounter with a forgiving and accepting authority figure, it can appear as a seemingly sudden decision (although an inner and largely unconscious debate may have been simmering for a long time) in response to an apparently minor experience—whatever it is, it offers a new source of positive idealization, an enrichment of a shifting, vacillating, unstable equilibrium, which now sets itself firmly on a path dominated by positive ideals. The former malcontent becomes compliant, the miscreant begins to behave himself, the drug user or drinker turns away from his habit, the failed scholar begins to work hard and to get high marks—the whole cast of personality seems to undergo a profound transformation.

Nor does this follow only positive encounters. Various survival and reality factors as well as changes in the family can make for equally dramatic transformations—the youngster who has gloried in his repeated malfeasance is suddenly arrested for the first time and must attend court. As he weighs the imperatives focused on him by the two ideal systems, he becomes aware that the mandates of the negative ideal can indeed lead him to destruction—and he flinches back from the abyss. Perhaps there is a shift in the relationship with his parents that strengthen his positive ideal—that in itself might help tip the balance. Perhaps there is a disillusionment with overvalued friends—who have left him in the lurch or turned against him in his hour of trouble.

All the warnings and the pleadings of his parents come back to haunt him—and strengthen his capacity to reattach to them and to their values—with a similar outcome.

Alternatively, the occurrence of a certain class of traumatic events can readily strengthen the negative ideal. This usually follows an experience of disillusionment—a moment when a former positive ideal is abruptly lost, deidealized, or converted into a negative ideal. Not infrequently this comes about when a youngster is told or discovers some family secret. A girl finds that her adored father is having an affair, and in short order she is exposing herself to pregnancy. A boy finds that his parents are breaking up, and the basis of his sense of security is suddenly shattered. Moreover, he cannot rid himself of the feeling that he is somehow responsible or that he should be able to bring them together again. His self-accusations grow apace, and presently he is engaging in provocative, punishment-seeking behavior.

References

Defoe, D. (1973). *Moll Flanders*. New York: W. W. Norton and Co.

Chapter 4

Music

INTRODUCTION

Carl Feinstein

This chapter introduces an entrancing and profound series of essays about the arts: "Music," "Visual Art," "Prose and Poetry," and "Mime and Dance." Writing about music served another purpose for Joe, even beyond explaining the origins of one of humanity's major cultural achievements. He uses it as an opportunity to immerse the reader in the sensory, affective, and social world of the human infant, the matrix from which, by Joe's vision, most of each individual's sense of self and psychological destiny evolve.

The chapter traces the origins of musical experience back to babies' innate capacity to transform sensory experiences from one modality to another (amodal perception). Starting from this foundation, babies mirror in movement and behavior the vocalizations and visual experiences of their mother and are soothed by regular rhythms and repetitions from within (biological) and without (by raptly attending to their mother). Babies are increasingly fascinated by novelty (the crescendos, decrescendos, accelerations, and slight pauses in the emotionally inflected patterns by which their mother engages them).

Joe states unequivocally that "...during the first half of our first year of life we are perhaps more intensely social than we will ever be again." For him, it is from the uniquely human developmental processes that lead us as a species to be socially and affectively communicative that music arises. While the intellectual synthesis of Joe's writing about the origins of music is unique, in this essay, as in the other arts essays, he draws upon the contemporary discoveries of Daniel Stern (1977), a great pioneer of infant developmental theory, who described "the first relationship" and was able to observe, using the microanalysis of mother–infant interactions, many of the specifics that Joe cites in this essay.

Evolutionary biology and research findings from modern neuroscience (primarily functional neuroimaging) have recently elaborated many of the details laid out in Joe's developmental theory of music. Indeed, in a recent review article, Mithen (2009) traces the phylogeny of human communication and demonstrates that musical and rhythmic interaction were pillars of social cohesion and affective communication that arose during prehistory, before verbal language evolved. Along converging lines from contemporary neuroscience, functional neuroimaging has elucidated the strong neural connectivity between the auditory and premotor cortex in the processing of rhythmic patterns and the synchronization of movements in social engagement movement patterns between people (Snyder, Large & Penhume, 2009; Chen, Penhume & Zataorre, 2009). However, the role of the vitality affects, so important a concept in Joe's theory by which human affective social engagement is achieved in infancy, still cannot be fully explicated by functional neuroimaging. In fact, it could be argued that the current state of understanding of human development, especially in the clinical arena, has yet to fully grasp—as thoroughly as Joe Noshpitz did decades ago—how crucial human social development in the first year of life is in the psychological development of human beings.

References

Chen, J. L., Penhume, V. B., & Zataorre, R. J. (2009). The role of auditory and premotor cortex in sensorimotor transformations. *Annals of the New York Academy of Science, 1169*, 15–34.

Mithen, S. (2009). The music instinct. *Annals of the New York Academy of Science, 1169*, 3–12.

Snyder, J. S., Large, E. W., & Penhume, V. B. (2009). Rhythms in the brain: Basic science and clinical perspectives. *Annals of the New York Academy of Sciences, 1169*, 13–14.

Stern, D. (1977). *The first relationship: Infant and mother*. Cambridge, MA: Harvard University Press.

MUSIC
Joseph D. Noshpitz

In approaching the connection between music and early human experience, it is appropriate to begin with an account of those aspects of early development on which this essay will focus. At the outset, the attempt will be made to draw the analogy between the nature of music and the form assumed by the sense of self as it exists in the very earliest weeks and months of life when babies are just beginning to undertake the work of constructing their worlds.

It is not quite accurate to say that a baby is born with no prior sensory experience. During the last trimester of pregnancy, the fetus will respond both to taste stimuli and to sounds in a very specific way. Indeed, during the last 6 weeks *in utero*, if the expectant mother reads aloud in a repetitious fashion, after delivery the newborn baby will respond unequivocally to the sound of the same material being read aloud. Babies remember what they heard before they were born.

More than that, once born, babies show a capacity to translate what they see into what they do. In particular, if you hold a baby and stick out your tongue at him where he can see your face plainly, presently he will stick his tongue out back at you. Now that may not sound like much, but in fact it is quite a remarkable phenomenon. If one but considers it for a moment, it implies that babies can see your behavior and that somewhere inside their psyche this visual image can be used as a model so that they can organize their musculature enough to respond in kind. How in the world do babies know enough to do that? How do they know where their face is, how do they know what their tongue is, where did they learn? Clearly they didn't learn that sort of thing anywhere; they were preprogrammed to be able to do that. And the crucial question is: how was this programming effected, what sort of internal arrangements exist within the newborn mentality?

The suggestion advanced by Daniel Stern is that we are born with a capacity to abstract elements of experience into a nonsensory realm. We can in our very nature transcend the sensory modalities and hold the essence of experience in an amodal form. Once we have it there, we can then reexpress it in motor form as an action or in some other sensory form. This has now been studied and demonstrated in a variety of ways. The easiest illustration to offer is babies' ability to translate the intensities of the light they see into intensities of sound they hear. Babies who are only a few weeks old can be conditioned to respond to varying intensities of one modality; when shown equivalent (as judged by adults) intensities of the other, they show the same kinds of responses. There are several studies of similar transfer of rhythmic patterns from one modality into equivalent temporal patterns in another. Somewhere there is a higher-order sense of rhythm, one that can find ready expression in any given sensory realm and in motor realms as well.

The amodal perception allows for the beginnings of organization. Organization is the key to an emerging sense of self. As infants begin to assemble a set of predictable outcomes in their universe, as they collect an array of memories, as they connect a sense impression with a cognitive grasp with a memory, they begin to construct an inner island of coherence. This follows that; this feeling follows that act. It will be weeks before these islands come together to form a continent, but that too will come to pass after babies are a few months old and the perceptual achievements and inner organizations mass up and increase.

It is worth noting that the basic capacity to transform experience, to change visual impressions to auditory ones, tactile sensations to visual recognition, or sensory patterns to motor actions, is one of the fundamental aspects of creativity. It is inherent in the very nature of emergent form. Moreover, when infants accomplish such a transformation, it heightens their sense of self and makes even the very early experience alive to their inner processes. It amounts to the fact of selfhood building on experience. There may well be a special quality of pleasure associated with this kind of transforming activity, the precursor to the pleasure that will later be experienced by persons writing music or painting or performing any other activity that changes their inner image to another and, ultimately, to a set of external symbols. It is the activity basic to later use of simile and metaphor, each of which is a means for doing just that—it transforms one kind of experience into another of different character via either analogy or identity. It allows for the possibility of symbol formation and is basic as well to the rendering of an idea or affect into a pattern of rhythm or a sequence of sounds or for the sounds to evoke the affect. Most of all, it gives babies a sense of the known, the familiar, the recognized. Thus the equation is: the inner capacity for amodal perception encounters sensations that give rise to the act of transformation. As this occurs, it becomes an act of awareness that now registers as a momentary feeling of selfness.

One of the easiest such recognitions concerns repetition. Such reencounters with the same stimulus at regular intervals is reassuring; one has an almost instant sense of mastery, one can predict the next event and it comes out as it is supposed to. With regular repetitions, infants are quickly in charge. The sense of self is alerted by the mastery feeling; one almost makes it happen. There is aliveness here, aroused sensibility, the solid security of knowing what will happen next. However, if this goes on for long and is in each instance the same, then babies more or less quickly habituate—and lose interest. If elements of variety are introduced, though—not too little and not too much—then each small difference is evocative and commands renewed interest and attention, and babies then stay satisfied and in touch. Each such element of variety is a new opportunity for mastery; each involves the work of comparison: Babies hark back to the previous image, note the basic similarity of the new one to the old, and distinguish the specific elements that have been varied. It is the game of theme and variations that allows for creativity in the midst of sameness, a sort of refinement of experience by artfully managed diversity where reassurance and mastery combine with novelty and surprise to produce a wholly new effect. Each such variation, if repeated a few times, becomes mastered in turn and will lead to a falloff in attention until yet another change is encountered—and so on and so on.

Meanwhile, as babies translate one kind of sensory experience into another, they are accumulating little bits of recognition and little bits of familiarity. The basic elements of selfhood are coming together. They go forward on many fronts at once, probably more fronts than we are yet aware of. However, for heuristic reasons I will divide them into three components: biological, affective, and cognitive. Of these, the most elementary level is the biological.

In a very real sense, all mentation—indeed, all psychic experience—is in fact biological. We are after all biological entities, and our thinking and feeling is no less biological than is our digestion. Each is an expression of the function of one of our organ sets. But we tend to think in dualistic terms about body and mind, so that assertions that distinguish the organic from the psychic are more natural to us than to consider the product of psychological work as biological. Hence the word must be used here in quite a different sense.

There is, however, one point of linkage between known biological experience and everyday human mentation that has a certain face validity. That is in the awareness of and responsiveness to rhythm. Rhythm, meter, temporal regularity—these are at the very core of all life processes. The jellyfish pulses, the swimming eel undulates, the cilia of the paramecium swing in synchrony, the heart beats, the digestive system exhibits peristalsis, the reproductive system ovulates and menstruates—short rhythms and long ones, throughout the wide array of living things, throughout their every vital act, the underlying phenomenon of rhythmicity is a continuous presence. It is profoundly important in the everyday processes of the human being. Our gait is a set of rhythmic, alternating, and carefully sequenced contractions and relaxations of integrated muscle groups; our respiration is a set of silent, regular, whole body movements; the tides of our blood ebb and flow in carefully pulsed, synchronous beats; our sexuality involves patterns of pelvic thrusts and recurrent waves of sensation; our speech has a basic cadence; our sleep–wake cycles, our endocrine secretion cycles, indeed, almost every element in our functioning all move to a hidden inner galley master who beats on his table and sets the pace of the oars of our being to rise and fall—or perhaps to a series of such masters whose activity is ultimately coordinated in the neuroendocrine system.

This pervasive biologic reality reflects itself directly into our conscious response to rhythm. I have but to snap my fingers in a regular way, thus, and I have you all; you are all vulnerable, all entrained, caught up in the pattern I have set up. You wait for the next beat. It is not a matter of choice—we are simply that kind of animal.

We can see it at work in the nursery. Wake and sleep times, elimination times, the very act of suckling—all are rhythmic. More than that, babies fret or fuss, and we rock them, we walk them, perhaps we speak to them in a repetitious way: "Nice baby, nice baby; there, there, there, there." Or we sing to them. If they are really hard to console, we might take them for a ride in the car; some babies who respond to nothing else are solaced by that. Under special conditions, some babies take over the rhythmic function themselves; they become rockers or head-bangers, as though there was an insufficiency of sensory input and they had to make up for it on their own.

This kind of repetition is one of the earliest forms of mastery and one of the basic elements in organization. The primary pleasure in achieving rhythmic organization will never leave us; one way or another, it will always be there. And one of the simplest kinds of organization is the sequencing of sounds.

Music is the sequencing of sounds. In its ultimate expression, it represents perhaps the most elementary form of this mastery through cadence. The sounds have no necessary meaning content (in the verbal sense of that word); they are an end in themselves. They are built upon rhythm; indeed, they need be nothing more than rhythm. If we listen to a steady drum beat, we hear elaborate but fundamental rhythmic patterns unadorned by minimal changes in pitch or in any other coloring quality; the rhythmic pattern is essentially pure and is an end in itself.

This then is the biologic component. The second element is the affective one. All of us are familiar with emotion, but there is an aspect of emotion that is relatively unfamiliar to most of us. Ordinarily, the very idea of emotion brings to mind the categorical affects, the feelings of sadness, elation, anger, envy, surprise, and the like. These are the basic elements that comprise our emotional life. But they say nothing about the way that emotional life is actually lived and is regularly experienced. We don't feel sad; we feel a pang of grief or a sweeping tide of sadness that swells and ebbs. We don't merely feel pleasure; we experience a burst of joy, a rush, a crescendo, and then a falloff, abrupt or gradual, a diminuendo. And so far all affect, we have both the quality and contour; of the two, we know far more about the contour, for it is with that that we live.

These rushes and rises and falls of emotion are now given a name by Stern. He calls them the vitality affects. They figure far more frequently in everyday experience than do the categorical feelings. It is these stabs and pangs and glows and fallings off that we know almost continuously, from moment to moment, as life makes its demands and offers it reliefs, and these are the major contact we have with the affects. So we are continuously engaged with the form and shape of these inner swellings and abating and thus are endlessly heedful of them and seek ever to master them.

One of the earliest lessons in mastery is the trick of objectifying, of placing a content external to ourselves so that we can encounter it not merely as felt and known but as perceived and considered: not something that happens to us but something we can make happen; not something that overtakes or surprises us but something we can turn on and turn off. We overcome our human helplessness; we deal with forces of which we have charge rather than those to which we must submit.

And so it is with the vitality affects: we want to have those too in a realm where we can know them, anticipate them and by that means control them.

With this we move on to the third component of early life: the experience of cognition. When we spoke earlier of the pleasures of the biologic component, we told of the mastery that comes with repetition, the comfort that emerges from predictability. And a regular rhythm is one of the most comforting and predictable experiences we can know.

There is, however, another side to this. For here we encounter the second essential of mastery behavior: the addition of variety. For young babies, the classic experiments in visual stimulation involve repeatedly showing babies a bull's-eye. Initially their eyes seize and hold on this novel presence and stare and stare and stare. But, with repeated exposure, babies give the target shorter and shorter periods of attention until presently they disregard the bull's-eye altogether. It has lost its novelty; they have become habituated. The initial representations were fascinating, but they serve for only so long. Once the stimulus has been mastered and encompassed, babies lose their interest; once they are known they no longer divert. Change some detail about it, however, and immediately attention snaps back and is riveted once more.

Mothers learn this quickly, and, as they play the games of infancy with the babies, they repeat many sequences over and over again but, to babies' delight, always with little differences, always with some element of novelty, not too little and not too much. And so it is with the sounds babies hear—they repeat over and over but always with the slight variations that make them interesting. Theme and variations—the most primitive and the most effective form of music, the basis of all jazz, the heart of the sonata structure.

We spoke earlier of amodal perception. This is the level of apprehension of the world that somehow passes beyond sensory perception, which moves to a realm of sensory absolutes where the essence of perception is grasped in a way that allows it to be realized in any other perceptual modality or converted into a muscle plan, into an action. There is no way to express this in ordinary terms; it is certainly not verbal and indeed cannot be rendered in verbal terms. Nor does it conform to the usual visual dimensions of space or touch—it is an abstraction that babies' minds are preprogrammed to form and that underlies all organization. Nor is it just formal qualities that are here involved; intensity, sequence, and affective elements get into it as well. I submit that this abstract psychological presence that can readily translate into image or feeling, into form or intensity—this aspect of mind finds its most proximate expression in music.

For now we come to the convergence of the elements with which we began. Biologic rhythms, the contoured vitality affects, the abstract qualities of intellect that underlie the map and plan of inner organization—taken together with the need for mastery they give us music. The formal qualities of melody are about as close as we will ever get to the nature of amodal perception, elements whose inherent configuration hangs together and feels good, feels right, feels pleasing. Nor do they have to be very elaborate. As melody, the opening notes of Beethoven's Fifth are extraordinarily simple, but no one has ever been able to achieve so dazzling an array of vitality affects as Beethoven—and the simplicity of the cognitive melodic component gives the extraordinary emotional creativity an enhanced thrust and intensified effectiveness. In contrast, the intellectual sweep of the opening of Mozart's 40th, with its complex—and satisfying—melodic (for which read cognitive) configuration is set off all the more sharply by the contoured vitality components when they come.

Now, we may ask, how does music heal? The first answer certainly involves the creation of organization. To listen to music is to reexperience our earliest encounters with sensation, to forge once again a set of random elements into a state of coherence, to weave together our surging affect-contours and our ineffable cognitive constructs into an orderly pattern of predictable regularities, all built on a firm foundation of biologic vitality and stability.

Each element of melody is a cognitive construct, an array of sound images that have been placed in some order, founded on rhythm and finding its way in a fashion that carries with it novelty and the element of discovery within a context of the tolerable and the acceptable. In infancy we are not acculturated, we have no acquired plan of the permissible that distinguishes immediately the syntonic and the familiar from the jarring and the exotic. But from the outset, we are geared to have certain preferences, and we learn rapidly to know the voice of our caretaker; it is, I think, music to our ears.

To understand this it is important to realize that during the first half of our first year of life, we are perhaps more intensely social than we will ever be again. It is a time when babies are avid in their hunger for interaction, a time when nothing excites and pleases them so much as seeing, meeting the eyes of, being held by, playing with, or in any way contacting the beloved caretaker. In effect, babies are head over heels in love with whoever tends to them, and everything about the significant other is absorbingly attractive. This includes the voice of the other; babies will recognize certain aspects of that voice at birth and by 3 months will have that voice and their mother's face firmly linked together.

Hence, the cadence and quality of the mother's speech and her singing (if she sings to baby) will be substantial and meaningful presences in the baby's acculturation. Ultimately, these experiences and those that follow on in subsequent years establish certain scale sequenced and preferred tonal intervals as the proper ones for a good sound; anything that differs too radically will sound atonal and strange and often enough unpleasant—so with some Asian music, for example, as experienced by occidental ears.

But music, of whatever variety, will draw a certain measure of its strength from the enormous value inherent in these earliest mastery experiences.

To understand musical acculturation, it is helpful to look at the fate of speech sounds. At about 6 months, babies begin to experiment with the laryngeal and nasopharyngeal apparatus—by proper manipulation of these muscles they find that they can make all sorts of noises. Indeed, the students of such matters have recorded babies as making just about all possible sounds during this interval; the clicks and gutturals and vowels of every known language come through at one moment or another. But this lasts only a short time. By 8 months of age, most of these sounds have dropped out. The babies are still vocalizing a good deal, but the character of the noises they make has altered in an important way. Now the sounds echo the qualities resident in the language or languages they hear about them. Now they are not merely making noises; in addition, they have begun to imitate. They are taking in the sound environment within which they grow, and they are seeking to emulate it and master its pattern.

This is a fateful moment for development. Here is a first great shaping of the communicative apparatus in the direction of genuine speech. First, one makes the sounds of speech; in time such sounds will be tied to meanings. We do not know whether the preliminary forms of music are coming into being at the same time. But we can speculate, and I would like to offer the following possibility. I would suggest that the underlying nature of verbal meaning and musical appeal are the same. Both come to lie inherently in the ability of the mind to construct organization. That ability is far more primitive than language; it allows nonverbal animals to use tools or to construct elaborate social organizations. At the heart of meaning are constructions, and the elements can be words, or signs, or symbols, or rhythmic patterns, or tones. The weaving together of tones into predictable patterns (made the more predictable—and the more satisfying—because associated with rhythm) is probably one of the earliest experiences of meaningful form. Infants apprehend order directly, in its very nature, right from the start. The mind is simply a context-former. Impressions, sensations, memories web together, and regularities are appreciated. One finds the pictures hidden in the drawing, something recognizable, something coherent.

After the primary grasp of rhythm, one of the easiest and earliest kinds of patterning is that of pitch. Different pitch sequences can repeat; in the beginning it's all music. Only later will speech differentiate out. And the music is functional. It soothes; from the very outset it offers a gratifying diversion. For babies to be rocked to sleep and sung to sleep—these are human universals, among the earliest forms of mastery. What they offer babies are regular, graspable organizations, context of connected sensations that fit together predictably and rhythmically and hence happily.

More than that, however, are the associated vitality affects. For the selection of tones, the sequencing, and character of the movement from tone to tone are designed to give the affective components a nonarousing form. By rocking and singing, the mother encourages a shift of state, from quiet alertness to drowsiness and sleep. But if she used other vitality affects that communicated opposite qualities, she would tend to cause the baby to shift toward active alertness, toward social engagement and playfulness. It is this elementary linking of vitality affects to state and tonal patterns to affect that gives music so much of its power.

It is this linkage as well that gives music its power as a healing agent. For here the elements of mastery, of cognitive structuring, and of affective engagement are all assembled in almost pristine form. And for the suffering ego, unable to bear the burden of its inability to master its world, both or either cognitively or affectively, the hearing of and the participation in musical formations can thus be a source of basic repair, something that really works. In particular, its connection with the profound biologic zone at the heart of human mental organization gives it a rootedness in the psyche that other forms of cognitive or even affective experience will not possess.

Chapter 5

Visual art

INTRODUCTION
Gilbert Rose

Written in the 1980s and never published, the following chapter on visual art is remarkable for its prescience in regard to thinking about art and the aesthetic experience. In down-to-earth language, Noshpitz tellingly emphasizes that (1) *motion*, rooted in rhythm, is a biologic basis of all works of art whatever the medium; (2) the various schools of art require *forms* to express and contain feelings; and (3) all aesthetic expression requires a coherent *sense of self* within one's body musculature to experience affect and agency.

The quality of early child–mother interactions is crucial as it becomes generalized into consistent representations that form the building blocks of the core self. Noshpitz holds that this distilled quality of early child–mother interactions is central to the aesthetic encounter—both the creator's and the viewer's. The best works of art force the observer to become emotionally engaged. This is because their forms capture the intensity and rhythmic coherence of early child–mother engagements and contain it within a frame—there to promote growth and greater objectivity of the self.

All this is congenial to the spirit of my own study of aesthetic form and experience and the ways they are relevant to growth and development (Rose, 1987, 1992, 1996, 2004). In briefest statement, my work places the creative process into a normative and progressive context rather than an aberrant—if privileged—one (like "regression in the service of the ego"). For example, aesthetic forms exploit the "creativity of everyday life"—enhancing perception by abstracting, highlighting, and objectifying its elements rather than primarily repressing and transforming them into unconscious material for dreams or psychopathology.

When we are exposed to a new aesthetic experience, there may be an initial shock at losing the safety of the familiar landmarks of ordinariness. The structure of aesthetic form provides the safety of containment—a frame wherein we may reawaken to dynamic aspects of reality and see them in a fresh way. The familiar is "reambiguated," and the strange is redifferentiated, enticing the observer into exercising a capacity for new adaptation.

After having allowed ourselves to be momentarily lost in the aesthetic moment we may refind ourselves affectively on levels of deepening resignification. A major aesthetic experience may include a transient sense of "unity" with what had been initially strange—even, perhaps, a mystical moment that William James (1902) would ascribe to relief from "the solitude of individuation" (p. 386).

In infant terms, brief loss and refinding the self reflected in the mother's eyes and responsive facial expression represent early tension, validation, and reassurance. Such peek-a-boo, to the accompaniment (universally) of the music of baby-talk, involves many sensory modes "orchestrated" to enliven the baby's experience with graded tension and relief. May such objective surprise, recognition, and embrace stand as an infantile precursor—a physical concretization—of empathic capacity? Further, may such empathy—internalized—subsequently become a subjective model of affect regulation?

If so, may this even provide a key to understand the enhanced affect regulation that ultimately accrues to the aesthetic experience? For, indeed, increased range and regulation of affect may well constitute an ongoing psychobiological contribution of art through one's lifetime.

What follows is a formulation that adds analytic insight to the structure of aesthetic forms and experience and expands the concept of sublimation to include nonverbal art. It requires that we accept a modification of primary–secondary process theory by assuming that, instead of secondary process replacing the primary process, there is feedback and interplay between primary and secondary processes; this assures that the primary process can undergo development (Noy, 1969).

In art, the interplay is between primary process perceptual forms and the delayed discharge of secondary process. This enables imagery from perceptual prestages to enter consciousness. Now the artist can play creatively and elaborate primary process forms within an overall composition. Modern art thus plays with figure–ground reversal, condensation, displacement, rotation, duplication, and so on.

Beginning in preverbal life, and given a favorable mother–infant ambience, feelings as well as primary process may begin to develop into sensibility. The capacity for feeling, as distinguished from secondary process cognition, may then eventually become an open-ended process of refined emotional sensitivity and taste, increasing discernment, receptivity, and responsiveness to sensory stimuli.

Turning to the significance of motion for both creator and viewer, it is less motion *per se* than imagined or *virtual motion*. Virtual motion is a representation of the essence of motion in the absence of the actual fact of motion. If somatic tension and release is the entry code of affect to the brain, virtual motion is the entry code of nonverbal art to the world of mind. Like the interplay of primary and secondary processes, it stimulates creative imagination.

Affectomotor sublimation transforms and transcends the somatic tension and release of the artist's expressive motions and emotions in making art. Such physical expression becomes inherently embedded in art as virtual motion. Viewers almost immediately retransform virtual motion into the somatic tension and release of their personal emotional response.

If virtual motion is the pivotal "hinge" among art, artist, and audience response, how does it work? Virtual motion creates an imaginative field of force that turns seeing (and hearing) into dynamic phenomena. An ordinary visual line becomes a stroke—according to Henri Matisse, a "disequilibrium" against the "indifference" of a white background. It imparts thrust and directionality. Analogously, in music mere acoustic sounds become tones that impart amplitude and thrust.

As a result of virtual motion, a work of art moves, works, breathes—in short, it becomes living art, taking its place among the life of forms in art irrespective of the various cognitive meanings that may be attributed to it in the course of time and where, above all, we are more alive in a field of motion and emotion.

References

James, W. (1902). *The varieties of religious experience.* New York: Random House.

Noy, P. (1969). A revision of the psychoanalytic theory of the primary process. *International Journal of Psycho-Analysis, 50*,155–178.

Rose, G. J. (1987). *Trauma and mastery in life and art.* Madison. CT: International Universities Press.

Rose, G. J. (1992). *The power of form: A psychoanalytic approach to aesthetic form.* Madison, CT: International Universities Press.

Rose, G. J. (1996). *Necessary illusion: Art as witness.* Madison, CT: International Universities Press.

Rose, G. J. (2004). *Between couch and piano: Psychoanalysis, music, art and neuroscience.* London: Brunner-Routledge.

VISUAL ART

Joseph D. Noshpitz

The next art form to concern us is the array of representational techniques involving drawing, painting, and sculpture. Although evidently of complex origin, the creation of such images, designs, and objects of art has been a facet of human behavior from the time of the dawn of man. One might prefer to draw a distinction between art as ornament (or adornment) and art as a means of depicting some aspect of the world. But in both instances, the central unifying idea is the creation of an image, whether it be the image of the self changed about by means of ornaments or an image drawn on a cave wall, scratched on bark, or painted on canvas. Hence, in the approach we are using, we must seek far the beginnings of imaging: so too for our ability to perceive the image as external to ourselves and in terms of our capacity to create internal images.

But it is not simply the ability to imagine or to visualize, to have a "mind's eye," so to speak, that we deal with here. For an art form to develop, it must be related to something a great deal more meaningful; it must be related to the growth of the sense of self. All aesthetic expression is in a sense a version of the intimate character of selfhood, and so it is to the study of such a developmental world that the present effort must turn.

From 3 or 4 months of age to 7 to 9 months is the era of the core self. It is the time when the emerging islands of self-awareness that had come into being during the first 3 months of life now come together, coalesce, and begin the formation of continents—continents of new awareness. These larger unities that now begin to take form are the senses of self on one hand and of the caretaker (or caretakers) on the other. The former partial recognitions become joined and confluent, and, bit by bit, a more coherent picture of one's self-in-the-world begins to emerge.

To accomplish this, infants are helped by a number of inborn characteristics. To begin with, there is the capacity for amodal perception (i.e., the ability to change sensory experience encountered in one sphere into an awareness of appropriate characteristics in an entirely different one). There is the readiness to experience affect and, in particular, the vitality affects (affective contours that change in some important way, that spring up or die down, perhaps abruptly, perhaps more gradually). There is the capacity to remember, present even before birth, and to respond differentially on the basis of recall. Then infants can construct organizations, stable inner versions of bits of experience that they will add to and enlarge and that form the islands of self and of other. As the weeks go on, these organizations become the constructs that underlie the sense of self and give it its first coherent form. Parallel with this is the emerging sense of other, similarly constructed but clearly known as, albeit like the self, nonetheless separate and different from the self. Within a few days after birth, babies can recognize the smell of their mother's breast pad as different from the aroma of another woman's. A few weeks later, infants can recognize the difference between a picture of their mother and their mother herself. The capacity for three-dimensional perception seems to be inborn, as does the ability to distinguish between the three-dimensional version and the two-dimensional image.

Still, to build a sense of self-and-other, a great many additional attainments have to be achieved. Stern (1985) lists a number of factors that contribute to the core sense of self. To begin with, there is the sense of agency, the feeling of self as having intentions, as willing to do something and initiating an action. To know such a sense of agency on some level, however primitive, children must be able to configure for themselves an inner image of the action they want to perform, they must in effect have a motor map of what it would take to execute their intentionality, and they must be able then to translate the map into actual performed behavior. They must in addition know the proprioceptive quality of action, the difference in the feel of someone else moving their limb compared with their own initiation of such movement. And they must have a sense of the effect of their action, its impact on their world. The fact that they can predict the outcome of their own actions but cannot predict the consequences of another's actions is an additional help in distinguishing self from other. These are invariants; they accompany every action and form the building blocks of the sense of agency.

In addition to agency, there is the sense of self-coherence. This includes a sense of place, the innate capacity to orient toward the source of a sound. It includes as well the capacity to see unified motion. Thus, a mother's unity is enhanced for her baby when she is regularly perceived to move as a unit. Beyond that, these elements, the parts of a mother's form as well as her voice, all move in synchrony, and they do so at a rhythm and pace different from that of the child. This pervasive temporal as well as situational character of the mother's presence, and the contrasts it offers to the equivalent aspects of her baby's presence, also help to differentiate the two and to define the selfhood of each.

Thus far we have studied the unity of locus, coherence of motion, and coherence of temporal structure as factors determining the sense of self. Add to these now items making for self-coherence. One is the encounter with intensity. To illustrate this, an angry or pleasurably excited mother carries with her a unity of movement, conveys a quality of intensity, voice, and facial expression that are experienced together and that are quite apart from her baby's intensity when the baby is hungry. Another is the awareness of the unity of form. Babies who are 3 months old know their mother's face as hers whether she frowns or smiles. In sum, all these add to the sense of self-coherence and give it added substantiality.

Along with the aspects of self afforded by the sense of agency and self-coherence, yet another definer of a sense of self is the presence of self-affectivity. Self-affectivity involves the awareness of one's own feelings and the contribution this emotion awareness makes to an enhancement of the sense of self. Feelings are known in several invariant ways: There is the knowledge of the change in one's musculature, especially one's facial expression, when in the grip of emotion; there is the factor of kindling of affect, the characteristic feeling of affective arousal, of moving from lower to higher levels of experience; and there is the quality of the affect as such, be it vitality affect or categorical in kind. This has a flavor all of its own, and in the experiencing of this, one is confirmed in the awareness of self.

Finally, and most importantly, is the manifestation of self that is associated with memory, namely, the sense of self-history. The capacity for recall is again inborn, an inherent given. Now, however, by 3 months, an extensive sea of impressions have entered memory—images of self-agency, of self-coherence, of self affectivity, and the parallel awarenesses of the activity, coherence, and emotionality of caretakers. Much of this is continuously and clearly available, and it is out of these recollections that a sense of self is constructed and is maintained and grows.

In particular, let us turn our attention to actual details of the process of recall: what are the elements babies use to construct inner images? It is evident that one of the elements of experience that has particular valence for babies is the encounter with the significant other. For infants, this 3- to 9-month period is a time of extraordinary pressure toward socialization. Another way of saying that is to state flatly that during this interval all babies fall intensely, passionately, head over heels in love with their mommies. They cannot get enough of her; nothing means as much. They yearn for her when they do not have her at hand, light up when they see her, reach for her when she comes near, and crow when they touch her. Smiling has appeared, social smiling in response to others' presence, with a special smile for the beloved mommy. Hence, in laying down memory traces, special emphasis should be given to these moments of intense interactive experience with the loved one as begetters of memories.

It is therefore not surprising that Stern suggests that the important units of recall are the occasions of repeated interaction. Thus, a feeding experience, a mother–infant play session, or some other such exchange between the two is the likeliest place to look for the groundwork of memory constructs. What happens then is that the interactions between the mother and infant become familiar; their quality is both anticipated and predictable. A feeding is a comparable sequence of positionings, holdings, lookings, sucklings, with a fairly standard pattern of overall conduct of self and other as the process continues. Babies lay down a memory trace of such an exchange, then add another of very similar character the next time, and then another, and yet another as time advances.

At this point, however, if Stern is correct, a remarkable thing happens. Babies begin to average out these experiences and to construct a model of how the experience *should* go. It were as though a generalized representation of the interaction emerged from the recurrent encounters, an image that can serve as a basis for predicting and judging the character of the next such encounter. Stern calls these representations of interactions that have been generalized (RIGs). These RIGs are the building blocks of the core self, islands of consistency that form and coalesce out of the welter of infantile experience. They provide the basic material for constructing a sense of self as well as a sense of other.

It is my view that these early generalized representations are a unique and precious achievement to infants. In effect, each one is a work of art, a creation, their own rendering of a series of intense and valued experiences into a concentrated and succinct whole. There is a quality here of recording unifying it, distilling its essence and capturing its quality, and this, I believe, is central to the aesthetic encounter with a work of art, whether as creator or as viewer.

It is important to keep in mind the central role of these RIGs. They provide the bricks to build the mansion of the sense of self. They give infants the agency, the intensity, the coherence, and the continuity that together make for a continuing awareness of inner presence, inner integrity. They are dynamic presences, constantly undergoing small changes as each new experience is summed into the average, yet they are static in the sense of being repeats of the same kind of sequence occurring over and over; this is what offers the sense of self the necessary stability and continuity and engenders the feeling of knowing one is there and who one is.

There are many RIGs because, in a reasonably stable household, many patterned interactions recur in predictable fashion. These averaged experiences then are constantly in mind. Indeed, it is likely that infants call them up and in effect replay them regularly for the sheer hedonic pleasure of the encounter, or in a striving for mastery, or both. In any case, these recalls offer an opportunity to use imagery in the service of personal growth, in the service of building a sense of self.

It is my thesis here that works of art or sculpture that have the greatest appeal for us do so because they echo or capture some of the elements that characterize our earliest RIGs. The works are always averages, distilled essences of numerous experiences, now frozen here for us within a single frame but wielding their power because they convey the immense richness of recurrent and repeated emotional experiences summed up and concentrated in this one image. In a sense, each encounter with a work of art, be it painting, etching, sculpture, woodcut, engraving, silk screen, or any other representational mode returns us immediately to the status of early learners, early experiencers. We see a presence that reverberates with our experience, which captures something of our own early formulations. Many variables can come to bear on such an encounter, personal idiosyncrasies, cultural conventions, recent traumatic events, the unique temperament and the individual development of the viewer, and the like. The better the work of art, the more effectively it can transcend these many variations on the principal theme and more truly reach in and touch the area of clamorous and resonating early experiences that never leave us. We are, after all, forever working with our core selves, forever reveling in our sense of agency. We can make things happen, forever studying our sense of coherence. We have assets and competencies; we command resources and maintain our identity, forever working with our sense of affectivity. We are swept by surges of emotion, or we contain all that we would or must. And finally, forever looking back to our sense of continuity, we have been somewhere and done some things; we go forward on a long path.

The sense of a core self is not usually very conscious; it is either unconscious (in the sense of unavailable to conscious experience on demand) or preconscious. In the latter case it is kept in our head like the times tables, ordinarily unobtrusive but available when needed. We think of our past, we attend to our emotions, we focus on our ability to make things happen, or we worry about the integrity of our bodies and minds; in each such instance we continue to be ever faithful to the demands of core experience. Or, as is probably more usually the case, we do not think of these things very often, and they continue to work away somewhere in the back of our minds to be evoked into full awareness only when something unusual occurs. And among the unusual things to happen is to become involved with a work of art.

At this point we can consider the theme of art from two points of view: that of the creator or that of the viewer. In the way we live our lives, most of us are both; we seek at times to create some meaningful art form (even if it is doodling), and we seek at other times to enjoy the objects of beauty that both man and nature thrust before us. Clearly, in our therapeutic work we encourage the creative component of art experience and seek to help both by freeing people to depict their experience and to tell their stories in nonverbal terms and by aiding them to understand the ineffable and unsayable and thus to grasp some of the meaning of what they have thus expressed.

But perhaps it will better illuminate the points to be made here if initially we come at the matter from the other approach, if we focus on the perception of art rather than on its formation, and attempt to describe its impact on the viewer rather than explore the mind of the artist. Moreover, the case of the spectator is probably the simpler situation and the more easily described; heuristically if not logically it deserves priority. In addition, if we set aside the complexities of creativity, the same essential elements will be present in both instances. Let us then begin from the viewer's standpoint.

To begin with, then, we might ask: What is a work of art; what distinguishes just any representation from the genuine aesthetic object? The average photograph, for example, is an image, but it is not a work of art.

It is a single impression, a cross section of reality; it has no quality of summarizing and concentrating many realities into a single image. Without the quality about it of a distillation of multiple experiences, it is imagery to be sure, but not art. To take the opposite extreme, let us consider for a moment the shadowed image of a Rembrandt. Here is a statement whose profundity lies precisely in its universality; it is the essence of all human suffering, all the struggles with the infinite ambiguities and ambivalences of life, all the efforts to contain and control the importunate strivings of the carnal and infantile, all the pain of injured pride and wounded self-respect, all captured in a single ultimately perfected image of light and shadow, of somberness and hope, of inner glow amid outer darkness. Another example: the madness of a late van Gogh is the churning twisting turmoil that at some moment in our lives all of us have known and to which so seldom we give voice; it is the torment of the breaking mind seeking to order what has become the chaos of everyday experience; it is ultimately all human torment drenched in bright sunlight and dancing color. And so for the sunglow of a Turner, the great sunlight he depicts is all the sunlight of the world, all the heat and glare of tossed light on water wherever we have seen it, captured for us in one frame, ultimate and forever.

What allows some to do this, to convert the barren materials and rather primitive paraphernalia of the artist into these glorious experiences of attained perfection? Well, the details of technique are far beyond me or my theorizing, and I will say nothing about those; however, we have but to look at the nature of core self to get a sense of at least some of the elements that must minimally be present. Let us start with the sense of agency. A work of art moves. That is to say, the eye moves; the work must be so constructed that it teaches the eye when to advance, when to retreat, and where and when to sojourn. With a photograph—with most photographs at any rate—there is a single item to be seen. No action on our part is required; we need but look. But with a creative work we cannot stand still. We must encompass, we must traverse, we must be active and engaged. We go forth, as agents, to meet the artist as agent; we explore the artist's themes, pursue the artist's ideas. All the elements of agency that give rise to self-feelings are there. We are forced, in the very engagement with the art object, to reach for it; it will not allow us to be passive. We must quest after it, seek its mystery, pursue its allusions—and come to know ourselves better in the very act of our seeking. We become aware of our quest, of the demand it makes and our attempt to reply; in the attempt to savor and to understand the cryptic message we are considering we become aware of ourselves as actors, doers, initiators. We feel the kinesthesia of our eyes, the effect upon us of our seeking—and our finding. Our action is rewarded. We stand quietly and contemplate, and withal we are enhanced, immensely alive.

Or, if we move from self-agency to self-coherence, here is where good art is master. Any creation of merit is profoundly together, profoundly one.

Each jot and tittle, each iota, each brush stroke, each dab of color or fragment of line, however minute, fits in. It belongs. It inheres in the work; it is part of the whole, contributes to the whole, takes meaning from the whole. Where art is at its best, nothing is superfluous; nothing can be spared. The sense of balanced belongingness of such works is a remarkable restorative to the human spirit; it catches our early efforts to summarize experiences and to pull out everything important to grasp the hidden essence in what happens to us and to keep every relevant detail in place and in order. Our RIGs seek such concentrated inclusiveness and achieve it, more or less depending on what we bring to the situation.

The coherence of locus, motion, temporal structure, intensity structure, and form are the invariants associated with self-coherence, and we find them richly present in works of art. To begin with, the overt boundaries of the work itself are a critical component of an artistic experience. No matter how chaotic or disruptive the image on the canvas, it always takes place within a bounded universe; the locus is set. It is like a tumult of passions and ideas rioting about inside the head. It is often important that they remain inside the head and is often difficult to keep them there. One of the defining burdens of the human condition is the problem of self-governance: putting limits to our drives and impulses. It is one of the dominating issues of the early epoch of development. It is then not surprising that the creation of frames has become something of an art form. It does not merely enhance the image within; it also contains it and keeps it in one defined place. It makes for at least the possibility of control.

The factor of coherence of motion is very alive in paintings or sculpture. Immobile they may be, but the several parts of the picture must nonetheless hang together, move together in relationship to other parts. Each sector, each subsection has its own patterns and regularities, and each plays against other patterns and rhythms in other parts of the work. For the really effective art object, the parts must move against each other, with each other, and with the whole. Moreover, the work never stands still; the movement is constant.

Temporal structure is visible in relation to rhythmic elements of the art object. This temporal unity is what contains the biologic aspect of the work, its basic cadence. For all works of art, of whatever medium, of whatever sensory modality, all share this rootedness in rhythm, all rest on this biologic base. And in painting or sculpture, this component, the pervasive quality of repetition, the internal mirroring and echoing, the resonance in the relationship of part to part and part to whole, adds to the unifying impact of the emergent organization. Surely that is one of the great functions of the RIGs: to give ever greater unity and coherence to the sense of self.

But beyond that both the RIGs and the works of art have the quality of intensity. Herein lies a factor that is at once elusive and fundamental. For good art commands; it requires and obtains concentration on the part of the viewer. Some of the sense of augmented awareness that accompanies the moment of contemplation, of indeed interaction with the art object, arises from the experience of heightened aliveness, heightened intensity, which is part of the experience. In responding to the demands of the image, we become more aware of ourselves. So indeed does it happen with infants whose sense of self is in part a function of their experience with their own RIGs; the greater the power of the image, the more perfect the balance among its components, the more evocative its inner structure, the greater its intensity, and the more alive babies become to their own selfhood.

Finally, form is all important in this kind of creativity, indeed, the purpose of it all is to create form. So powerful and so dominating is the presence of form at this juncture that whole schools of art have arisen around the extolling of particular varieties of form and, in more recent years, around the defiance of form. Cubism, Dadaism, abstract expressionism, and a host of other movements of one kind or another have taken up cudgels against form or have espoused particular kinds of form or in any case have attempted by one means or another to alter the existing and accepted modes of artistic expression. There is, however, no evading form; to the extent that one is an artist one is forced ultimately to cope with this even if it means merely to substitute one form for another. One may well fight against traditional concepts of or prevailing preferences for particular varieties of form; there is nowhere to flee from form itself. It is necessary for us, too necessary in these early crucible months when we are just gaining the first rudiments of a sense of self, to allow any such possibility of flight to exist. We are hungry for forms, and we will have them.

Let us study a Kandinsky or a Miro. We see a play of forms; playfulness indeed pervades the work. Clearly the artists are busily avoiding anything that could be called representational art. But the criteria of coherence in locus, in motion, in temporal structure or rhythm, and in form are all remarkably well joined. The elements are not random; they are intricately and beautifully structured together. Most important of all, perhaps, is the unity of intensity structure that pervades throughout. The playful quality previously noted is everywhere. It is apparent in the choices of colors, in the design of the selected configurations, in the situating of the various elements in relationship to one another and to the whole. It is apparent as well that the playfulness conceals a more serious goal, an attempt to take us back to the earliest preverbal times when the meaning of the many images that impinged on us was not yet evident, when experience was largely with images that lacked cognitive significance but were nonetheless orderly and coherent and delightful and diverting in their own way. In the beginning the world we as babies put together was probably very unlike the world that now we know. Perhaps the elements were less familiar, less formed, then, than they would later become. But these ancestors marched to the same drum as would their later descendents; they had to cohere, to stay within the RIG, to be satisfying and intense and together, and to merit recall. And so with these later artistic creations, they are about nothing at all; they tell merely of artists' love of their work and quest for its essence.

Self-affectivity is closely linked to intensity. It involves the emotional message conveyed by the work of art, a message induced both by its form, its content, and the level of its demand on the viewer. This probably works in two ways. The first involves the matter of amodal perception. Certain colors, certain linear arrangements, certain patterns will transform themselves into amodal forms that in turn can be felt as affective experience. A jagged line excites one kind of affective stirring, a gentle flowing line another. Bright colors against pastels, clarity against ambiguity, shadow against light, coarse texture against fine grain, crude and massive form against delicate or sophisticated outline, clustering forms against those that seem to fly from each other: these and an infinity of additional possibilities all speak to the universe of vitality affects. By dint of amodal perception they "translate" immediately into inner stirrings of affective rejoinder. They are lines; form and colors become movements of feeling and emotion, not yet moods, not states of categorical emotion, but full of vital arousal nonetheless. Explosive patterns, or soothing ones, surges and stirrings and calmings and quietings, a sense of gusto or a press toward inwardness: all these can flow from the way light encounters darkness, the boldness of drawn lines, or the surface finishing of a carved or molded form. An immense variety of responses can flow from appropriate arrays of such parts. Not everyone will be affected in exactly the same way; not everyone responds in the same way to any of the visual art forms. The good artists find the means, however, that have general applicability and to which many respond. The heavy palette knife of one painter and the tiny watercolor brush of another are both but means to that end, to instill the vitality affects essential to the overall emotional message of the work.

The categorical affects, sadness or rage or joy and the like, will emerge as well. These are more global in character, the resultants of many details acting together. Such overall emotions and moods are more closely tied to the massing of elements than to any single factor among them. These larger affect bundles would include the content of the work in the sense of its explicit story, plus the vitality affects hidden away in the kinds of lines, patterns, and color play employed.

But the categorical affects are even more dependent on the second major factor making for self-feelings: the affective content of the RIGs. For the RIGs, as elements of memory, carry with them potent lacings of the emotional experiences that accompanied the events thus remembered. This is particularly true after the RIGs for painful and stressful events have been established; anything that acts to evoke such a RIG will carry with it the disturbing affects that are resident in that recalled generalization. Babies learn early of tears and crying and hurt, and if they recall the event sequence that involved such pain they recall the pain as well. They recall the content of the experience, what their face felt like as they cried, what tears felt like, what their feelings were, what happened in the actual interaction with the caretaker, what caused the pain to mount, and what brought relief. Thus, the content of the RIG, the generalized recollection, also includes the generalized version of the affective response. Later, when an appropriate stimulus evokes the RIG, these affects are there to be reexperienced.

Let us consider an infant whose mother is depressed. Such a baby learns early that when his mother is tearful, protest though he may, he will feel his hunger mount for a long time before she acts to bring him relief—and any subsequent experiences with tears may have enormous meaning to him, far beyond what would usually be evoked by such an encounter.

The capacity of good artists to capture the impact and the sense of early RIGs is one of the great phenomena of creativity. Let us look at such a painting as *Le Cri* (*The Scream*) by Munch. Here the combination of vitality affect arousing components with a content of imagery, suggesting aloneness, abandonment, and overwhelming fear, have enough of the indistinct about them to fit the generalized recollections of many, many people. In particular, these will affect people who have known traumatic experience at some point in their lives. So powerful and so effective is the work that there are individuals who cannot endure this painting; they admire the greatness of the painter but are unable to cope with the level of disturbing affect the work itself arouses. I would speculate that the degree of disturbance such people experience is a direct function of the level of development involved; those who have been traumatized at earlier times, who have fewer defenses against the overwhelming character of such early emotions, are more likely to find this not so much a work of art as a breach into the outline of the self, an opening into themselves of unendurable character. A similar pattern of responses is to be found in the macabre painting by Goya, *Cronus Devouring His Children*. Once again we face a combination of vitality affect evokers and a sufficiently indistinct, generalized gigantic devourer of a small, helpless human figure to arouse the RIGs of early childhood fears. All the complaints we hear from little ones of being afraid in the night, that "something will come and eat me up," all the pure infantile terror enshrined in these RIGs, is there to be recalled by the content of this terrifying image. Again, I would suggest that many of those most vulnerable to this painting's message will have had an especially difficult time at these early epochs when oral fears were so omnipresent and so strong.

All of this belongs as well with the final category of core self-experience, that of self-history. This is in a sense self-explanatory; one of the surest guarantors we have of the reality of our selves is the knowledge of our past, the ability to look back and recognize that we have come from somewhere and that we are continuing a pattern of the past as we build toward the future. It is so fundamental that in fact we do not ordinarily consider it;

we simply accept it as a given. The elements of personal history are stored somewhat untidily as a set of memories occupying the back of our minds and open to recall on request. In effect, much of the earlier experience amounts to a series of RIGs, not individual memories so much as generalized reconstructions of many memories, serving now the functions of allowing us to prepare for new experiences by consulting the summary statements of our prior encounters.

So too does art affect us. It summarizes our past, brings out the essence of our interactions, be they compassionate, erotic, or horrific, and offers them to us as yet another occasion to experience our link to that past, another occasion for enhancing our selfhood. We sense a kinship with a good work of art; what its creator knew, we know too, what he felt, we feel too. Among other things, we share a common past. And this can transcend time and culture; truly good art captures the dimensions of human experience (as we have seen) that are true for us because of our preverbal humanity rather than because of our social affinities. To be sure, if we understand the culture within which art objects develop we will know that much more about the intention of the artists, the forces that shaped them and perhaps compelled them to work as they did, and the intended meaning of the elements of their work. But we can look at the Lescaux cave paintings whose creators have vanished totally from the world leaving no other account of their passing than these very paintings, and we can know something of their work and their lives, their feelings and their dreams, their greatness and their primitivism.

We now turn our attention to the creative aspect of artistry and perceive immediately that the most salient and evident dimension of self that accompanies the creative effort is that of self-agency. Nothing makes us more alive to ourselves than the act of creation. We tune in to our inner processes with a closeness and vividness that are unique. For many people this is a source of curious and specific pleasure, and for many it is a troublesome kind of awareness; however, for all people it is an encounter with the sense of self as actor, the self as initiator, the self as willing that something happen—and then making it happen. It is a moment of great aliveness.

This perhaps more than any other feature of artistic activity defines and enhances the therapeutic impact of art therapy; patients engaged in this way are not blocked and helpless and thwarted; inherently, they become persons who can do something. Perhaps it is not what they would most wish to do and dream of doing—but something. The self is there as agent, to be reckoned with, to express what it would. The very act of creation adds to their wholeness.

And as agents they know their inner schema for the effort, their action plan, and they know too their sense of movement in the actual accomplishment of the work, the physical involvement in the performance. And then there is the reward of the product; they produce something, have an accomplishment to show for their efforts, and their uniqueness is inevitably more clearly defined.

The several elements of coherence implicit in such work are especially helpful for heavily burdened individuals. Stressful emotional difficulties make for a sense of being overwhelmed, with a resultant loss of outlines and a blurring of the margins of their identity. The augmentation of the sense of self-coherence that accompanies creative acts is reflected in the sharpening of boundaries with the consequent strengthening of controls (the crayon may not go outside the line or the pencil off the paper and onto the table). The need to master at least the rudiments of technique makes for a more unified sense of self as mover; they must focus their effort and act in a unitary rather than a fragmented fashion. Then, the elements in the work ask for some kind of rhythmic treatment, even if it is merely filling in the color on a particular patch or, more subtly, catching the rhythm of the figure they seek to produce, its bilaterality (if that is applicable), the symmetry of its placement on the page. Balance and equilibrium both play a part in any drawing or painting or carving or molding; they are inherent in the very essence of form.

Then the need to cope with intensity brings to the fore the mode of expression and the mastery aspect of creativity; by the very depiction of some of what one feels inside, by its externalization in a bound and sublimated fashion, these individuals are less burdened by the power of the inner stresses, less their victim. This easing of pressure, even if momentary, can be a source of significant relief at a time of intense and explosive inner turmoil. In the nature of things, the readiness to express and the capacity to do so will vary enormously from person to person, but even miniscule creative efforts are likely to offer an element of basic support to the management of internal pain. Finally, as the last component of self-coherence, the creation of forms has peculiar and powerful meaning to the sense of self. There is a quality of conclusive closure, a sense, and, indeed, a reality of accomplishment that accompanies the achievement of any created form. We do not doodle by accident. We do not build collections or undertake crossword puzzles by happenstance. We seek and need to have a task done and speak often of doing it right, doing it well. Moreover, we select and devote ourselves to such relatively easy and innocuous tasks as antidote to some of the more burdensome and toxic tasks with which life so often confronts us. Form is very fundamental to the inner sense of self and is given such names as identity or personality, the sense of wholeness. The attainment of form is reassuring, completing, and to offer someone in need the opportunity and the means of attaining form, in any sense, is to offer a substantial assist indeed.

This has meaning as well for the self dimension associated with affectivity. The vitality affects in particular, with their eruptings and explodings, their recoilings and deadenings, tend to make for extremes of experience, including inner encounters with hurtful and distressing sensations; to the extent that these can be translated as such into lines and planes, colors and surfaces, textures and images—in short, into communicable sensory modalities, it opens the door to a greater measure of objectivity than we had before. By studying what we have expressed, we can approach a better and more rational view of the nature of our problems and thus come nearer to an improved possibility of self-understanding. This more objective view of the inner dynamic forces allows as well for the beginning emergence of better coping strategies for their management.

We close with self-history. Each achievement of form, each accomplished task, is a marker in the growth and solidification of the sense of self. Factory workers look back to the cars they have helped build, or laborers at the railroad, or construction workers at the building; it is a milestone, a sign post that validates their existence, a building block in their sense of self. Babies have their RIGs, their important moments of excitation and interaction that they recall and relive and that assure them of their continuity from past to present. And patients have their moments of insight and understanding, of relationship opening and achieved expression to mark the stages of their struggle with their pain and increasing grasp on their problems. For those who are helped by the use of art, the ability to create forms that were once taboo, to communicate themes that could not be previously expressed, and to share emotions that were once too dangerous to approach are landmarks of worth and substance, and their attainment too can be facilitated by the work of the attuned therapist.

References

Stern, D. N. (1985). *The interpersonal world of the infant: A view from psychoanalytic and developmental psychology.* New York: Basic Books.

Chapter 6

Prose and poetry

INTRODUCTION

Theodore Shapiro

The following essay draws on many themes that I am sure Joe Noshpitz enjoyed investigating. He tells of the loss of the seamless self of infancy that fades with the acquisition of language; of the domains of feeling that can never again be accessed once the child takes on verbal capacity; of the malleability of language in use as prose and poetry. These themes are all discussed within the idiom of developmental theory and as a remarkably sophisticated parse on Freudian ideas concerning inner and outer life as well as a commentary on infantile mirroring and its effect on the growing child's capacity to experience, tolerate, and express emotions.

Each of these areas has been elaborated by more specialized scholars such as Lev Vigotsky, Heinz Werner, Daniel Stern, Peter Fonagy, and Sigmund Freud and those who followed him focusing on object relations.

From a linguistic standpoint, the earliest developmentalists indicated that expression precedes the appeal function of language and that in the end we can dissociate the utterance from the thing and declare at a physical and temporal distance from the experience. Language is a coded reference system. Thus, we finally are able to create narratives that refer to both description of the past and present and future world and also to fantasy and emotion. Someone once noted that babies are "overheard" and from that initial recognition of the shape of words use their new words to appeal—thus the word *Mommy* can have the appeal function that designates "pick me up," "hold me," "feed me," and then after some differentiation more words are added that create new and more articulated stories and out of sight references. Vigotsky boldly said that once the knot of prelinguistic thought is tied to language at about 3 years, it is firmly established as the human communication system.

Werner, in addition, refers to the growing distancing between word and its referent, the thing that parallels the distancing between mother and infant during development. Mahler's practicing subphase depends on locomotion and language, both enhancing the act of removal from the mother.

Stern's exploration of the development of self, from core to linguistic self, offers a broader description of Joe Noshpitz's lost inner self, the synscitium of feelings and convergent states of mind and affect that alienates the language competent child from the nonverbal infant. Joe too suggests that the words of our language are never adequate to describe inner states well; indeed, he goes so far as to say that, even when parental mirroring permits an accession of knowledge of one's own and other's mental–affective states, words are weak communicators.

I would suggest that Joe is talking about the difference between communion and communication. Poetry, in turn, is the closest arbiter of feelingful discourse. The condensations and rich allusions and displacements in metaphor in poetry remind us of the tropes in the dreamwork that Freud used to decipher dreams derived during sleep from the impact of the day residue and the workings of drive and defense on the image of representation.

The effectiveness of dynamic therapy that Joe espoused is an amalgam of affect designation in the context of human interactions boiled down to a narrative that has salience. That is why Fonagy insists on reflective function and Joe carries his removal of the word from the thing to a more generalized narrative that in all its specificity in the therapeutic hour also can be generalized for use in life and reflected on at a distance.

Joe Noshpitz had broad experience with indigent children who did not have adequate grasp of the names of their feelings and were not mirrored well or accustomed to using feelings as signals that helped modulate and delay motor discharge and impulsivity. He knew also that words could be delivered with precision and that some words are laden with affect and appropriate for certain rhetorical speech acts and that others could be delivered with tonal prosodic accuracy to display feeling in the music of the discourse. He was a master at oratory.

I will end by citing an incident that I witnessed. Joe was introducing an esteemed colleague, Jerry Wiener, who had just completed his stint as program chair of the American Academy of Child Psychiatry. He described the complexities of the work using the metaphor of the construction of a cathedral—the suspension of the apse, the construction of the archways and the buttresses. All were described in grandiloquent language and with much enthusiasm and love. Jerry thanked Joe for the lavish introduction but cautioned that while he was ever thankful he was not certain what his Jewish mother would say on learning that he was spending his time constructing a cathedral. Everyone enjoyed Joe and learned from his breadth of knowledge. His capacity for joy in learning was universally recognized.

PROSE AND POETRY

Joseph D. Noshpitz

The sense of verbal self appears at approximately 15 months of age. This coincides with the elaboration of language and opens up a remarkable epoch in child development. For with the coming of language, all the former structuring of self is forever altered and will never regain its previous state.

Put in simplest terms, words bring with them the ability to denote, and that in turn enters into the previously sensual wholeness and unity of experience and begins to fractionate it. Under optimal conditions, preverbal children know their affects, movements, initiatives, and memories as a smooth connected flow of experience without seam or fissure. Things happen to them, and they respond, they recall, but they do all this consecutively and in an undulating, continuous fashion. Their feelings, all of their feelings, are more or less continually available to them as they study their world and move around within it, communicate, and interact. To be sure, where conditions are less than optimal, disturbing emphases may already have been put on one aspect of self or another, and a sense of concealment may be in place even at this early epoch. Children whose mother cannot endure dirt or spit or noise, or too much excitement, or tears, or pleas for attention will have already communicated to them that some part of them is undesirable, that they must forbid themselves the expression of certain natural responses if they are to remain on good terms with their mother. And during this age of social drivenness, nothing is more important than to maintain those good terms, and all too often an aspect of the self is given up in the hope of retaining their mother's favor.

For example, a youngster may ascertain by too many repeated experiences that any effort on her part to reach for what interests her automatically involves frustration, and sometimes confrontation. After many such daily experiences she simply stops reaching. She may yield her capacity for agency; all spontaneity and initiative are lost. She becomes sad and passive, unwilling any longer to try, waiting for the decisions to come from the outside. Thus, such communication patterns with their massive effects can begin early in life, long before the verbal self appears. Somewhere within the child's self, we can speculate that the wishes and impulses have not altogether disappeared, but now their form is hidden, they are contained, they have become secrets. Where and how they are walled off, we do not yet know; however it happens, it means that the integrity and overall continuity of self has been ruptured.

Let us abandon this image for the moment and return to the ideal picture. Let us assume that the sense of self has been well treated and well supported throughout and that the child has come to the period of verbalization with no sense of fragmentation or inner division. Then language begins to become central to the child. Now it is important to note that language is specific, it is not general. The child's caretakers respond to elements in his makeup, but not to its totality. Out of the mix of movement and intent and emotion and image, the words select one feeling and speak only to that. There is no way to capture the fullness of experience in words. A little shake of the baby's bottom, a pat on his head, a game—those need exclude nothing, they are experienced as empathic reflections and responses that confirm both the act of the moment specifically and the child generally. With nonverbal responses, wholeness is preserved.

Once words enter the picture, however, they cannot convey the same totality; in the nature of things they are too specific. This precision is both their greatest asset and their major problem. They denote an act, a feeling, a part of babies, a point in reality; they can subtend somewhat more of babies' self by adding rhythm and gearing the choice of words to an optimal level, they can add mock emotion and playful affects of all kinds and take in even more—but ultimately, they must leave out much. As babies begin to rely on words, their mother's reactions become far more specific and her responses leave out as much or more than they blend in.

At first, the excitement of the word game, the ability to name things, the gladsome reward of the elation that comes with each new word, each new utterance: these override all other feelings; they dominate the experience. This is Mahler's practicing phase, the first flush of discovery, the first entrance into a new world of interactive exchange, the ecstatic response to novel encounter.

Presently, however, the novel becomes the everyday, the word that was worn like a jewel dazzling everyone becomes a functional tool that is taken for granted. In particular, instead of enacting their feelings, children turn more and more to these new instruments to make their case. And so, they find them woefully lacking. Whole rushes of emotion cannot be articulated, quick blends and tinges of feeling come and go, subterranean floods of affect that form a background to a particular affirmation or denial have no ready way to come into the one- or two-word sentence currently available to them. They can offer a strident "No!" to certain overtures, a complex directive that tries to express many levels of meaning at once. Ultimately, however, much is inherently omitted.

Perhaps more to the point is that all prior experience, all preverbal encounters, were always in the form of contexts. One took in a context with feelings and images, with smells and movements, all combining to comprise a totality. Words also create context; indeed, every sentence is a new context, and within that framework even half-heard words or incomplete grammatical structures can convey meanings. They grow out of the context; they are carried by it and convey their modicum of understanding even though they are impaired or imperfect or have even omitted parts. But it is in the nature of words to have about them a rather sharp boundary, a delimited specificity that cannot truly capture the wholeness of the inner milieu. The part that the words describe is depicted wonderfully, perhaps pulling the inner mixture into a form and setting around it a boundary that gives it a sharpness and definition it can achieve no other way. But at best only a part can be thus articulated, and the rest remains hidden. This is the great paradox of language: it reveals elements, items of inner experience, threads drawn from the pattern that in themselves are fuzzy and relatively soft-edged, flowing into the rest of the pattern of inner experience, hard to extract, hard to delineate. But once named, once designated by word, once removed from the flowing state of inwardness and made into a verbalized entity, that strand of thought, feeling, image, dream-like association, in any case inner experience now assumes boundary and definition, has been given title and delimitation, can be shared and mutually examined. And it can be questioned and challenged, studied and tested, compared and contrasted, and ultimately made common property of the many.

But, in doing so, we must recall its origins—it was taken out of matrix, abstracted from concept, parted from wholeness. What then of the matrix or context itself: what happens to it? It is inherently damaged. One cannot leave out a portion of something and just get away with it; there is always a price to pay. We humans pay the price for our precious gift of speech; it loses us our inner integrity and divides us from one another's empathic and subjective connectedness. It forces us to reestablish new wholenesses on the outside, as it were, to create new contexts now, verbal contexts, where a certain soundness and totality, a sense of contextual wholeness, can be reestablished by words, by language, and by the use of verbal instrumentalities of one kind or another.

More than that, it drives us to find new ways to connect with one another, verbal ways, ways that transcend or at any rate replace the former empathic state, that require that the shadings of affect be named, that the multiple and conflicting intentions be made explicit, that the glints of memory and the many, many contexts formerly created, formerly known and felt, all be arrayed in order and specified in detail.

In fact, it cannot be done; it cannot even be done partially. Only fragments of that endless and turbulent inner flow can ever be captured, and only tiny bits (sampled from prior experience) can be recaptured. There is no way to grasp the majority, no way to say it all, and, within the interpersonal context, no way to express it all. In the nature of things within human communication, much must remain allusive and implicit. And within the individual mind, much—most of its contents—will remain forever unexpressed, a truly inner world.

What, then, of the connection between this inner world and the outer universe of experience? This is one of the key tensions of human existence, conscious and unconscious. It has two great interfaces, the one between the full flow of the inner life and the attempt to formulate it and to frame it in language. This is roughly the censor between preconscious and conscious. The other is the gateway between conscious awareness and action, in particular, the action of speaking. Individuals pull their thoughts together, capture the elusive concept, the fugitive image—and find language for it. Then they must pass the final censor and communicate.

Or, they find a way, by means of word, to hark back to the original inner milieu, to restore words to the great flow from which the idea was torn, to indicate—by verbal structures—that things can be put back together, made whole again. The rent in fabric can be mended; the flow continues within with a sense of healing and wholeness. How can words—the great specifiers, the inherent dividers of consciousness—repair? The answer is simple. There are two great modes of word use: the prosaic and the poetic. The prosaic divides the self but constructs the verbal and conceptual world on the objective nonself. The poetic, to the extent that it succeeds, is always a self-experience. The truly prosaic is inherently objective and at odds with the self-milieu. There are many shadings in between.

Let us look at some examples. Perhaps the ultimate in prosody is the technical statement, the bare account of an objective datum. For example, let us take the statement: for any right triangle, the square of the hypotenuse equals the sum of the squares of the arms. Here we can see the truly inhuman, the statement that stands despite all subjective experience, indeed outside of subjective experience, and utterly uncaring of whether it connects with such experience. It belongs to the outside world, and in encountering it subjectivity must divide and flow around it. It cannot affect such a statement; it can barely connect with it. To understand it requires technical knowledge, in other words, nonself-related knowledge, and the words bear the hallmark of such knowledge. Such language draws people outside themselves; it immerses them totally in the world. It can thus be used in the service of flight from the self. Once buried in their work, people turn from inner experience to the kind of outer involvement offered by the technical, the completely external. Perhaps they fight with themselves to remain in this realm, to avoid pain or fear by turning their back on inwardness, to lose self-awareness by committing to thing awareness, by keeping these worlds apart.

But this is the easy kind of example, the commonplace experience. A better illustration comes when people try to talk about their feelings. How difficult this is for so many. How inarticulate they become when they try to describe some aspect of inner experience, especially within an interpersonal context. They suffer from two problems. One is that they do not know how to sector out a part of the flow of consciousness and put it into words. For them, that remains always a massive undertaking, one that baffles and defeats them. They cannot give name to their feelings; they do not know them and may experience emotions as threatening always to escape control, dangerous inner entities they strive to submerge rather than identify.

By the same token, they are deeply concerned, sometimes terrified, that whatever way they do express the feelings will fail, will not be understood, or, worse still, if understood, rejected. Or perhaps rejected because misunderstood, and how to repair the ensuing breach, how to set things right? They have to identify the misunderstanding as such and to reexplain the hard-to-describe feeling. It is all so complicated, impossible—and these individuals are stopped, frozen. There is no way to say it and get it right, no way to be sure one will remain in control, no way to be sure one will not be misunderstood, and absolutely no way to correct things if they do go awry.

Then, suppose they do say it; can it ever be said right? Is it ever the full context that is conveyed? No, prose does not allow for that; language isolates elements, abstracts particular issues, fails to convey context. To be sure, there are a few, a talented few, who can tell everything, describe the whole context, render the full experience in enough words to capture it all. But it took James Joyce many hundreds of pages and many truly extraordinary flights of language to tell the story of a single day in the life of one man—how many words, how many pages are needed for a single moment? For a single feeling? And at best it can be only part of the flow.

Prose is like a camera. It stops a bit of experience, catches a frame, part of a moment. Most photographs—as most people take them—are not works of art; they are merely prosaic accounts of what is, interruptions in the ordinary ordering of human awareness, inherently incomplete, inherently transitory, a single frame of memory, usually with most of the affect left out.

In therapy, the proper use of prose is to build cognitive structures. There are several kinds. One is the establishing of links, building bridges of words and of understanding. These connections can occur in a variety of areas. They can relate the past to the present, they can link up the emotion to the idea, they would tie together one part of current experience and another, they serve to connect the unconscious and the conscious. There are thus a host of potential linkages that escape us or that we need to keep hidden or that we know but cannot face (cannot express), and the pronouncement of these linkages, especially if we can be led to make the connections ourselves has a unifying effect, restores at least a modicum of wholeness. In effect, what was fragmented can, at least to a limited extent, be given to repair through words.

There are inherent limits to this. Since we cannot as a rule knit together contexts, and the words themselves capture only fragments of background, even our best efforts are necessarily incomplete. So long as we confine ourselves to prose, we can undo some of the damage. But we have no tools to get at it all.

Poetry, on the other hand, is not divisive and explicit. It can be, but that is not its nature. Poetry is the effort to use language not constructively, as does prose, but reconstructively. Poetry is always an attempt to heal. To achieve its goals, it uses a wide variety of techniques.

To begin with, poetry is anarchic. In the seeking of wholeness it tries to approximate the fluid unity of inner experience, and it therefore is unbounded and amorphous, striving to lose itself in us, to have us lose ourselves in it. This carries with it the threat of chaos; it can slip over into the boundless, the amorphous, the use of language without identifiable referents in experience. In its truest sense it is inherently enigmatic, attempting as it does to use words to express the ineffable. Hence it is driven to many strange devices.

To begin with, poetry is profoundly biological. To the extent that it seeks the wholeness of experience it is close to how the brain works. This is visible in its structure—basic to poetry is the presence of rhythm. This is critical; it is probably true that without rhythm we are not really dealing with poetry at all—that is one of the characteristics of prose. Not that prose lacks all rhythm; it is likely to be there on some level, but it is far less central to the prosaic experience and far less salient.

With poetry, in most instances, the rhythmic component is marked. It is called meter and at one time was divided into many varieties, each with a classical Greek name. This was usually considered a contrivance, a device to add richness and beauty and power to the poem and indeed it does all that or can do it. But it adds something else as well—a biological base on which the work is built, a connection with the earthy and the primitive. It is one of the great unifiers we know and keeps the basic context of the poem allied with the context of the working body, of life.

A second dimension of poetry is form. Perhaps in reaction to its potential for chaos, much poetic expression has been confined within the bounds of strict formal requirements. This included the number of feet per line, the character of the rhythmic pattern employed, the number of lines required, the rhyme pattern appointed for this structure, even the distribution of meanings. Thus, the Shakespearean sonnet had to have three four-line quatrains, which stated a troubled proposition, and a final couplet that reflected back on all the 12 preceding lines and illuminated them, casting, as it were, a sharp beam of light into the semidarkness of the poem so that its contours stood out with power and clarity and the meaning of the whole was thrust home.

Within this context, poets would then allow their yearning to capture and connect with inner experience, to provide a sense of inner restoration, to reach for wholeness, to convey something of the multipotentiality of inner experience, and to communicate it to readers or listeners so they were enlarged and unified, understood more, or, even without understanding, were better knit than they had been. The goal of the poem is to send a message to the preverbal and unutterable inner core of the person, a message of discovery and novelty, of mounting tension and achieved resolution, of fear of fragmentation and the restoration of unity. It tells of chaos encountered and disorganization surmounted. No state of entropy, no gravity death of a universe here, not in a poem. By its very nature, a poem must tell of the human capacity to cope with randomness and meaninglessness and loss; however much they tell of suffering, however much the suffering of which he tells, the poets have coped by placing it within a poem and thus having it mesh back into and heighten the integrity of the human condition. It is a way to give the unutterable voice and at once to convey and to affirm the wholeness of human experience. It is a way of bringing words out from their natural place as dividers and restrictors and so employing them that they become supple indicators of where feelings and thoughts blend and coexist.

This undertaking is inherently mercurial stuff; it is turning words against themselves—or part of themselves. It is making them do the opposite of what they usually do. By specifying, words highlight their subject but detach it from its inner place. In a poem, words may be murky and quirky and multipotential, but their allusive arrangement and biological rooting give them access to the hidden and convey meaning that opens out rather than closes in and that mingles well and joins the subjective continuity of experience rather than sundering it and detaching one segment.

Let us consider a poem, something small and simple—"Fog" by Carl Sandburg:

> The fog comes
> on little cat feet.
> It sits looking
> over harbor and city
> on silent haunches
> And then moves on.

Here is a poem where a minimum is asked of a very few and those rather simple words. There is no rhyme. The rhythm is there, powerful and basic, but not salient and obvious. The form is primitive, reduced to its minimum, something in the character of a Japanese haiku. Yet the form is all important; in some mysterious way the spacing of the lines on the page matters, and the effect of the poem is in large part achieved through this means. Let us return to that presently.

The content of the poem is delimited and external. No human reference is employed directly, although "harbor" and "city" are clearly human constructions. Yet it is an expressive poem, even a powerful one. Certainly it is very well known. It must be an effective poem—where then, we may ask, is all the effect derived from? In particular, how does it fit in with the present thesis?

To begin with, we must consider the poem's allusiveness. It is fog, yet within the poem it is alive. Immediately the universe or animism is opened to us, the normal outlook of the small child to whom everything is alive. Fog, as a phenomenon of nature, can have a variety of meanings, but fog *alive*—here is the link with the spectral, the undistinguishable inner presence that may have so many implications—frightening perhaps, fascinating certainly—rich in its potential for any form, many forms. To the poet, it comes catlike, and cats have their own mystique, their own unknowable purposes, their own inscrutability. What does it think as it looks over the city—at people, at everyone, at the reader—what is configuring within, what will it do? What do I, the reader, think as I look at people; what does that preverbal, ineffable part of me think as I look out on my people world; what do I want of them; what does that infant within me want? For many people there will be an ominous hint here and a sense of great powers beginning to awaken, to uncurl, to stretch themselves, perhaps to reach out—but the poet saves us, from the fog, and from ourselves. It moves on. The tension state is broken. We have been led to inwardness, we have known ourselves a little more deeply than before, we have known ourselves perhaps too well—but we are contained. We have learned that we can allow ourselves a moment of inwardness when perhaps the banshees howl and the witches wait yet emerge from it all and move on. An unnamable thought has stolen to the surface and looked out of our eyes, and then it has moved on—and we have survived and our world has not been affected. The words have evoked the unnamable and the indescribable and have made us a little more sure of ourselves, a little better at the mastery of what we have within. The poem has done its work.

Chapter 7

Mime and dance

INTRODUCTION

Esther Rashkin

In this thoughtful and artistically insightful essay, Joseph Noshpitz elaborates the key elements that lead a preverbal infant to develop the capacity for intersubjectivity during the second half of the first year of life. By intersubjectivity, Noshpitz means infants' ability to recognize and experience the feelings and intentions of others, beginning with the mother or primary caregiver, and to convey nonverbally their own feelings and intentions. This reciprocal attunement, which is a necessary precursor of infants' capacity to develop empathy and compassion, requires the mother to respond with appropriate intensity, content, and timing to infants' constantly shifting preverbal signaling of emotional states and desires. Only through the mother's "resonant mirroring" can infants feel understood, intuit what the mother experiences and means, and learn to communicate their internal feelings and intentions.

Recalling aspects of the work of Donald W. Winnicott, Heinz Kohut, and Daniel Stern (to whom Noshpitz refers), the essay is especially fascinating because of the parallels it draws between infants' development of intersubjective communicative capacity and the effects generated by truly artistic (not just technically proficient) performances of mime, puppetry, and dance. Talented performers not only convey their inner thoughts and intent to the audience but also activate the audience's sense of sharing in a felt human experience by physically embodying and silently transmitting a sense of pleasure and aliveness.

For example, Noshpitz states that mimes not only have to communicate their intent to climb a staircase in a way that audience members can intuit and grasp; they must also use movement, posture, and expression to create the staircase itself so that the audience can fully share in their imagined experience. I would add that the power of a master mime like Marcel Marceau also comes from his ability to construct and make visible for the audience the space in which he is climbing and the weight of gravity upon him as he tries to ascend. He thereby invites the audience to experience the tension and subtle but present threat of failure inherent in the situation and to share the sense of relief and release that comes from overcoming gravity and climbing upward.

Mimes' silence is equally crucial to conveying the presence of an inner world of thought and desire with which the audience can resonate and also offers a chance to experience the pleasure that comes from grasping these performers' unspoken intent. We can relate this to infants who gain a sense of aliveness and connection from discerning the unspoken thoughts behind their mother's silent movements, touch, and expressions and who thereby begin to develop a sense of cognitive competence that reinforces the ability to identify with and imitate their mother's way of thinking.

Marceau's famous "Walking Against the Wind" mime (an inspiration for Michael Jackson's moonwalk) is a good example of this interplay between intentionality, tension, and release. Marceau engages the audience by transcending the display of mere bodily agility and control to convey the idea of a struggle to move forward—a metaphor of survival that Jackson, too, explored in his performances. The same is true, perhaps more acutely so, in "The Cage," in which Marceau mimes being confined within the walls of a box whose sides relentlessly close in on him. As Marceau's silent movements and expressions arouse the audience's anxiety at being trapped and ultimately crushed within the shrinking space, he must also measure the intensity and duration of the illusion so as not to exceed the audience's affective tolerance. Having stimulated audience members to feel with him, in other words, he must also attend closely to their response—as mothers must do with their infants—so that the pleasure of intersubjective connection and unspoken complicity does not turn into painful misattunement and overstimulation.

Dance is another art form in which the sense of self and aliveness is intensified through movement, rhythm, and nonverbal communication of affect between performers and their audience. Noshpitz suggests that dance also has a therapeutic function, since it can evoke feelings that may not be verbalized but whose communication engenders a sense of intimacy with others. Focusing on ballroom dance, he notes the predominance of courtship and coital fantasies, involving dramas of pursuit and escape or dominance and submission, whose effects are heightened by rhythmic movement that arouses a sense of relatedness in spectators. We can readily recognize this in Latin ballroom dances such as the rumba, samba, mambo, and tango. I would suggest that we can also see the courtship ritual enacted in the more decorous Viennese waltz whose strictly codified positions and choreography resonate with the developmental phase of infant/mother intersubjectivity with which Noshpitz is concerned.

The Viennese waltz is danced in closed position, with both partners' bodies facing each other, the man's right arm embracing the woman around her back, her left arm and hand lying atop his right arm and shoulder. The man holds the woman in frame, constructing the space in which she will move synchronously with him, as their lower torsos are pressed against each other as if literally joined at the hips. However, while physical contact below the waist is maintained throughout the waltz, the dancers make virtually no eye contact. In fact, their heads are turned away from each other at opposing oblique angles, while their upper bodies arch backward in what is called a "leverage" or "tension connection."

The excitement for the audience comes from identifying with the seamless intimacy of the attached torsos—counterbalanced by the muscular tension of the cambered upper bodies—as the dancers turn around the floor, rhythmically rising and falling to the music. The sense of enlivened relatedness that the dancers experience and that the audience intuits and shares is reminiscent, developmentally speaking, of the rapport between nursing mothers and their children. Just as the dance couple need not look at each other to maintain contact or to adjust to nonverbalized changes in direction, speed, posture, and expression, so infants need not keep visual contact with their mother to feed (although both gaze at each other from time to time). Held securely within the frame created by their mother's body and literally attached to her torso, infants intuit their mother's intentions and respond to shifts in posture, position, and expression, just as mothers read and respond to their infants' physical and emotional shifts. The synchronous flow of this nurturing waltz, in which each partner grasps and responds to the changing bodily and affective rhythms of the other, heightens the infant's sense of connectivity and intersubjective awareness and lays the foundation for an emergent sense of identity.

A similarly powerful dynamic occurs in ballet and modern dance. Noshpitz observes that the basic goal of both is to imbue the audience with a sense of vitality and that resonating with the patterned movements and rhythms heightens one's sense of self. I would add that both forms of dance play with and work out tensions between autonomy and partnership, isolation and interconnectedness. We experience a release of tension when the ballerina successfully rises *en pointe* in sustained balances and descends safely, when she completes 32 *fouettés* without losing her balance, or when she is lifted high, dropped, and then caught by her partner inches from the floor. These exhilarating moves toward individuation and independence are in constant tension with the stable, secure holding environment provided by the framing and containing relationship with her partner.

Modern dance, while eschewing ballet's classical lines, formalized technique, and codified steps, is also characterized by increases and releases of tension as space, movement, gravity, and emotions are explored. With a freer sense of self-expression and a more malleable concept of the body than ballet, modern dance explores the nature of motion, the shifts, asymmetries, and stresses in physical and psychical relationships, and the body's connection with the dance floor itself. In fact, the floor in modern dance functions less as a platform for flight and illusions of weightlessness (as in ballet) than as a dense surface whose gravitational pull holds dancers in a grounded, more realistic space in which motions like crawling, rolling, and dragging the body replace ballet's emphasis on elevation and the lightness of being.

Viewed from this perspective, modern dance could be said to resonate with the tensions that infants experience between expanding their world through gravity-bound motions like crawling and rolling and the risk that comes with leaving a safe holding environment to explore unfamiliar territory. Infants' sense of groundedness and secure attachment to their mother or primary caregiver is central to their capacity to assume such risk. Modern dance, despite its long history of varied choreographic content and shifting esthetic goals, is an art form that consciously, or more usually unconsciously, stages and engages with this drama of self-definition and world discovery and that not only invigorates its performers but also vitalizes its audience.

Noshpitz's essay makes clear that he appreciated the animating power of these performing arts and their relevance for deepening our understanding of infants' internal world. It also invites us to reflect on why dance and mime affect us so viscerally and spontaneously and on how they awaken in us our most primordial yearnings to feel alive and held in the world.

MIME AND DANCE
Joseph D. Noshpitz

The next stage of development to concern us appears at some 7 to 9 months of age and heralds the beginnings of human intersubjectivity. To explain this, let us consider an analogy. A man becomes aware that something is the matter with his car; it doesn't steer properly or makes a funny noise. His awareness is based on his detection of an aspect of its action and his cognitive grasp about how and why it works—or doesn't work. He might consider the car in human terms and say, "Poor old Bessie, you're not feeling so good," but that is semijocular, and in fact he has no illusions about the car's "feelings." Not so with a person, however; for most of us, we take for granted the fact that any given human being does in fact have feelings, and, what is more, we have the capacity to sense how that other person feels. We do not judge this merely on the basis of that individual's posture, or acts, or facial expression, or statement; it is the totality of what the person conveys that arouses within us a subjective sense akin to what he experiences and thus informs us as to what his inner state must be like. We resonate with his concern or suspicion, sadness or elation, rage or anticipation, joy or apprehension—we feel it directly.

The capacity thus to experience another's feelings is not a given, however. It is a developmental emergent that appears only under conditions of wholesome growth, where the combination of genetic potential and environmental support has made for its production. It comes about as a normal stage in growth and fills the gap between the formation of a sense of a core self and the later appearance of a verbal self.

This quality of intersubjectivity is in the nature of things preverbal. It is a development that is basic to later human empathy and makes for the firmest and most integral social bonds. It allows for the development of compassion; because of its presence, people will care for one another not as they care for their cars or their equipment but as they care for fellow human beings, with some capacity to feel with the other and therefore act for the other. It is for this reason that they will care for infants or the helpless or the sick; they can sense what it is like to be helpless or bereft, and this awareness becomes a powerful motivator. To put it briefly, intersubjectivity has enormous survival value.

Given its importance, intersubjectivity clearly merits careful study. Let us ask first: Where does it come from? How does it appear? Under favorable conditions it arises spontaneously, sometime during the second half of the first year. Its presence can be sensed by the new quality in babies' interactions. Mothers point to a toy, and babies look not at their finger but toward the toy. Babies have now caught on to the fact that their mother has about her a quality of intentionality; when she acts, it is not only her behavior that counts—something is going on inside her mind. When she points, it is not only an act in itself; it has an additional quality, signals an intention, a thought. In responding to her gesture, babies now catch the sense of the thought and look to the toy. But it is all pretty new; they are just catching on, so they look back to their mother's face a trifle anxiously, or at any rate inquiringly, as if to say, "Did I read your intention correctly? Is that what you had in mind?" and how very gratifying it is when they have—what a great discovery.

This newfound capacity to indicate works both ways. Prior to this, babies have indicated wants by reaching for things, or by crying, signals that were either too specific (they were not really signals so much as attempts to get what they wanted) or too general (i.e., they would simply cry and wail, without additional information as to why they were doing so or what was the matter). Many parents have gone through considerable stress because their baby was crying and they could not figure out what was wrong. Now, however, things have changed. True signals appear, babies begin to point to what they want and perhaps to make noises—"eh, eh"—in an attempt to say something about their state of mind. All of a sudden, it is a lot easier to understand them. And the relationship with the caretaker takes a new turn, one that is deeper and richer than the existing bond, one based on mutual understanding.

It is this capacity for intersubjective communication—for signaling and conveying, for perceiving and intuiting the content of another's mind—that is basic to many aesthetic forms. Some of these include mime, puppet theater, and dance.

The mime can be thought of and can function as a set of images capable of being appreciated for grace and technique and artistry. But a good mime and the effective puppet master do something more complex. They tell something about the inner state of people, about their love or shyness or suffering, and they do so by means of a sequence of nonverbal indicators that collectively construct an integrated image of a condition of human consciousness, a segment of felt human experience, which the mime and the mimicry convey. This is typically augmented by the presence of more than one performer, with the collectivity elaborating some aspect of human exchange. The success of the montage will be measured by the profundity of the experience.

What are the basic elements involved here? There is first a quality of shared attention: both performer and audience participate raptly in a communicative experience. The entire structure of the stage—lighting, setting, backdrop—all create an experimental matrix, a message-laden set that engages with the audience and prepares the way for the subsequent mimicry. It is the equivalent in the nursery of the initiation of play; whatever the cues, whatever the preliminary steps, the stage is set for the ensuing exchange.

Once attention is shared, the next great interactive step is the sharing of intention. The design, the goal of the action, has to be conveyed by the one and grasped by the other for the display to succeed. The mime grasps the bars of a cage, tugs at a kite string, climbs a staircase, all without visible props, all constructed and implied merely by gesture and posture, gait and attitude—and, to the extent that it is well done, inferred and understood by the attentive audience who now shares the mime's intention and studies his skill in conveying it.

This, for babies, is an enormously meaningful discovery. To be able to think of ways to communicate something on their mind and to begin to grasp what is going on in someone else's mind is a marvelous bag of discoveries. It is the beginning of a process that will never go away; nonverbal communicative cues will play a part in all significant human exchange for all the rest of the life span. For some individuals, these nonverbal devices will become and remain their most important expressive modalities; they will never be successful verbalizers. To the extent that they send messages about their awareness of others' inner worlds and their wish to transmit something of their own subjective experience, it will have to be in this way. Most people are not so limited, yet the degree to which such behavioral components are vital elements in their way of making significant statements will vary enormously.

In any case, shared attention and shared intention are the first two of three central factors. The third is shared affectivity, and in infancy this one is the most important and persistent element in intersubjective awareness. It is in the richness, the subtlety, and the precision with which he can kindle affects and define their individual qualities that the mime excels, and it is in his capacity to do this well that the merit of his performance is measured.

How is this affectivity shared? There are two important dimensions to this. The first is best illustrated by an ingenious experiment. A 1-year-old is placed on a table on which the appearance of a sharp declivity has been created in one area—an abrupt fall-off. It looks for all the world as though, if she advances beyond the apparent edge, she would surely take a tumble. An attractive toy is placed beyond the margin of the fall-off and the child is left to make the decision: Should she try for the toy and risk the fall? Or should she wait, perhaps cry, for it to be given to her?

What happens, in fact, is that the child tends to advance to the "edge" and then looks apprehensively toward her mother. If she smiles encouragingly, the youngster picks up her mother's feeling, is reassured, and proceeds forward over the "edge" to get to the toy. If her mother frowns or looks worried, the youngster retreats and may begin to cry.

It is evident that this process of "social referring" is a vital component of human exchange. How we feel about something is likely to be a function of how we feel, in particular, about the significant others in our life. We seek for clues about their state of mind, about their emotions, and our inner life reflects and mirrors and resonates with that state of mind. The nature of human social organization involves a constant interplay of such affective cueing, with messages of approbation and approval, or criticism and disapproval, of fear and concern, of joyous reward and gratification—in short, of a huge array of affective states constantly being intuited and reacted to in the everyday flux of social exchange.

For the mime, the problem is to conduct himself in a way that creates and broadcasts a quality of affective meaning that will be intuited by his audience. The mime can use a variety of means to do this, but they come down largely to the reality that what typically gets exchanged in the course of this process are the vitality affects. And this both simplifies the task of the performer and places special demands on him.

For the vitality affects are the acceleration components of emotional life, the rate of change of emotion and velocity as it were. If the categorical affects—sadness, surprise, rage, amusement, and the like—are the steady-state aspects of the progress of emotion, then their crescendos, diminuendos, abrupt onsets, crashing conclusions, shifting and swellings, ebbings and weavings all comprise the vitality affects and form a universe of experience very much their own.

These lend themselves well to the motions of the mime. The gesture, the grimace, the sudden body bend or turn, the sweep of a limb, the toss of a head, the shrug—all these are translated by amodal perception into shifts of feeling, gusts of emotion, upwellings of affect. The basic tactic employed is affective attunement. This is the means by which mothers convey to infants (at this end of the first-year stage of development) that they have sensed where their infants are emotionally and that they feel it too. But the communication of this feeling is not done by imitation. Mothers carry out a version of the feelings as it translates within them; they perform some pattern of responsive reaction that signifies their awareness and empathy. A baby puts a form correctly into the mold surface and, with explosive satisfaction, exclaims, "Ha!" His mother reaches over and gives his bottom a shake. But it has to be just the right shake at just the right rhythm and with just the right force—not too fast but not too slow, not too vigorous but not too gentle. Or another mother might sing baby a little song at such a moment, or she might shake her own body and do a little dance in resonance with her baby's reaction. A wide variety of messages could be sent, but they all involve the same thrust: I know how you feel; I feel it too. Whatever the means employed, it is the mother's way of catching the quality of her baby's affect.

Having said that, we might consider the nature of affective exchange of this sort and wonder: What goes into affect expression? If one is indeed to do this kind of resonant mirroring, what is it that must be echoed? What must the mother's behavior in fact accomplish? And in considering this, Stern suggests that mothers' behavior must resonate with at least three aspects of babies' emotions: intensity, timing, and shape. Let us begin with intensity.

When mothers respond to babies, the amplitude of mothers' reactions must be carefully measured, and the quality of their energy must match that of the babies' in a reasonably synchronous way.

To illustrate this in a bit more detail, let us observe that one of the common disparities in the intersubjective experience occurs when, as adults, we try to excite a certain level of response, perhaps of enthusiasm or amusement or outrage, by something we say—and the thing falls flat. The reaction is there, but its intensity is far less than we had attempted to evoke. People smile politely at our joke instead of laughing, or we occasionally note the opposite—that someone laughs too much or responds in some other way that strikes us as excessive and out of proportion to what we had communicated. This is always confronting and somewhat disturbing. For us to feel understood and appropriate, there is a need for a certain range of intensity to be evoked, one that matches what we feel. And so it is with babies. They need to perceive their mother's response as not too strong and not too weak.

It is interesting that when their mother's response is right, babies may show no reaction and merely continue what they are doing. But should their mother's response be in fact too much one way or the other, then babies do indeed respond, perhaps by turning toward her with a questioning, what's-going-on look.

The second dimension of responsiveness involves timing. Here again, the rate of the mother's response needs to be in keeping with what babies are experiencing. The beat, the rhythm of the reaction, is another subtle dimension of affect expression; it must catch the quality of babies' inner state.

And, finally, the shape of the affective exchange is all important. For herein lies the true nature of the vitality affect—its activation contour. This rests in its rising or falling or wavering, its suddenness or gradualness; in its very nature such an affect represents a particular outline of change, and this shape is characteristic of the transformation of that moment. Hence, in catching and echoing it back to babies, the shape of the response must be commensurate with the outline of babies' affective experience. The more accurately this shape is rendered, the more precise—and satisfying—the sense of emotional accord.

The same principle holds true for the mime. The most powerful component of the impact made by the mime's behavior will be the validity of the emotional message he conveys. To be sure, this will be modified and given substance by the rhythm of the behavior and by its intensity, but these are qualities of the shape; they emphasize and modulate it, but they do not give it its basic form. What supplies the critical component is the character of the vitality affects as such, or, more precisely, the essentially unceasing flow of these affects as they continue to be elaborated. They give life and character to the image the mime created; they take the elementary cognitive content of the performance and change that from the flat and mechanical—or even from the clever and ingenious—to the vivid and evocative. The mime who is skillful in portraying content may come through as dexterous and acrobatic; it does not become a truly meaningful performance until the range and richness of affect attain a certain critical level. For it is only at that point that one passes from core self-experience to the intersubjective. The technical competence as such speaks for mastery of the other-than-intersubjective factors; it is the addition of vitality affects that adds the critical spice. It is what makes the members of the audience resonate inwardly and experience what is portrayed as a self-enhancing event rather than merely admiring externally the skill they see.

Similar considerations apply to puppet theaters. Many levels of ingenuity and decorative brilliance can be achieved by skillful and able design, adornment, and artful manipulation of the puppets. But only the truly outstanding puppeteer can so imbue her figures with movements that translate into vitality affects to give the audience a sense of genuine emotional arousal. Nor is it easy to define precisely how this is done; it is the essence of artistry to manage her medium in a manner that will excite the amodal perceptual capacities of the audience into the desired translations. Undoubtedly, there are a series of complex rule structures, action formats, and discovery procedures involved according to which patterns of gesture, posture, facial expression, and body movement will achieve the desired effect. Indeed, it is at this point that cultural conventions become of central importance in defining the significance and the emotional impact of given moments.

This point needs a little elaboration. Each culture tends to develop a universe of nonverbal patterns and actions that have significance within the context of that ethnic realm. This implies both overt and covert elements, down to such details as characteristic postures and facial expressions. In particular, however, it applies to the regulation of interpersonal behaviors. Thus, when Japanese meet they bow, as a sign of respect; when certain groups of Amerindian boys address their elders they do not look them in the eye; it would be disrespectful to do so. In a thousand ways different cultures, and different casts or socioeconomic groups within a given culture, comport themselves in keeping with models that are at once distinctive and demanding. It would be a breach of propriety, a departure from the expected, to act in any other fashion. This is likely to be vividly highlighted in the schoolyard, where the acquisition of appropriate stereotypes is relatively new and fragile—and hence the more highly defended and where, by the same token, any departures from the norm—be it in gesture, garment, gait, speech, or appearance—will be responded to by name-calling, teasing, or proscription.

Such ethnic patterning of the motor and postural components of behavior surely begins at the earliest moments of social exchange. We take in these models with our mother's milk, and by the time we become alert to intersubjective realities, the likelihood is that we are already beginning to show the stamp of our culture.

In particular, the patterns of reinforcement, the unconscious but omni-present sequences mothers deliver in response to the nuances of behavior they seek in their infants and value, the behavioral organizations they look for as culturally correct, as confirming the propriety and the belongings of their babies to society all act as profound inducers of the culturally dictated styles of comportment and address. As the intersubjective state proceeds, social modeling is added to the reinforcement paradigms, and babies begin to adopt and emulate and imitate not only the behaviors of the valued caretakers but their way of thinking as well, so additional defi-nition is given to the norms and communicative modes of the particular society. All of which is to say that the power to excite the sense of self-related meanings, which is so vital to the effectiveness of nonverbal art forms, will be modulated and qualified by the critical layer of mutually shared cultural superimpositions.

That this is a layering will become evident as we come to consider the next art form, the varieties of dance. Dance is universal; every society, no matter how primitive or how sophisticated, has some form of dance. It appears to be a pan-human form of expression and hence of special interest to us. Let us then consider some of its constituent elements.

To begin with, dance is built upon rhythm. Like music, then, it stands very close to its biologic base. It also stands very near to music itself; indeed, so close is it to music that the presence of music as an accompaniment to or part of dance is almost universal. Whether there can be dance without music is an interesting and somewhat tricky question. Let us consider for a moment a squad of soldiers marching in formation, receiving different orders from the drill master, wheeling and reversing on command, and then given the order, "Count cadence, count," whereupon the soldiers break into a rhythmic chant of some kind. One version went something like this:

> One two, one two,
> One two three four,
> You'll never get home on your left, your right,
> You'll never get home on your left, your right,
> One two, one two...

or some such doggerel. This has about it much of the quality of dance. It is certainly not defined so, but it does involve rhythmic, patterned movement performed in keeping with a definite beat and following regular rules and a preformed model. For that is the core component of dance: the alert-ing and intensifying of the sense of self by the enactment of set sequences of rhythmic movement. For the soldiers, the movement and chanting in unison is designed to reinforce their reality as a functioning unit. The unearned capacity for rhythm and the trained-in response of the march movements combine to heighten this effect and to increase group coherence, self-awareness, and thus morale. This is probably only one instance where the peculiar nature of the work experience allows for such emergents; something of this kind is not unusual with many kinds of labor involving rhythmic activity. A group of men pulling up a long cable will swing in unison repeatedly back and forth, forward and back, and begin to chant or to sing as accompaniment of—and support to—their efforts. As a result, instead of a boring, stressful, and tiresome form of toil, it all becomes a kind of dance. Instead of being threatened by the meaninglessness of repetitious and laborious activity, their sense of self is heightened by the pleasure of the muscle play in rhythm and the sense of unity that comes with shared communal action.

A similar example is to be found in various kinds of exercise classes where the pattern of shared rhythmic group action becomes for the participants a kind of dance experience. In many instances, of course, such group activity is quite literally set to music. Many tribal peoples today continue patterns of dance accompanied by nothing but a drum beat or by the chanting of onlookers or of the dancers themselves. Hence, there are levels of and varieties of dance with little or no formal musical accompaniment.

But at its best, dance is more than a set of patterned actions designed to reinforce the sense of self. Dance is, or can be, a very powerful kind of communication—in particular, affective communication. Ultimately, it can act to bring about a heightened sense of self in the audience. And it does this by exciting their rhythmic selves, their cognitive selves, and most meaningfully, their affective selves.

Thus far, we have said little about the cognitive component. All dance involves some level of fantasy. In effect, it is an enactment of some inner vision or some felt state that seeks an action component. It is perhaps no exaggeration to say that dance is a form of mime set to music; in its very nature, it tends to tell a story. Often enough the story is submerged beneath the proprioceptive pleasure in the movement itself; rhythmic movement is inherently gratifying for most people, so they will give themselves over to the swing and the sway without much conscious address to the implicit content of the action. But content there is nonetheless, and one usually does not have to look too deeply to discern the underlying message.

In that connection it is important to note that dance can be both a type of performance and a site for participation. Let us consider the participatory variety first. Perhaps the commonest form of engagement in dancing in our culture is the experience of ballroom dancing. In such couples dancing, the underlying fantasy is probably that of courtship, up to and including the act of copulation. There may be elements of pursuit and escape, of dominance and submission, of enticement and evasion, and of overpowering and yielding. There may be pelvic rolling and thrusting of explicitly coital character.

Depending on time and place, social definitions and stylized modes of inter-action, any or all of these may be present and, in the course of their enact-ing, may produce a pattern of reciprocally shared and exchanged fantasies. One of the greatest bonds between people is the awareness of participation in such mutual fantasies, and shared dancing patterns with their powerful biologic rhythms and the releasing power of their movement components are prime evokers and engenderers of fantasy imagery. Hence the potency of dance: the rhythmic movement heightens the sense of self, the shared patterned action heightens the sense of group or couple unity and selfhood, and the message of the dance as communication leads to sharing of inter-subjective awareness.

It is in connection with this last component that we can now shift our site of observation to contemplate the experience of viewers who attend a performance of ballet or modern dance. For there, the basic goal of the performance is to imbue the viewers and listeners with a powerful sense of affective color. The sights and sounds of the performance are designed to address the amodal perceptive capacities of the audience in such a manner as to be recorded as a continuing stream of vitality affects ornamenting a more limited group of categorical affects with or without an accompanying cognitive recounting of some sort. Since dance offers so much in terms of skillful and technically demanding mastery of performance, it is sometimes difficult to know when mere admiration for superb craftsmanship gives way to a deeper sense of emotional engagement and enrichment achieved by the character of the performance. It is here, perhaps, that modern dance comes into its own; most of it is designed explicitly around the concept of arousing emotion and stands or falls on its success in achieving that goal.

Perhaps something else plays a role as well in the impact of dance. The very nature of the costumes and settings, let alone the extraordinary com-portment of the performers, makes the world of dance into a sort of imag-inary, idealized universe of its own, set aside from ordinary reality and opening the doors to possibilities without end. Performers are infinitely, inhumanly graceful, impossibly adept at leaping high, able to remain up in the air for what seem like extended intervals, capable of whirling in a fashion mere mortal flesh could not endure, and thus on and on. These are not real people carrying out a planful activity—this is fairyland, the world of make-believe. And for a brief time, viewers can join them there, be part of these wonders. This too offers its rewards.

It is important to recognize the nature of dance as multiple: It often (though not always) tells a story in the course of which it creates its illusory world; it takes time out to show the technical wares of the individual art-ists; it seeks to impress the viewer with sound, color, form, lighting, tex-ture, garb, staging, complexity, or even gorgeousness of setting, multiplicity of actions by several performers at once—indeed, only opera presents an audience with more intricately worked images (with dance not infrequently employed as part of the overall message). With so many elements at work simultaneously, it is not easy to give special credits to any one. Withal, however, the lavishness, the splendor, the complexities will serve to heighten only one aspect of viewers' perceptual worlds: the aliveness that comes with encountering the sensuous and the spectacular. These are not trivial dimensions, and, for many people, they are the *summum bonum*; the viewers would ask for nothing better.

But some people will seek still more. They look for the humane and the interpersonal; they visit the theater seeking a sense of shared subjectivity, the excitement engendered by the stimulation of their intersubjective affectivity. This is so important for them that they appreciate even the arousal of sad affects, even of tragedy. When they feel such arousal they are more alive, they have been "reached" and elevated, they feel closer to their inner selves and to other people, they feel more emotionally whole. They feel like the baby when the mother, in a bad moment, holds him especially close and the baby senses some of what mother feels. The sadness is painful, but the aliveness is wonderful. Dance, with its remarkable capacity to portray vitality affects, can generate such responses; when it is well done, it is a powerful means of human expression and communication.

These latter qualities are what make it suitable and indeed an effective medium for therapy. In essence, any truly serviceable therapeutic tactic must possess a number of qualities. It must in itself have a quality of gratification that would make the troubled person take to it at all; specifically, it must provide some answer to the two great human needs that pervade all psychological treatment. First, in and of itself it must bring with it an element of primary gratification that it can offer to a life with all too little healthy sources of pleasure; second, it must supply some measure of release and relief from the pain patients regularly bring to therapeutic encounters when they come seeking for help.

In addition to gratification, a useful therapeutic modality must offer an opportunity, or even more, an invitation, for wholesome self-expression. In making this observation it is important to repeat the obvious: Not all self-expression is good. Violence is a form of self-expression that individuals must work to contain; the flooding of anxiety and its expression in the form of a panic attack is a dreadful human experience against which therapists seek to protect patients. Or the outpouring of psychotic mentation because patients' controls have broken down is a signal to join them in their failed efforts to dam back and repress and to help them shore up that particular levee. But even in these instances, the dilemmas posed by such inner threats to individuals' life and happiness, the fact that they live such a precarious and uncertain existence—these psychological realities do need expression, and the search for adequate and constructive means to communicate these is one of the key tasks for all the helping professions.

It is in this sense that dance has so much to offer appropriate individuals. There is the primary pleasure that so many people get in rhythmic body movement, the biological given with which we are endowed. This can offer a measure of direct gratification that has immediate appeal. The experience of joining with others, sharing in the larger group pattern, makes for a factor of socialization that can be very precious to isolated individuals who feel so cut off from humanity. The relief of tension and the expression of affects through body movement is a variable that serves many people. But of the greatest importance, the chance to express in motion what might be so hard to say in words is a boon of great price indeed. For some, dance is the best if not the only way they can tell about their individual emotional snarls and stumbling blocks; only in this way can they attain a sense of self-understanding or of being understood. Or only in this way can they begin to make up for what was left out in that dim forgotten epoch when the necessary intersubjectivity was so desperately needed and was so definitively denied them. For such individuals dance is their only second chance—it offers them a unique and specific form of help.

Chapter 8

Infantile narcissism in the grade school years

INTRODUCTION

Efrain Bleiberg

Plunging in pursuit of his beautiful image turned Narcissus into a ready symbol of the perils of self-absorption. Joe Noshpitz, by contrast, plunged into a life marked by generosity and yearnings to live up to ideals and standards of decency and fairness, a yearning rooted in a keen sensitivity to the plight of others. His was a life that provides a ready model of the "healthy narcissism" he explores in this chapter, as it is shaped during the crucial formative period of the grade school years.

Examining the narcissistic pursuits of young children was one of Joe's abiding interests. He used this exploration to open a window into key mechanisms to attain healthy self-regulation—the internal limit-setting and direction—giving mechanisms fueling "the yearning to live up to an ideal" and strive "to behave in accordance with standards." He identified these mechanisms as a crucial foundation of children's resilience in the face of adversity and of the capacity to repair the psychic damage inflicted by biological vulnerabilities or environmental assaults.

Over 10 years, from the early '80s to the early '90s, Joe chaired an annual symposium at the meeting of the American Academy of Child and Adolescent Psychiatry that included Paulina Kernberg, Anna Ornstein, and me. These symposia were dedicated to making sense of the diagnostic and therapeutic challenges posed by children and adolescents entrapped in pathological configurations of narcissistic regulation. It was Joe's gift to guide this highly opinionated group of panelists in the direction of searching for how basic developmental-adaptive mechanisms of self-regulation, protection, and repair go awry and result in troubling behavior, arrogance, defiance, and manipulation that effectively conceal pain and anguish.

The themes and formulations discussed during that decade of discussions find their way into Joe's notes on "infantile narcissism in the grade school years," including our reliance on Joffe and Sandler's (1967) conceptualization of narcissism in normality and psychopathology. Joe used Joffe and Sandler's conceptualization to build his formulation of the tension between the "ideal" and the "real" self, as this tension is negotiated during the grade school years.

Joffe and Sandler (1967) proposed that self-esteem—or narcissistic well-being—is the affective experience that results from people's sense of *matching* or bringing about a convergence of the "actual self" (defined as the mental representation that integrates people's conscious and unconscious sense of their own characteristics, physical appearance and body self, psychological traits, dispositions, talents, limitations, goals, intentions, and overall capacities to meet internal and external adaptive demands—the "me" I believe I am) on one hand, and the "ideal self" (defined as the "shape" of people's self-representation associated with a sense of safety, satisfaction, pleasure, sustaining connections with others, and effective coping with internal and external demands—the "me" I would *need to become* to feel safe, loved, gratified and in control), on the other. In Joffe and Sandler's view, the tension or distance between ideal self and actual self is a measure of persons' narcissistic vulnerability, a vulnerability signaled by a particular affective experience, the affect of shame.

Joe draws our attention to the vicissitudes of the development of narcissistic regulation during the grade school years. This is a stage that forms a critical bridge between the laying out of the building blocks of the mechanisms involved in narcissistic regulation taking place between birth and age 6 on one hand and the unique narcissistic challenges of adolescence on the other hand.

Joe would have appreciated the current explosion in developmental and neuroscientific research into the basic sociocognitive mechanisms that underlie *how* we generate, organize, and represent experience of self and others and create representational models such as those he described. This research is beginning to provide an empirical foundation to Joe's clinical impressions and conceptualizations.

Such impressions and conceptualizations anticipated that social cognition and the disposition to represent social experience as means to develop self-regulating capacities are biologically prepared (Frith, 2007; Frith & Frith, 2006) but that the development of these capacities depends on the quality of attachments, particularly (but not exclusively) early attachments. Early attachments reflect the extent to which children's subjective experience was adequately attuned and contingently reciprocated by a trusted other. The quality of attachment attunement and contingent reciprocity impacts, in turn, the development of affect regulating and affect representing processes and self-control (including attentional effortful control and self-limiting capacities), which lead to the symbolic–representational capabilities that give rise to coherent self-structures, such as a well-integrated autobiographical narrative and ideal self (Fonagy, Gergely, & Target, 2007; Gergely, 2004).

It is during grade school that cognitive–representational capacities allow for the formation of a composite representation of self-states—built of episodic and procedural, implicit and explicit memories—that can generate a sense of continuity of the self—the "autobiographical narrative" that provides the framework of the "actual self." Cognitive–representational capacities also come into play in the construction of a second composite reflecting self-experiences of achievement of mastery, pleasure, sustaining attachments, and satisfaction that become organized with the aspects of the mental representation of gratifying, protective, supportive, and regulating others and with fantasies built on such experiences of self or others.

Joe Noshpitz was uniquely attuned to how grade school children negotiate the tension between ideal and actual self and experience states of narcissistic vulnerability that propel them to develop effective self-regulation by creating an internal roadmap they can seek to approximate.

It is only fitting to conclude this introduction by noting the degree to which Joe's passionate commitment to help children break the grip that vulnerability fastened on their anguish, their despair, and their loneliness provides us who seek to help children with a model, a roadmap we could only hope to approximate.

References

Fonagy, P., Gergely, G., & Target, M. (2007). The parent-infant dyad and the construction of the subjective self. *Journal of Child Psychology and Psychiatry, 48*(3–4), 288–328.

Frith, C. D. (2007). The social brain? *Philosophical Transactions of the Royal Society of London B: Biological Sciences, 362*(1480), 671–678.

Frith, C. D., & Frith, V. (2006). The neural basis of mentalizing. *Neuron, 50*(4), 531–534.

Gergely, G. (2004). The role of contingency detection in early affect-regulative interactions and in the development of different types of infant attachment. *Social Behavior, 13*, 468–478.

Joffe, W. G., & Sandler, J. (1967). Some conceptual problems involved in the consideration of disorders of narcissism. *Journal of Child Psychotherapy, 2*(1), 56–66.

INFANTILE NARCISSM IN THE GRADE SCHOOL YEARS

Joseph D. Noshpitz

Normal developmental functions of narcissism

For grade school children, narcissism serves three major functions, namely, regulation, resilience, and repair. Regulation arises from the yearning to live up to an ideal and to behave in accordance with some preconceived notion of perfection; for normal children, this is a significant element in helping manage temptation, impulse, rage, the seduction of peers, and other such urges to engage in deviant behavior. Resilience implies the presence of an inner feeling of worth and self-love that buffer these children against the everyday experiences of teasing, confrontation, and correction that might otherwise result in feelings of sadness and personal devaluation. And repair consists of ameliorative fantasies that follow experiences of humiliation or injury to their sense of personal worth; the youngsters so afflicted are likely to engage in a sequence of imaginary scenarios that allow them to escape the ravages of the pain and to emerge less wounded by injurious experience.

Pathological narcissism in these early years has been dealt with by a number of authors (e.g., Bleiberg, 1984; Kernberg, 1989; Rinsley, 1988). However, to address the problem of normal narcissism during this epoch, we enter relatively uncharted waters. It therefore seems reasonable at the outset to touch briefly on some of the inner structures of mind that give rise to the phenomena associated with narcissistic experience. To begin with, there is the realistic awareness of how children look, how they come across to others, what their competencies are, and what form their vulnerabilities take. All this together forms a layered set of images of the self that are collectively called the self-concept. For normal children this tends to be both rather concrete and fairly accurate.

In a different area of mind, where the superego is solidifying, there seems to be quite a distinct set of functions that collectively form a contrasting organization. This involves an inner core of specialness and grandiosity that to some extent almost all of us harbor; in our heart of hearts, we all see ourselves as unique, meritorious, deserving of more recognition than has so far come our way, capable of yet greater attainments that have so far been our lot, and yearning for more praise and recognition than are normally forthcoming from the usually rather grudging environment. For most youngsters this comes down to an inner sense of a perfected self, an ideal self enshrined as part of the conscience somewhere in the inner recesses of human awareness. What we deal with here is the residuum of all the unresolved yearnings and wishes of earlier years, all the specialness awarded by loving parents, all the wished-for recognitions and capacities created by a fertile childhood imagination. It is an image of the self that has been glorified and idealized; it makes sense then to designate it as the ego ideal.

The realistic self-concept of which we have already spoken stands in a kind of tense equilibrium with the ego ideal—the ideal component offers a prompting and a press toward achieving a level of competence, attainment, romantic attractiveness, interpersonal grace, social importance, and overall status which the self usually never attains but toward which it always strives.

The characteristic outcome of the tension between these two elements of mind makes for the state of affairs we call self-esteem. This is the subjective experience of feeling good about ourselves (if self-esteem is high) or feeling bad (if it is low). The index that measures this is the distance experienced between the ego ideal and the self-concept; if individuals feel they are not anywhere near to living up to the ideal, self-esteem plummets. If, on the other hand, they have come very close to behaving as the ego ideal postulates they should behave, then the inner feeling is the warm glow of meeting their ideals, a sense of satisfaction that, in its more extreme forms, can become a feeling of elation. The maintenance of a good feeling about themselves is very much a function of how the gap between their self-representation and their ego ideal is managed.

A somewhat similar set of factors holds true for our view of significant others in our social world. On one hand, we can make realistic estimates and judgments about the people around us. We see them, interact with them, and form inner images of who they are and what they are like. This inner picture comprises the real object representation. Alongside this is the image we form of the significant others as we would wish them to be: beautiful, generous, giving, loving, supportive, exciting, romantic, and interested primarily in us. This comprises the idealized object representation. This can be observed in particularly vivid form in the way we regard someone with whom we have just fallen in love or in the adulation young people extend to cult figures such as rock stars or other entertainers. The loved or venerated one is larger than life, by several orders of magnitude.

By the same token, when we are hurt by others, we can form very negative images of what they are like. In effect, we devalue them, view them as mean hostile, malicious, untrustworthy, perhaps even filled with venom. They become for us thoroughly wicked and evil as their idealized counterparts are noble and rewarding. If we should happen to be more primitively organized, perhaps with a ready tendency toward paranoia, then the negative images of this kind become demonic in character, totally malign and implacably hostile.

Nor, alas, does this process of devaluation stop there. It can apply with equal readiness to ourselves, and, parallel with our realistic self-representation and our ego ideal, we can (and all too often do) maintain an inner image of the self as no good, filthy, worthless, and meriting only criticism, humiliation, and punishment.

If now we set this array of inner presences up against our model of development, we can study how these elements of mind elaborate during the grade school years.

The oedipal period is a time when, for the normal child, fantasy runs riot (Freud, 1953/1905). It is a period when little 4- or 5-year-olds think expansively of ousting one parent and taking over the other—an inherently grandiose notion. Moreover, all this is taking place at a developmental moment when wish and the magic of word and thought are at their highest pitch in the life cycle. For such a child, wishing will make it so; it is merely a matter of wishing hard enough, getting the magic right, imagining with enough intensity, playing it out as though it were true—and poof, it will happen.

Part of the work of leaving this epoch behind and moving into the grade school period is the transmutation from preoperational thinking to the level of concrete operations (Piaget, 1954). Within the Freudian canon, it is the advance to the second of Freud's (1958/1911) two principles of mental functioning, with an accompanying shift from the pleasure principle to the reality principle. In making this transition, one renounces not only the bodies of the parents as objects of erotic and aggressive thinking but the whole style of thinking that accompanies this oedipal stance. Now a new relationship to fantasy supervenes. Fantasy is no longer the means for coercing reality to do one's bidding; fantasy now serves as a refuge from reality, a retreat and safe haven, in effect, a means for repairing the damage encountered in the real world. It is a site where one may dream what one wishes with no one the wiser. Many grade school children are great daydreamers, but they are all too aware that such images are merely second-best alternatives to their true business, that of acquiring the skills and competencies requisite for their time of life. This is a complex, multifaceted business. At this moment in development, youngsters must learn to get along with peers, to deal appropriately with nonparental adults, to master the context of school lessons, and to become proficient at the games, sports, crafts, and usages of their age group. Moreover, within their homes, they must become familiar with extended family members, with the intricacies of the familial social hierarchy, and with the religious, cultural, and subcultural practices of their immediate milieu. In addition, both at home and away from home, there are important issues to be addressed (e.g., they must learn to define and defend a personal territory, must encounter and come to terms with the social expectations for their gender-related behavior). As they begin to deal with these multiple demands, some areas will be more challenging than others, and some areas will all too likely be sites of failure. In the face of the ensuing frustrations, many youngsters cope by making up wished-for scenarios where they reverse their misfortunes and drift into daydreaming states where fantasies of achievement and success take the place of the frustrations and disappointments. In the daydreams, they achieve startling scores of the same ball field where they recently struck out. The boy enchants the little girl to whom he was attracted but in whose presence he was tongue-tied. The failed scholar knows more than the teacher and dazzles her classmates, and the youngster who could not finish his piece at the student recital plays masterfully at the imagined keyboard. The grandiose fantasy serves in some measure as reparative: Instead of failure one achieves success, instead of depression one experiences an elevation of one's spirits, an elation. Such flights are, as a rule, transient states, temporary respites before one picks up the burden and goes on.

Despite their transience, however, these fantasies can be curiously intense. The youngster may walk along the street, barely aware of what is going on about him, making odd noises as he dramatizes the various situations he imagines, sometimes calling out *sotto voce* his defiance or triumph, sometimes changing his facial expression or posture, and all in all swept up to a remarkable degree in the living out of these dreams. This is often called "building castles in the air," since the foundation of the dream rests on nothing more substantial than the wish—but the proportions of what is dreamed of—ah, there is a castle indeed, with all of its grandiose pretensions. Within the daydream, little boys think of strength, of daring rescues, of great escapes; little girls may well think of such adventures too, but they are also likely to have additional dreams of alluring beauty, or of motherhood and child care—or both. The degree of overlap and variation is considerable. It is not surprising that what is true of fantasy is also characteristic of play in general. Much of the play of childhood is an attempt to deal with narcissistic issues. It involves combat and trials and contests, wherein good guys and bad guys in one guise or another meet in some critical arena and battle to the death. For a previous generation it was cowboys and Indians on the Western plains; currently it may be the intergalactic warfare with Darth Vader as the dreaded foe. Little girls may have similar play sequences and may in addition with oedipal battles, have their own babies, trade places with teacher and conduct school, or otherwise achieve triumphs and experience glory. The fact that it is all in play gives permission for the expression of themes of grandiosity that could not otherwise be accepted either by people around the children or the children themselves. The outcome of some of this work is the creation of a set of idealized versions of the self that maintains a dynamic equilibrium with the real self. These emerge alongside the sense of self as one realistically knows oneself to be. Under optimal circumstances there is not too great a gap between the images created by these two functions of mind. Under more unfortunate circumstances, there may yet be a third element present: a sense of self as troubled and troublesome, as unlovable and worthless, even as horrid and disgusting. This is a departure from the norm, and we note it only to include it among the potential factors that may be at work in a given child's inner organization.

In parallel fashion, children will have similar images of the important people in their social world. The parents may be idealized and often are: My dad can beat up your dad; my mom is the most beautiful lady in the whole world; no one could be sweeter than grandma. Alternatively, one may fall in love with another child, and that object of first-grade love may then become transfigured in one's eyes. The mechanism for idealizing the other is already established; it now becomes a question of who will be selected, under what conditions, and for how long. Sometimes the idealizations are fleeting businesses, ephemeral, transient, lasting a few days to a few weeks. In other cases, the process is deep-rooted and prolonged. This is especially likely to occur where the child has known a good deal of deprivation and where the idealized fantasy serves powerful ameliorative and defensive purposes.

The associated process of forming a negative inner image is less well understood, in part because the associated phenomena are typically unconscious. But the fact that debased and devalued images are formed, both of self and of significant others, has played a major role in various theoretical approaches. Kernberg's (1976) formulation, for example, has amounted to saying that the demonized self and the demonized other are expelled from the self by means of projections and externalization; the child is thus left with only the vainglorious idealized self and object representations retained as parts of the self. Because of the warping effects of development, these components of self lose their discreetness and become inextricably fused with one another. The result is enormous self-centeredness and self-aggrandizement: in short, the formation of a grandiose self.

In normal children, however, these several elements retain their discreetness. The realistic awareness of self and the reality of others, the idealized self and the idealized other—each has its niche. Children's conscience functions in a normal way. The ego ideal is operational but does not place immoderate or impossible demands on the self, and a punitive conscience is present, but it is not so primitive and sadistic as to maintain a constant need for suffering and expiation. The primary issue then becomes a matter of living each day with some awareness of how close they have come to living up to their ideal, or how far they have departed from that preferred state.

To be sure, healthy children may well suffer an occasional lapse in comportment, but conscience will take over, and often enough children will confess their misdeed or will act in some way to expiate the wrongdoing (apologize, ask for forgiveness, accept or even prescribe a suitable punishment, or agree to pay some sort of indemnity). Living up to their ideal means a great deal to such children, and maintaining their self-esteem depends on acting in an acceptable fashion. This system functions as a major regulator of behavior, and it is further reinforced by the threat of a bad conscience if they continue to misbehave. For normal children this is a potent set of inner controls. Hence, normal narcissism acts as a powerful regulating force in their life.

Beyond that, however, the ego ideal, in particular, shapes many children's aspirations, the choice of models, the setting of goals for the self, the kind of degree of dedication to work, and the efforts expended to win the positive regard of significant authority figures. The common phrase "my dad (or mom) would kill me if I did that" bespeaks less a fear of destruction than a sense of the boundary between the acceptable and the unacceptable and an awareness of the painful consequences of embarking on a dubious course of behavior. What children often mean by such a statement is that they would be in big trouble within themselves if they were to depart from their ideal to that extent. Even the anticipated unhappiness of their parents might be felt more keenly in terms of the inner sense of having disappointed these idealized figures. In brief, it is the combination of guilt, shame, and the bite of anticipated low self-esteem to which children turn to help resist temptation.

On the other hand, the dreams of glory that can figure so largely in the lives of these children are derived directly from the ego ideal and can act as remarkable motivator toward exemplary performance. In particular, where children manifest some talent, unusual IQ, an innate grasp of mathematics, a gift for performing on some musical instrument, an unusual ability in athletics, a precocious coordination in the enactment of gymnastic feats or the execution of demanding ballet routines, the dreams of mastery and achievement that then ensue (aided and abetted, one may be sure, by parental encouragement) can become powerful shaping forces in the youngster's life. It is because of this narcissistic drivenness that these children can so dedicate themselves to long hours of grueling practice and, in effect, total life commitment. The ego ideal elements have received enormous reinforcement by the combination of these children's awareness of their ability and the environment's designation of them as special. Where the narcissism is too great, they will become excessively demanding and unable to tolerate any frustration, and the effort will fail. But for essentially normal children, there is enough healthy ego ideal and functioning conscience to make for a pattern of great and serious effort, sometimes with extraordinary results. Many great artists have begun their careers in just this fashion.

In brief, normal narcissism has many gifts to offer children. It is a major factor in behavioral self-regulation and helps maintain the everyday self-esteem (or, more simply, happiness) of children. It plays a role in helping children set goals and formulate aspirations for their life and future. And it acts as a cushion and preserver of self-confidence in the face of adversity. There is a reparative quality to many of the daydreams of childhood; when life is stressful and depriving, these can be a refuge and a preserve. Like so many elements of mind, these factors can be either helpful and rewarding or problematic and disruptive, depending on context and quality. When not excessive and when set within a basically healthy personality organization, narcissism can be a source of major constructive potential for children's further development.

Fantasy heroes and superheroes: Birth of the superego

Our culture is rich in powerful figures to serve as models, inspirations, and objects of identification for youngsters. There are, to begin with, certain perennial favorites, classic images that culture carries forward. Specifically, parental recollections, the school system, the comic book publishers, and makers of movies and videos support one another and continue to keep these presences alive. Currently, for example, a Robin Hood series appearing on television comes in the wake of the new, recently released movie version of *Robin Hood*. There have been any number of Robin Hoods in the past, and there probably will be others in the future. This keen-eyed shooter of phallic arrows lives with his peer group in the woods and regularly confronts the parental authority of the Nottingham police force; he thus has a great many things going for him that obviously contribute to his continued appeal.

An earlier example of nobility and chivalry, King Arthur and his Round Table, is still in the running, although he does not seem to be doing as well. Yet another perennial favorite is Tarzan. He too lives in the woods, although his peer group consists largely of anthropoid apes. Notwithstanding, however, it is present, and its function is preserved. There are evidently many such figures, some of them curious blends of fantasy and reality. For certain girls, the American Indian held a particular fascination. The notion of living close to nature, making one's own habitat, riding horseback everywhere— these were inviting images and, when physical circumstances allowed, the youngsters could live them out in some detail. Quite a different category of fantasy is the superhero. Here the conceptualization is less real and more infantile; accordingly it is at once more expansionary and capable of even greater distortion. The ensuing images are usually a picture of the primitive superego aborning. Here there is a perennial battle, good fights ever against evil and the story never ends; there is always another chapter. The figures involved are often quite inhuman. They can be super robots, or androids, all sorts of weddings of flesh and mechanism (as the youngsters sense their capacity to think and feel changing within). The evil ones are an equally varied array of monsters. The characteristics of both sides are their extraordinary (magical) powers. Force fields, ray guns, tractor beams, heat rays, freezers, lasers, powers to change form, or read minds, or hurl objects by mental force alone, the ability to transfix or penetrate with a look, the capacity to fly through the air at will. All the fantasies of the pre-genital and phallic child, now in more dressed-up versions to be sure, more sophisticated, better described, but filled with the same fiery malevolence of sadistic fantasy, the same transcendent sweep of phallic grandiosity, and the same primitive morality of early conscience structures—all are in place, and all give their characters a powerful allure of the young mind. For the earlier grade-school group in particular, the role of emotion is a key agent in the invoking of magic. The yearning for change to take place in response to one's feelings—does ones heart skip a beat when an exciting other passes by? Oh to become something great, impressive, remarkable, at that very moment. In the actual situation, one stands riveted to the earth, but within, ah, how fantasy soars! When the emotions rage, how much one might wish to become a puissant, all-powerful figure who sweeps all before him or her.

The culture was not slow in responding to these yearnings. Television, that most malleable and responsive of media, spawned a host of embodiments of this set of wishes. One of the most illustrative figures that was a long-time popular favorite with the younger set was the Hulk. The hero was a very average young man who carried within him a special germ of change. In the course of the stories he would encounter stresses that provoked fear and rage. At this point a change would come over him and, in a trice, he would grow a head taller, huge muscles would balloon out all over his body, bursting out of his clothes, his face would transform into a Gorgon mask of ferocity, and his skin would turn green. He was now *deus ex machina*, a new entity, the Hulk, uncontrollable and irresistible—and he would proceed to undo the bad guys, thwart their evil designs, and make everything come right. The younger grade schoolers loved this—it matched their wishes exactly.

Parallel with this was the appearance of a set of toys called Transformers, to which many of these grade-school children became very attached. These playthings would be innocent-looking cars, trucks, buses, or even articles of furniture, which, with the rotation and manipulation of their innocent-looking parts, turned into heavily armed futuristic robots with a host of super weapons to turn loose on enemy forces. Such a transformation had been adumbrated by Superman (who changed from bumbling Clark Kent to the soaring super being he was), by Captain Marvel (who had but to say "Shazam!" to effect the necessary alterations), and by Wonder Woman (who spun around as the trigger for her transfiguration). Now, instead of merely watching the change from a plebian figure to a heroic one, children had a world of change at their fingertips; the little Transformer toy became an overt expression of the wish. It allowed for the sudden acquisition of enormous powers or, more exactly, for the sudden revelation of powers that had always been present but that had heretofore been concealed.

Thus far, we have addressed the images of super strength or superpowers. Both boys and girls will play with these toys. But with toys that are closer to the immediate realities of children, there is often a good deal of difference between the interests of the sexes. Thus, that perennial favorite, the

Barbie doll, is largely the plaything of younger girls. By and large, the boys who prefer such items as their playthings are likely to be regarded askance by their communities and to be considered effeminate. For little girls, however, Barbie becomes a site for the wreathing of considerable swaths of fantasy. Whether it be dress-up play or any sort of body adornment (hairdos, jewelry, sports outfits, or elaborate costumes), Barbie is there to allow their dreams to come true. Through the figurine, an endless panoply of domestic and romantic issues get relived and reenacted. Glorious erotic fantasies are realized, conquests achieved, sinners converted to virtue, and every manner of wish fulfillment attained. For several generations of American women a Barbie doll, or several Barbie dolls (along with her male counterpart, Ken, and several girlfriends), has been an essential element in their growing up.

For more maternal girls, the Cabbage Patch doll has served to offer endless diversions and satisfactions of all manner of child-caring impulses. There is a great variety of these rather ugly infant replicas now available (e.g., a preemie), and they have been tenderly nursed, fed, changed, pampered, spanked, sung to, and mused over by literally thousands of little girls.

The closest correlate for boys, and for some girls, is probably G.I. Joe. This modern soldier, the archetypal American fighting man, has been armed with everything from standard combat gear to the most futuristic and elaborate laser emplacements. Brave, fearless, intrepid, aggressive, intrusive, powerful, and sweeping all before him, he allows for all kinds of grandiose, warlike play. Endless scenarios of combat and conquest are the child's for the asking. This remains a perennial favorite.

For the older latency-age child, the naïve fantasies of the prior years often no longer sufficed. The nature of the developmental thrust of the time was to move from fantasy solutions to more concrete and practical ways to attain fame and glory. More and more individual proclivities would find behavioral expression, and the youngsters would begin to strive for achievement in many arenas. They would learn athletic skills and seek to excel, and they would then turn to the great athletes of the day and model after and idolize them. These figures are evidently quite different from the strictly fantasy images of which we spoke. Sports heroes may be television idols, but more than that they are real, human, current, an individual one might see in the ballpark or even meet in person—even approach for an autograph. The role of such a figure in development is also rather different. The fantasy superhero is a flight from reality. Once the world is too painful, one takes refuge in dreams of glory. In it an enclave of blissful make-believe that allows some respite from the less rewarding, often gritty context of the everyday.

The real-life hero or heroine is something else again. Here is a model for identification. It is out of recognition of this aspect of development that so much emphasis is placed on the probity of the public figure. The classic appeal addressed to a shamed baseball player by a disillusioned child—"Say it ain't so!"—bears witness to the intensity of the pain youngsters experience as their ideals are shattered. This theme reverberates with particular intensity in the Black community, which is today struggling with powerful regressive forces affecting its children. Each time a Black athlete or civic leader falls from grace, youngsters struggling to survive and to grow in the inner cities experience a blow to their ideals and self-respect. The maelstrom of gangs, rackets, and escapist activity sucks down all too many of these vulnerable youngsters, and the powerful model of a respected and successful achiever is perceived as a material presence for young people to hold on to, something to help them resist the tug of the troubled community life.

Not only athletes serve as heroes. More bookish boys and girls might turn to intellectual giants like Albert Einstein, to master poets of their day or of bygone days, or creative musical performers or musicians, as avatars of triumphant achievement. One may dream of meeting them, knowing them, impressing them, or possibly transcending them. Depending on earlier fixations, many residua from earlier stages of development may color the fantasy life of a particular youngster. Thus, some deprived children have extraordinary daydreams about food and eating. There is a terrible innocence to these powerful, primitive images. Not infrequently they will spin off thinly disguised stories about being themselves the victims of the oral gorging of some monstrous, fanged entity.

There are children fixated at a sadistic level who may be fascinated by torture and dream of inflicting pain on helpless victims or of being the subject of some torturer's ministrations. Often the significant other is some figure from the movies or from the video images of the day. There are quite an array of such monstrous presences to choose among—Freddy Kruger, Jason, and the like. More anxious children may be tormented by the fears such entities create, especially when a bout of television watching or attendance at a horror movie has evoked the child's inner vulnerabilities and given form and immediacy to the imminent but heretofore contained terrors lying in wait in that child's mind. (Even a movie intended to be a spoof on horror films, *Attack of the Killer Tomatoes*, was able to send a 6-year-old patient whom the author treated into a year-long bout of anxiety attacks. Evidently the sense of a large, soft body pressing down upon its victims and destroying them echoed enough of this child's own experience to evoke an enduring panicky reaction.)

Then there are grade-school children who never enter latency at all. They are overstimulated either by seduction or by an unaware pattern of child rearing that exposes them repeatedly to adult nakedness or sexual activity. In any case, the majority of such children will not fantasize these events but will seek to enact them, much to the detriment of their psychological development as well as to the well-being of their playmates. However, some of these youngsters (probably those with a more internalizing constitutional endowment) maintain their fixations on a strictly fantasy level. Their inner life recapitulates the things that have happened to them as a kind of theme and variations; they are endlessly preoccupied by a sense of eroticism, and they imagine all sorts of adventures involving highly sexualized interactions.

Toward the end of the grade school years, one of the inevitable emergents is a partial deidealization of the parents. Children have now lived long enough and matured sufficiently to see that their parents are all too human, with the faults and foibles of all human beings. The adults begin to lose some of the sheen that protected them from childhood critique, their several faults are perceived and beginning to be understood, and they are found wanting in a number of critical areas. Children then begin to dream of other parents, their true parents, not like these deficient people with whom they live at home but people of nobler, purer stuff, or more sterling qualities, of greater wealth and importance, people who know they are theirs and who will someday come to claim them as their own. At that point in the fantasy, these youngsters will see themselves driving off in a blaze of glory and leaving behind these pedestrian clods with whom now they are compelled to live.

This is the family romance made famous by Freud (1959/1909). Many people can recall this particular image in later years and remember it with a combination of humor and pathos. In summary, then, early grade-school children are dominated largely by the struggle to finish consolidation of the superego and to shore up the means to contain the oedipal yearnings. Later in this epoch, the interest turns more toward the ego ideal, toward realizing what the ego can do, toward the setting of goals and the achievement of aspirations. Toward the end of the grade school years, with the family romance, there is a beginning thought of separation from the parents, leaving them behind to find a better way of life. And with this foreshadowing of puberty, the grade school era comes to an end.

Although the concept of self-love had already been considered by several authors, Freud gave it the name *narcissism* and focused both theoretical and clinical attention on what it means and where it comes from. For psychoanalysts, narcissism became a seminal idea, and patients were presently classified as having a narcissistic condition or a neurotic one (i.e., they could not be analyzed, or they were appropriate candidates for such treatment).

In the second half of the twentieth century, an entirely new dimension of classification and technique appeared. Margaret Mahler had already broken away from the existing developmental schema of oral, anal, and phallic–oedipal level and had introduced a new conceptual approach based not so much on analytic reconstruction as on direct child observation. She saw children as going through autistic, symbiotic, differentiation, practicing, rapprochement, and separation–individuation phases. Without intending to, she nonetheless opened the gates to the object relations theorists. Otto Kernberg developed a schema in which an ideal image of the self and an ideal image of the parent would flow together, fusing in the patient's mind, often sweeping up and joining with the more realistic sense of self so that a blurred self-idealizing, grandiose mass of internal images held sway in his or her mind. Presently the individual would be living independently in a distorted world. Heinz Kohut, who was developing his own ideas apart from those of Kernberg (although parallel in time), saw these conditions not so much as a product of trauma and conflict but as a sort of deficiency disease. Kohut placed a powerful emphasis on empathy, the empathic mirroring infants need, the sense of value and support and responsive attentiveness that had to be offered them in response to their hunger for recognition and interaction. When this empathy failed either through absence or through inadequate responsiveness on the part of the caretaker, the infants took refuge in themselves—and a narcissistic line of development ensued. Subsequent theorists have developed a psychology of the self, and narcissistic pathology is now thought to be within the framework of the disturbances of the self.

Disturbances of narcissism are present in many conditions (e.g., mania, depression, paranoia). To the extent that the major form of pathology is in the narcissistic component of the disorder, then a diagnosis of narcissistic personality disorder (NPD) is made. The term *narcissistic personality disorder* first appeared in the *Diagnostic and Statistical Manual of Mental Disorders,* third edition (*DSM-III*). It emerged with the work of Kernberg and Kohut; many of the original descriptive terms were written by Theodore Millon. Millon emphasized the close relationship to exhibitionistic personality disorder; in effect he regarded the narcissist as an exhibitionist with grandiose tendencies.

Meanwhile, with the universe of disorders of childhood, a number of authors had begun to explore the dimensions of the condition. Offer, Madin, Bleiberg, and Rensley, to mention only a few, were presenting the initial picture of the disorder. It was evident that one could detect the presence of precursors from toddlerhood onward. To begin with, there is a normal anthology of narcissistic grandiosity that finds varied expression at each of the several developmental levels. The 2-year-old can have wild tantrums where through screaming and kicking and drumming his hands on the floor he will *make* the adult world submit to his will. For the moment he feels powerful, huge, compelling. The 3- to 4-year-old has dreams of glory; she will drive out one parent and take over the sexual connection with the other; small as she is, she will nonetheless win the battle and come back in triumph to claim the bed of the absent parent. There is something inherently grandiose within. As for the grade-school child, a host of heroes and superheroes—everything from ball players and wrestlers to Superman and Wonder Woman—form a rich pantheon of fantasy figures where they can join in their magnificence by collecting baseball cards or playing with the figurines. Thus, each developmental level has its own mode of expressing the normal grandiosity of its epoch.

Clinical aspects of narcissism

Overt signs and symptoms

Narcissists at any age show the cardinal combination of pronounced self-centeredness, an exaggerated sense of their own importance, a feeling they are not bound to fulfill the usual social requirements, and an expectation of unique response on the part of whomever they come in contact with. There is often a quality of profound vanity; they see themselves as exceptionally interesting and important. They are special; ordinary rules do not apply. There is often an associated feeling of entitlement, a very intense response to any frustration or disappointment, a profound preoccupation with concerns about shame and humiliation, a total devotion to maintaining an image, and a need to receive attention, recognition, and praise beyond all others. Often there is a very "thin skin" present, a readiness to have their feelings hurt by the most trivial slight and an intensive defensive response to any possible criticism or even question; should this transpire, it is experienced as a loss of face or wound to their dignity. In some instances there are additional complicating factors like the need to make up stories that are substituted for the truth. This redoubtable lying is one of the hallmarks of the condition.

In some instances, youngsters behave in this way when there is no evident need to do so. Despite this, however, not all narcissistic children are antisocial. Many are quiet and retiring, preferring to live in a haze of grandiose fantasy rather than to engage in the painful give and take of the schoolyard. On the other hand, when an antisocial syndrome is present, it usually arises in connection with an associated fixation at a sadistic level of early development. These children may then seek to live out a fantasy of domination, with a need to obtain abject submission from their victims, as a means of validating their grandiose stance.

The play patterns of narcissistic children are often quite striking. They do not cooperate well, and they compete with even less success. It is difficult to cooperate when they want to do all the best, or the easiest, or the most interesting parts of the task and, moreover, feel entitled to do so. It is impossible to compete if only winning is allowed, when they feel it is intolerable to lose and if they insist on cheating where winning is in question. Narcissistic children do not do well with the rules; rules are for others; they should be a privileged exception to the rules—otherwise they feel wounded and misunderstood and are likely either to sulk, withdraw, or explode.

Much depends on the degree of talent or giftedness with which these youngsters are endowed. Thus, children with a knack for music, with an aptitude for gymnastics, or with a high IQ may do striking work in their area of special competence. The hunger for praise is so great that they will work hard and strive mightily to build on their talent to be all the more outstanding. At the same time, they may do little and exert only indifferent effort in areas where they do not excel. In general, narcissistic children work in uneven ways, striving not so much to learn or to please the parents or teacher but rather to achieve the kind of ready recognition on which this personality organization thrives. Where that reception is not immediately attainable, the quality of the work is all too likely to suffer.

In their interpersonal relationships, narcissists are often said to lack empathy. This observation needs a good deal of qualification. In fact, many such youngsters are very apt at tuning in to the feelings of others and can indeed be remarkably empathic. At the same time, they are often uncaring about others' responses, not so much because they are unaware of these reactions as because these feelings dwindle into insignificance by comparison with their own. Not infrequently they use their sensitivities to enhance their own position. They can become very manipulative, twisting the truth, rationalizing in extraordinarily facile ways, and responding with great perceptiveness to the reactions their stories evoke. People often remark on how extraordinarily charming and ingratiating such children can be—when they are not being selfish, grandiose, and impossible.

Relationship to other disorders

Not every display of vanity or self-centered grandiosity implies that the basic personality organization of that person is narcissistic. The narcissistic stance can be a temporary or a transient defensive position that is adopted briefly only in the face of some pressing stress. On the other hand, the expressions of narcissistic grandiosity can figure in as part of some other serious disturbance of mental health, and in that case we diagnose the major condition and accept the grandiose elements as part of the spectrum of the basic illness. Let us review some of the conditions where narcissistic elements are to be found.

To begin with, as noted, some degree of narcissism can be a component of normal adaptation. Normal individuals can certainly have dreams of glory, build castles in the air, and treasure the idea that in some way they excel others in appearance, empathy, sexual appeal, beauty, good taste, or in respect to some other virtuous dimension of experience. The key variable is the matter of degree. The treasured fantasy, the self-centeredness, the boasting, the vanity—all these may be present, but it becomes a matter of degree. In the normal, they are not the dominant aspects of self;

indeed, they may be regarded as charming weaknesses in an otherwise sterling individual.

When we consider psychopathology, however, it is evident that there are important narcissistic dimensions to many serious conditions. Hypomania and manic disorders are almost invariably accompanied by expansive, grandiose feelings, a constant need to attract attention, a tendency to tell dramatic tales for self-enhancement, and other such elaborations, all too suggestive of the narcissistic state. The relationship of narcissism to borderline personality disorders is so close that some others consider the two syndromes parallel or overlapping conditions. In particular, the personality structure of borderline patients is layered around a core of profound disfigured anxiety; these youngsters experience a constant preoccupation with the danger of losing the object by abandonment or because their hostility has destroyed it and with the danger of losing the self because it has been fused with or engulfed by the object. Such patients are given to deploying a large number of defensive patterns. At moments they seem anxious and neurotic, at other times they are somatizing in dramatic ways, at other moments still they present themselves as overly psychotic, and then, recovering, they may plunge into sequences of serious acting out. Interwoven among these transient defensive patterns, there is often a tendency toward grandiose self-centeredness as they seek to shore up in the face of their great concerns about crumbling defenses and their inability to maintain a stable sense of self. This grandiose stance can simulate a classic narcissistic personality patterns, and many frequently recur or persist for long periods.

Many conduct-disorder patients, too, display multiple narcissistic elements. Group experiences make for a set of reinforcing fantasies, which collectively project a quality of arrogance, contempt, superiority, condescension, and, in a word, grandiosity. Individuals with one kind of superego deficiency may seek to prevail over their peers or neighbors by manipulation, swindling, or conning. Others, with a different kind of superego design, may display a more primitive need to be the terror of everyone who knows them, the toughest, meanest, most feared individual in their milieu. Some disturbed youngsters combine both proclivities. In any case, the narcissistic elements can be striking.

Paranoia is often associated with construction of a grandiose system of some kind; it thus shares some elements of megalomania in common with the pure narcissist. The primary role of projective mechanisms and the delusional quality of the ensuing ideation serve to distinguish the two conditions. The connection linking exhibitionism to narcissism is so close that it may require careful diagnostic work to distinguish them. The key to resolving this lies in the fact that exhibitionists are interested primarily in display. Narcissists, on the other hand, will be moved by a desire for praise that might indeed lead to some display but that need not require showing off as such to obtain that. Narcissistic children are possessed by many powerful impulses to be special and grand, but this can exist on a largely ideational level and need not take the form of exhibitionism. Such children can be content with fantasies of how much better and smarter they are than the people around them, or they can act in arrogant and supercilious fashion in contexts where they feel safe enough to "be them-selves"; unlike exhibitionists, however, they are not driven primarily by a need to show off. However, the inordinate need of many narcissistic children to be the center of attention does make for a good deal of overlap in the two conditions.

Sometimes people with multiple personality disorder have one alter who is intensely narcissistic. It were as though the narcissistic condition is pres-ent but is sequestered and confined to one area. Gamblers are usually quite narcissistic. They challenge fate with the fantasy of conquering it, of out-witting it, or of facing it down. Their basic impulse is ultimately toward self-destruction, but the superficial appearance they present may be one of arrogant superiority as they compare themselves with all the poor suckers out there who work for a living.

Patterns of peer relationships

One of the pressing urges of narcissistic children is the need to fill all available relationship space. They would have all attention centered on them, emanating from them, included within them. Their playmates presently find them bossy or domineering. They insist on having things their own way; others' interests must give way to theirs. If they are smart and talented and strongly convinced of their own special worth, they might become leaders and fulfill their personal mandate in that fashion. In particular, less secure youngsters will be drawn to others who are so sure of themselves.

If they are less able, they may resort to clowning, to making noise, or to giving directives to others to gain the attention they seek. Sometimes they will strive to attach themselves to members of the in-group, the popular kids, so that they can share in their elevated station.

The end result is that these youngsters are often outsiders who are con-sidered too stuck-up or too demanding to be good companions. They do not share well, they are sore losers, and they do not play fair at games. Moreover, they are quite ready to criticize others but unable to tolerate their criticism. In particular, narcissistic grade schoolers are intolerant of teasing. With their exaggerated sense of self-importance, even gentle gibes are experienced as cruel assaults, and they will react with intense emotion to everyday schoolboy pranks. Thus, the schoolyard experience is for them a dangerous jungle they tread warily or, more commonly, avoid.

Patterns of adult relationship

Often these youngsters prefer the company of adults to that of peers. Not infrequently the children feel, and act, like miniature adults. They seek to enter into adult conversations and readily voice opinions and fire advice or directions to the adults. The parents may complain that there is an incessant battle for control in the home. These youngsters challenge the parental rules and argue constantly about every direction; more than that, some of these youngsters constantly make up their own rules and want to know why they are not carried out. All in all, the parents (who may have thought these traits cute in the preschooler) find this kind of behavior in a grade-school child to be trying to the extreme.

Patterns of fantasy

The fantasies tend to cluster around themes of being powerful, in control, and even in a position to mete out punishment. An example from a current clinical case involving an 8-year-old boy goes as follows (reported to a psychologist in response to a request to have dolls act out a family story):

> Everyone constantly bangs on each other, knocking the figures around. He describes himself as the winner, because he finally knocked everyone down. He says: "I'm Superman. I'm on the couch and Mom and Dad are talking. My brother and sister come in, everyone looks at me. I wave my arms and everyone falls down. They get up and say: 'How did you do that?' Now all of you versus me." He thereupon knocks them all down again. He told of doing this at school too.

References

Bleiberg, E. (1984). Narcissistic disorders in children. *Bulletin of the Menninger Clinic*, 48(6), 501–517.

Freud, S. (1959). Family romances. In J. Strachey (Ed. & Trans.), *The standard edition of the complete psychological works of Sigmund Freud* (Vol. 9, pp. 235–241). London: Hogarth Press. (Originally published in 1909)

Freud, S. (1958). Formulation on the two principles of mental functioning. In J. Strachey (Ed. & Trans.), *The standard edition of the complete psychological works of Sigmund Freud* (Vol. 12, pp. 213–226). London: Hogarth Press. (Originally published in 1911)

Freud, S. (1953). Three essays on the theory of sexuality. In J. Strachey (Ed. & Trans.), *The standard edition of the complete psychological works of Sigmund Freud* (Vol. 7. pp. 3–122). London: Hogarth Press. (Originally published in 1905)

Kernberg, O. (1976). *Borderline conditions and pathological narcissism*. New York: Jason Aronson.

Kernberg, P. (1989). Narcissistic personality conditions in childhood. *Psychiatric Clinics of North America, 12*(3), 671–694.

Piaget, J. (1954). *The construction of reality in the child*. New York: Basic Books.

Rinsley, D. B. (1988). A review of the pathogenesis of borderline and narcissistic personality disorders. *Adolescent Psychiatry, 15*, 387–406.

Chapter 9

Teenage mutant ninja turtles

INTRODUCTION

John McDermott

In the chapter that follows, as Joe Noshpitz analyzes a popular children's film of the 1990s, *Teenage Mutant Ninja Turtles*, you can see both the breadth and depth of his thinking. Describing the essential characteristics of pop culture, he skillfully takes us beyond the obvious good guys versus bad guys themes, combining insights from Carl Jung and Sigmund Freud with his own, as he delves into the hidden crevices of the inner lives of our children. Specifically, he penetrates the unconscious minds of teenagers in a way that we (and their parents) can accept—and come away with a better understanding of their oft-annoying behavior.

Teenage Mutant Ninja Turtles, he tells us, can best be seen as a developmental drama, the representation of a life journey, one that focuses on getting through a particularly difficult phase of growing up. This was back in the '80s and '90s, a time when parents wondered whether the then-current "Turtlemania" was a cause for alarm. They were perplexed about the possible harmful effects of these four sword-wielding, wisecracking, pizza-grinding turtle characters as role models for their own teenagers. Meanwhile, the movie was breaking all records at the box office.

Let me provide some important background that the author skips when he wrote this piece about the movie. After all, the Turtles are old stuff now, and Turtlemania was at its peak 25 years ago.

The *Teenage Mutant Ninja Turtles* story begins when a rat named Splinter (yes, that's right, a rat), who had once been a ninja master (a kind of super samurai warrior, expert at martial arts, coupled with a deep spiritual philosophy), escaped from an evil force called Shredder by hiding underground in a Manhattan sewer. A terrible accident aboveground caused four baby turtles to slosh into his underground hideout along with a radioactive spill that evidently caused their mutation. The old ninja warrior adopted the baby turtles, naming them, of all things, after Renaissance artists—Raphael, Donatello, Michelangelo, and Leonardo. He raised them in true samurai tradition, teaching them skills in martial arts and the samurai philosophy. But as they grew up, they began to behave like typical teenagers everywhere, desecrating the samurai code they had been taught, turning their underground home into a typical teenage clubhouse, and scarfing down pizza. At night they would sneak out to learn about the real world above. Soon they encountered Shredder and his gang of thugs. The gang captured and held their mentor, Splinter, prisoner until our Turtles, aided by their friend in the real world above, a newspaper reporter named April, rescued Splinter, and all was well again.

Teenagers loved the story, of course. But what about younger kids, the preteens who flocked to the film and bought all of that commercial turtle paraphernalia to be like the Turtles?

The late Bruno Bettelheim, in his classic book *The Uses of Enchantment* (1989), described how traditional fairy tales were really hidden morality tales that allowed children to process their fears and worries. But these fairy tales dramatically changed form with the explosion of the modern media. Themes changed, too. Noshpitz adapts Bettelheim's method to the Turtles saga, analyzing the hidden theme and offering us reassurance, not just about teenaged sloppiness and eating junk food but about other themes like flaunting independence from parental guidance.

Noshpitz shows how *Teenage Mutant Ninja Turtles* still used the upside-down world of opposites and reversals to disguise the message. The hero is a rat, at the same time a mentor and leader of adolescents. The good guys live in the sewer and the bad guys above ground. Of course, the old fairy tale lesson is the same—hard work pays off in the end. Along the way, though, Noshpitz discusses the changing historical roots of fighting and violence, once a reflection of achieving manhood and now a prohibition. But the fighting is really a side issue, he claims. It is on the side of righteousness. And after all, the Turtles fight together as a team, not against each other. That's how he gets to his main theme—how a boy arrives into manhood these days. The history alone is worth the read. But the developmental theme is the key.

Joseph Campbell also wrote about the stuff of legend and myth adapted by Hollywood. Old wine in new bottles? Perhaps. But when I would give a presentation on one of the *Star Wars* film series at the annual meeting of the American Academy of Child and Adolescent Psychiatry, I could count on Joe Noshpitz sitting right there in the front row. As you can guess when you read the essay that follows, he couldn't wait to be the first to raise his hand when I finished. Joe would ask, "But Jack, isn't it really basically an oedipal theme?"

"Yes, Joe," I'd answer, "but it's *more* than that, too." And off we'd go.

Recently I was honored to present the Joseph Noshpitz Lecture at the annual meeting of the AACAP. The paper was titled "Harry Potter: Passing Fad or Children's Classic?" As I looked out into the audience, I imagined Joe Noshpitz sitting right there in the front row, his hand ready to shoot up with the first question.

It must be that I miss him—as all of us do.

Reference

Bettelheim, B. (1989). *The uses of enchantment: The meaning and importance of fairy tales.* New York: Vintage.

TEENAGE MUTANT NINJA TURTLES
Joseph D. Noshpitz

Popular culture is an important and fascinating phenomenon, perhaps the closest thing we have to a group mind or a tribal consciousness. It pervades our lives, its usages find their way into our language, and its figures have presence in the inner life of many children and adults. One should not overestimate its importance; it does not compare, for example, with the significance of parents or siblings, but during late latency and early puberty its effects run a close second to the psychological import of school. For some youngsters it may be more important. If nothing else, studying the nature of pop culture is likely to tell us something of the prevailing emotional hungers and yearnings of people, for it is in response to those that pop culture exists, and it is in its influence *on* those that its significance lays. Pop culture is endlessly dynamic, as performers and creators seek to read the public's mood and interest and to feed that public what it wants. And, as the public in turn grows and develops and responds, now to this, now to that, selecting its themes with quicksilver shifts of topic and mood, there is a certain cumulative effect to the way that things evolve so that, over time, major alterations in public taste and values can take place.

The way it works is that something catches on—hula hoops or Cabbage Patch dolls or the Beatles—and spreads like wildfire through a particular segment of the population. For a time the flames burn brightly and light up the social sky, and then something happens; some other presence commands the public horizon. For children and younger adolescents, the Teenage Mutant Ninja Turtles have been such a phenomenon; they have had their interval of glory, and they are only now beginning to pass the crest of their popularity and to start the long and steady slide into oblivion that has characterized so many of their notable predecessors. Or perhaps they will follow the Beatles and Elvis Presley into sainthood—who can tell?

Let us consider some of the characteristics that I think contribute to make a particular item offered by the creators of pop culture likely to be accepted. First, it has to address some deep-seated existential problem in society. Often the problem is associated with uncertainty or an area of public stress. Our feelings toward gender issues and male–female interactions are perennial favorites. But husband–wife tensions, the honesty and dishonesty of police, the wisdom of children against the wisdom of their elders, all sorts of challenges to the official—and often the euphemistic—address to emotional issues are likely to be at the core. As we shall see, the theme of coming into manhood is one such that is integral to this movie.

Second, it has to simplify the issue. One of the great bugaboos of humankind, certainly of civilized humankind, is the extraordinary complexity of at once their inner experience, interactive relationship, and civic, larger community adaptation. The yearning that emerges, among all of us sometimes and among young people much of the time, is for things to be simple. "Lighten up," "take it easy," "cool it" are among the common injunctions aimed at least in part toward shaking off the yoke of our complexity and acting as though life were something other than the tangled snarl it so frequently becomes. What a relief it is to know the good guys from the bad guys, to be sure that in the end virtue will triumph over evil and that the hero will get the girl. One need not untangle byzantine motivational intricacies with all their changeability, uncertainty, and ambiguity. As long as the story goes on, one is free from the burden of complexity.

A third characteristic of pop culture is arousal. Such consumable stuff must feed the instincts, must be evocative, and in effect must massage the id. Fight scenes, chase scenes, sex scenes, or merely simple pie-in-the-face, pants-falling-down kinds of slapstick are cases in point. There has to be at least some such payoff.

Allied to that (and number four in the sequence), there is often rather a special kind of morality. Sentimentality, bathos, scenes of reconciliation, all are there, some kind of fairly obvious moral choice has to be made, and, *mirabile dictu*, it is on the side we know is right. The hero is tempted but stands firm and resists the siren song. The errant one strays but is troubled by conscience, and finally, at the critical juncture, he does the right thing. With this, we all mist over and come away with a sense of uplift.

Finally there is the associated aesthetic. Here we stand on shakier ground because the variety of pop culture's expressive forms is so vast. Basically, it comes down to how best to tell a story. Accordingly, the means of telling, the coherence of the tale, the skill of the creators in employing whatever media they works in—all these will help determine how well it all comes together. If it is a cartoon, how well is it drawn, how convincingly do the depicted characters convey the intended message, and how well told is the tale of their efforts? If it is a printed story, how good of a wordsmith is the author? If it is a movie, how about pacing and sequence and soundtrack and camera work—all the necessary elements—let alone storyline, acting, sets, and directing? We should never forget that Utagawa Hiroshige designed prints to put on tea wrappers and that Charles Dickens wrote chapters for a weekly serial. This work can be done poorly or well—and to considerable extent that matters too.

With this, we move from the general to the specific work we are here addressing. For purposes of our work, I propose to focus in particular on adolescent development.

First, a few preliminary observations about the style of the telling. The story of *Teenage Mutant Ninja Turtles* is told largely in darkness. It is the stuff of dream, myth, and legend, with a repeatedly recurring image of idealized and demonized figures coming out of concealment—that is to say, out of the unconscious—and interacting in various ways during night-time encounters. The heroes live underground and come to the surface only at night. The villains live in a large warehouse and have their own inner world, which is artificially lit. The darkness emphasizes the mythic tone of the story, a tale of good versus evil, of darkness against light. It is altogether reminiscent of another recent fairy tale adventure, *Beauty and the Beast*. In this story too, the beast-like hero lives in dark underground spaces, comes out only at night, rescues a girl, and brings her down to his world of make-believe.

With so much said, let us move to the main theme. Before the movie begins, the preliminary lead-in tells up something of the character of the ensuing interplay. A young newswoman announces on television that a crime wave is currently inundating the community. Then, as she walks the darkened street, she is frightened by a rat and begins the transition into the world of myth. It is a world of reversals where the good guys live in darkness and the bad guys in light, where the unpleasant rat becomes the revered mentor, and where the deformed and potentially monstrous Turtles are the heroes, and the human followers of Shredder are the villains. In that extraordinary realm, she is accosted by the evildoers, the bad youths. Before they can harm her, however, the lights go out, and these aggressors are attacked by a group of invisible assailants. The mysterious rescuers overcome the bad youths quickly, tie them up, and leave them bound on the sidewalk.

Thus, virtue triumphs, good overcomes evil, the safety of the girl is assured—and the movie begins. This simple morality play is further enhanced by the basic theme that now develops and that will run throughout. It is the story of becoming—how the boy becomes a man. It is one of the conundrums of our time that that everyday sequence, the elementary transformation of the male child as he moves into and through adolescence, has become muffled and confused to the point where masculinity has become an amorphous concept and even a disreputable one, where what was once a self-evident change everyone took for granted has now become one of the most poorly defined passages in the human lifespan. Hence, one of the great appeals of such a movie, albeit symbolically and to some extent in caricature, is that it nevertheless portrays a vision of boy becoming youth becoming man.

To be sure, in this tale, the notion of manhood is defined as being able to fight—and that requires some explanation. It is not so long ago that a real boy was expected to come home from school now and then with a black eye. The important issues then were: Did you fight fair, and did you give as good as you got? Nowadays, a fight by a middle-class boy in a middle-class school would be totally unacceptable and might very well become grounds for a lawsuit. The expected level of decorum and the forms of acceptable miscreance have both changed dramatically over the last two generations. Along with this, there has been a radical revision in the definition of manhood. Or perhaps revision is the wrong term. There has been an abandonment of the former conception not jeered at as macho, without any very clear formulation emerging to take its place. The fathers are perplexed as to what model to offer their sons, and the sons are even more baffled. The culture has turned its back on direct violence as a virtuous or even a permissible form of expression, and, despite the fact that they have been shaped by millennia of violent experience, the males in our society now find themselves chastened and in some corners excoriated for any such interest. But no cultural taboo can make all of that phylogenetic pressure simply give way. The hunger for more simple and direct expression of aggressive, competitive and combative impulses is rampant. Those who write and produce media materials respond to this demand and make hours of violence viewing available in every possible form: cartoons, movies, videos, television, and so on. No wonder, then, that the theme of the *Ninja Turtles* packs a great deal of combative stuff.

The specific ideal extolled in this presentation is very simple: it involves excellence in fighting as long as it is on the side of righteousness. This is a very old tradition, deeply engrained in our culture, and readily evoked in times of war or national stress. Indeed, once upon a time the notion of fighting was an honorable one. We have but to think of the model of knighthood and chivalry, the knights of our storied tradition did very little else *but* fight. Indeed, we always think of them as clad in their somewhat grotesque garb—their own Turtle get-up, the suit of mail, designed to protect them during their many battles. Our Old Testament rings with accounts of battles and alarms, prophesies about war and tales of bloodshed. The games of male childhood used to be cowboys and Indians, or some other version of good guys against bad guys. It is only in our time that things have changed and that the notion of the boy growing into man, the fighter, has fallen into disrepute. Hence a story based on fighting skills and filled with fighting sequences will meet wide appreciation among our action-hungry young. Paradoxically, as the acceptability of fights has in fact diminished, the frequency and intensity of violence and combat in entertainment (e.g., movies, television, video) seems to have increased proportionally. Hundreds of hours each month are devoted to scenes of violence—primarily because the market demands it. That is what the young like to watch—in particular, what young boys like to watch.

The notion of growing up to be a successful fighter in some realm is one of the dreams of boyhood. Hence, a story depicting the training and preparation of fighters is bound to be interesting to young viewers. The question of *how* one is prepared for such a future is a subtheme of this story. The concept of the ninja is, of course, one of a super fighter, a master of the martial arts. Presumably it involves a good deal of training and years of practice. Thus, the preparation for becoming a man, a fighter, involves a lifetime of hard work and discipline. But that is only part of the story. For it involves a teacher and a special kind of student–teacher relationship. With this, another of the main themes appears: the role of the man as teacher, mentor, parent, or model in the rearing of the boy.

The father–son relationship is of peculiar moment for the story we are studying. The theme of the old man of the tribe as instructing the young boys is as old as mankind itself. No great wonder then that it is central to this story—and indeed offers the major relationship the movie portrays. Again and again, in one form or another, the theme returns to the link between father and son in numerous permutations and combinations.

Leaving that for a moment, there is another theme, prominent and pervasive throughout, that I feel needs address, and that is: The Turtles are grotesque. How does that link with development? It seems to me that in some version or in some limited way, the Teenage Mutant Ninja Turtle is the inner self of every teenage boy. Such a youth has moments when his head is filled with egregious lusts and forbidden images, he masturbates in secret, he may be experimenting with forbidden substances, he hides things from his parents. As a result, there are times when he regards himself as grotesque, misshapen, bizarre. If his inner self were seen, people would shrink away in horror from his ungainly contours; hence that must always be hidden. But, at the same time, he has other moments when he is strong, noble, virtuous, and good; in his heart of hearts he dreams of himself as grand, magical, and gifted with great prowess. He is full of ardent appetites and is basically lovable but is sadly misunderstood by an uncomprehending world. His only recourse is to turn to others who are in similar case, equally deformed within, equally pressed and hagridden by their drives, and to mingle and interact with them.

Now let us consider the oddity of the Turtles in a more general way. According to Harvey Greenberg (writing in *Psychiatric Times*), the idea of Teenage Mutant Ninja Turtles was conceived as a kind of half-mocking commentary on some of the current or recent fads. Shredder, the bad guy of the piece, looks an awful lot like *Star Wars*' Darth Vader, and all sorts of other borrowings are scattered throughout. The idea of Ninja Turtles as such is, to say the least, far-fetched; in fact it is zany and way out. Evidently it is a pastiche of some prevalent concepts mixed together in an original way—but characterized more by its grotesque peculiarity than by any inherent grace or universality. Yet, that in itself should give us pause, because in recent years the grotesque has come to assume rather remarkable proportions in the realm of teenage entertainment. We have but to consider the garb and behavior of many popular band leaders, and we find ourselves confronting some strange images indeed. It is not so many years ago that one such voice-that-sang-to-youth included a procedure of throwing the entrails of slaughtered chickens in gobs and handfuls out to the uproarious audience, apparently to their frenzied delight. Bizarre posturing, extreme hairdos, oddly formed beards, offbeat costumes, suggestive imitations of perversity, in a host of ways those who stood before and chanted to our youth strove to render themselves as deviant, as unconforming, as distant as possible from any hint of mainstream acceptability. Shock value was sought, and the grotesque was courted.

Even the affective demeanor of these performers was devoted to excess. They strove to portray an individual brought to the very limit of emotional endurance and then pushed beyond. They were frenzied, ecstatic, abandoned, amok; they flung themselves about in a very extremity of pseudo-passion. They tried to do with song and music what they sensed the youngsters both sought and feared, to feel deeply, to test newfound emotions to the limits, to search for the borders of their control. And they sensed as well that some experimentation with alienation from the culture into which they were growing was a pervasive interest among the young.

The creators of the Turtles, however, did them one better. Instead of enacting the extremes of emotion and depicting the overwhelmed ego, they chose instead to report an image of mastery of all that. To do this, the authors chose to resort to humor as their chief mode of coping. The Turtles are inherently funny, they are given to joking, wisecracking, punning, they are greedy, and they indulge in endless mutual teasing. They are also odd-looking, droll, ungainly, essentially ugly and, best of all, apparently unaware and not self-conscious about their oddness. And therein lies one of the powerful secrets of the Turtles' attractiveness. Albeit grotesque, they are not a whit disturbed by their oddness. They know they must keep concealed but betray no trace of self-consciousness about their deviance. If anything, they are filled with macho good humor; they kid around, banter, tease, and carry on as though they were altogether regular guys. They are akin to the taxi driver who tells his astonished passenger: "It looked like a big toitle—where to, folks?"

What a model for the young teenager who is in the midst of his own awkward body changes and who feels so keenly the inner grotesquerie of his passions and imagery. Here are individuals with even more to worry about than he, and look how cheerful they are—they don't let it phase them, any of it, and they embody and live out all his fantasies of righting wrongs, combating evildoers, and impressing girls, and all within a framework of spoofs and rollicking good humor, quips, and cranks and wanton wiles galore.

As noted, one of the threads that binds this story together is the theme of coming into manhood. This is a powerful and universal motif that every culture must face and that has evolved some of the best-known and most elaborately developed human rituals. In tribal contexts, it often enough requires an experience of mutilation, such as the pectoral lacerations of the American Plains Indians or the circumcision and subincision of Australian aborigines. Almost always it necessitates some form of ordeal, some stressful undertaking that demonstrates the prowess and mastery of the youth seeking manhood. This is true even in less warlike societies. The 13-year-old *bar mitzvah* boy must demonstrate his learning before he can say, "Today I am a man." There is usually a period of intensive preparational training that precedes the ordeal and prepares for it. To be sure, in fairy tales, no training is required. One acquires the competencies of manhood merely by growing from the process of development itself. Thus, in the tale of the prince and his companions, there is a tower in which a prince's beloved is immured by a wicked old wizard. As the story opens, the prince is going there to rescue her. On his way he meets a series of odd characters—a very tall man, a very strong man, a man with big eyes, and man with big ears—each of whom seeks to join him. He thus arrives at the tower with a host of competencies he has acquired along the way. Each of the companions assists him, and with their help he defeats the wizard, rescues the maiden, and claims her for his own. Thus, with the additional capacities added by the process of development, he is enabled ultimately to conquer the father figure and to achieve the longed-for oedipal victory. The journey itself is his ordeal and prepares him for the direct oedipal confrontation.

But the usual story in human culture is that of a more or less extended period of training and preparation followed by a ceremonial inflicting of pain, stress, and suffering in the service of achieving manhood. One way or another, the youngster must learn the secrets of the tribe as part of his preparation for the transition to come. Often enough, when he has succeeded, he earns the right to a name. The names accorded the Turtles—Leonardo, Donatello, Michelangelo, and Raphael—are obviously spoofs, another of the reversals, where their ungainly contours are associated with the creators of the most beautiful of all human forms and appearances.

The Turtles, too, had to go through a long period of training. We do not see much of that, but it is described graphically, and they are demonstrably skilled performers at martial arts. Indeed, the themes of hard work, preparation, and acquiring the fitness to perform good deeds are so intrinsic to the Turtles that, as I have noted, their story has about it the elements of a morality play. This is no small part of their appeal; after the relative quietude of latency, teenagers are reencountering their superegos. They are discovering the ambiguities of human motivation and the complexities of interpersonal relationships, so that simplified morality themes, where good guys and bad guys carry evident nametags as to their polarities, are a great relief—and a subject of profound interest.

To continue the discussion of the transition into manhood, let us return to the theme of the father–son relationship. Evidently this can have many derivative forms. There might be a teacher–student interplay and grandfather–grandson, uncle–nephew, even therapist–patient equivalent. As the story gets played out, however, the father–son theme gets reworked in a variety of ways. It is the essence of the interaction between the Turtles and Splinter. It is stated formally as the connection between Shredder and the youngsters who surround him. It is encountered directly in the interplay between Mr. Pennington, the newspaper editor, and his son, Danny. One way or another, it weaves itself into the story and lends an intense emotional tone to the unfolding events.

The Turtles are depicted as rather heedless, inattentive, and wisecracking as their mentor tries to speak seriously to them. At one point he looks up in mock despair and says, "Kids!" Yet despite all the kidding around, when the chips are down and he is spirited away by the bad guys, the Turtles lament his loss and seek him with such fervor that ultimately they reach him telepathically and achieve a sort of mystical union. His particular form of parenting involved training, discipline, and the pronouncement of many wise saws. This stands in contrast to the rearing styles of Shredder, whose message to his young protégés is: "You can have anything you want whenever you want it." This theme of hedonism unlimited does not seem to encourage much discipline, but without laboring the logic of it it turns out that Shredder, too, offers martial arts training and has his own corps of bully-boys to serve as foils for the Turtles. Both the upright Splinter and the debased Shredder exemplify symbolic versions, caricatures if you will, of child-rearing systems. The most realistic father–son relationship, seen only in fragmentary glimpses, is that between Mr. Pennington and his miscreant son. This boy is disobedient, steals, runs away, and joins forces with the bad guys but falls under the sway of Splinter's benign wisdom and is eventually reunited with his father. Here, then, is another of the morality themes: the matter of choice. The young are confronted by both exhortations to do the right thing and obey their parents, and temptations—drink, drugs, cigarettes, theft, gambling, and spending money in profligate fashion—and they must sometimes make hard choices about which course to pursue. This is dramatized once by Danny's struggles with himself and a second time when in the course of rescuing Splinter the Turtles confront the youngsters who have fallen under the sway of Shredder.

Finally, since we speak of development and becoming a man, what about the presence of a woman? And, indeed, the woman, April, is present more or less throughout—only one woman, to be sure, but still quite a significant element in the story. In fact, it is no exaggeration to say that the network of relationships around this figure serves as the essential armature on which the story is mounted. Psychologically, at any rate, the theme of coming into manhood involves the seeking and interacting with an appropriate mate. Accordingly, the unfolding of the story of the Turtles is built around a core of romantic attachment. To be sure, the Turtles, as such, are not romantic. Although early on they make a few feeble remarks and token gestures to suggest some arousal by April, there are no true female objects of their passion, and there is no hint of sexual interplay in their interactions. Instead, their efforts are devoted to righting wrongs, protecting the innocent and, most prominent of all, combating evildoers. When in the presence of April, they strive to entertain her, but they do not become drawn to her or aroused by her; their primary affiliation is with one another and with their mentor. When they deal with the woman, they do so as small children might. They eat her food, they stay in the living quarters she provides (she is the only one in the array of good guys who seems to have any material possessions that amount to anything), and finally, as noted, they act to entertain her. They put on skits and imitations to divert her and make her laugh. The one nonchild element in the relationship is when they act to protect her, both at the outset and subsequently. For them she is a kind of pregenital mother about whom they might harbor rescue fantasies but nothing else.

The romantic attachment does not involve the Turtles. Instead, it is rather sketchily developed between April and an intermittent young male character who keeps appearing at unexpected moments and whose presence is never really explained. This young man is named Casey Jones and, as such, adds to the mythic character of the story by bringing in the theme of the great American railroad saga familiar to every schoolboy. It is a ballad, a song, about the railroad engineer who was one of the models of male vigor and fortitude for an earlier generation; in the Turtles' story it suggests youth and adolescence coming of age and growing into manhood.

As he appears in the story, Casey is at first perceived in a somewhat ambiguous light. He has the same mission as the Turtles, he too battles against the evildoers, despite the fact that he is without the blessing of ninja training, he too is a formidable master of martial arts. His competence derives from the American equivalent of the ninja, namely, he is a former hockey player, a sort of hockey ninja as it were. (There is an old quip: "I went to a fight, and a hockey game broke out.") Indeed, we first meet him opposing Raphael and besting him at hand-to-hand combat. But it soon develops that Casey is a supporter of the Turtles' mission. He is a vigilante of sorts, who with the notable exception of clubs, golf sticks, and cricket bats can somehow outninja the ninjas. He tips the balance in one of their battles with the bad guys, covers their retreat, and is a crucial participant in their final victory. His role is a muted one, in some ways minor; he does not appear in the final battle with Shredder, and one may wonder why he is necessary to the story at all. Paradoxically, I would suggest that the underlying dynamic is such that in fact it is *his* story we are seeing, the story of his meeting, courting, and ultimately joining with April. Indeed, I would go further and say that, despite their centrality, the Turtles are in fact an aspect of *his* growth and development. They represent the qualities that coming into manhood requires. They are actually part beings—the virility, steadfastness, faith, brotherly caring, filial devotion, protectiveness, and *joie de vivre*—that manhood includes, or should include. They are also wise guys, punners, sometimes irreverent, and hence all the more typically male—by this culture's standards. Their part-being status is epitomized by their mentor, whose name, Splinter, testifies to the fragmentary quality of their nature. Even their opponents have a part-object name, the Foot. Hence, in contrast to the storyline, it is not the Turtles who acquire Casey Jones as a companion. It is Casey who, with the help of the characteristics the Turtles represent, by acquiring *them* as it were, is eventually able to mature enough to get the girl—or, more exactly, to be acquired by the girl. In addition to being the only one in their cohort with any possessions, she is the one who says at the end "Kiss me!"—and thus initiates their sexual engagement. As is inevitable for part beings, the Turtles really cannot develop any sort of fully mature relationship. They go another route; they join to Splinter and to one another in mutual symbiosis. Together they quite literally become one—and it is this mythic group that encounters the equally mythic Shredder and overcomes him and thus allows Casey to move into manhood, to come together with his girl, and to make it possible for the film, and this paper, to end.

Chapter 10

Nancy Drew and *The baby-sitters club*

INTRODUCTION

James Lock

Depicting gender role development, whether in pictures, film, or literature, poses problems for the artist and the observer or reader of such works. For the artist, decisions about gender presentation reflect values, beliefs, and social norms about gender, usually derived from the sociocultural context within which the artist is operating. Gender roles are neither universal nor static even within a culture (Ringrose, 1993). Although most Western cultures present only two gender roles, other cultures have for a variety of reasons found the need for a third gender that falls somewhere between the two biological sexes (Herdt, 1993). The Berdache in the Navajo, Hijras in India, and the Sworn Virgins in the Balkans are examples (Bem, 1993; Grémaux, 1993; Nanda, 1993; Roscoe, 1993).

In child psychiatry, gender identity and its relationship to gender roles are the subject of some debate in the context of the diagnosis and treatment of gender identity disorder (GID) with some arguing for supporting behavioral or psychological treatments that promote the adoption of the gender role of the assigned sex (Zucker & Bradley, 1995), whereas others argue that these gender roles are social constructs that should not be imposed upon a developing child who appears to be severely uncomfortable in taking on the role assigned (Bartlett, Vasey, & Bukowski, 2000). Gender role is not to be confused with gender identity. Gender identity refers to the fundamental match of psychological *identity* with biological sex, whereas gender roles are socially condoned roles composed of *behaviors* associated with a particular sex. It is noteworthy, perhaps, that anxiety about gender identity and gender roles in Western society is much greater in males, at least in childhood, and that the majority of children diagnosed with gender identity disorder are males (Zucker & Bradley). This does not suggest that girls escape from the dilemmas of gender confines, but their dilemmas are often related to problems that arise from conflicting versions of female gender roles that they must navigate rather than problems with gender identity *per se*. Thus, in terms of adopting gender roles congruent with biological sex, girls are often asked to be both assertive and demure, successful but modest, independent but socially related (especially to other females), attractive but not preoccupied by appearance. In the last 50 years in the West, girls have struggled to find a way through these conflicting expectations. Fiction directed at young girls and teenagers, it might be suggested, could provide models for gender role development and in this way provide examples of how to manage these conflicting expectations.

Reading fiction, Joe Noshpitz contends, is a domain that many, though not all, children enjoy. Fiction readers as a group are more often females (55% for women compared with 38% for men), especially by the adolescent years (National Endowment for the Arts, 2004). Thus, fictional accounts of female gender role models may be particularly relevant to young girls and women. The imaginative participation in the "as if" world of fiction that reading involves allows the reader to try on roles, to take imaginative risks, and to explore options that the real world does not always permit. Developmentally, the use of fiction to explore identity and social processes is particularly pertinent. Thus, child therapists have every reason to be interested in the types of fiction that patients might be reading as it may well indicate their preoccupations and concerns. As Noshpitz points out, the fictional analogue of the self may serve as a role model for the self and the internalized self-ideal. Therefore, it is of interest when fictional gender role models change or conflict as appears to be the case when he compares the different ways gender roles are taken up in the *Nancy Drew* series and *The Baby-sitters Club* (Ann M. Martin) series, both sets of popular books for girls.

Starting with the titles of the two series, differences emerge between these competing ideas about how to be a female. The focus in *Nancy Drew* is always Nancy Drew and what she is doing and accomplishing; hence, every title refers directly to her person. *The Baby-sitters Club* focuses on a group of young girls and the dilemmas they face together, as a *club* rather than as as single individuals and their achievements. As Noshpitz describes Nancy Drew, she is a kind of Athena figure—bold, rational, and in many ways only reluctantly female. Her father is her ideal, and no boy or girl can compete or displace him. Nancy's own phallic status is confirmed by her father's gift of a "blue sports car." At the same time, her attributes of fearlessness (in fact seeking out danger), analytic thinking, and emotional control appear to interfere with the development of deeper interpersonal relationships. In any event, her friendships and romantic relationships are superficial and are not the focus of the narrative. She is valiant and self-reliant as opposed to caring and cooperative. It is of more than casual interest that the *nom de plume* of the author Carolyn Keene was originally a "skirt" for the male author of the series, Edward Stratemeyer, the prolific creator of many children's books including *The Hardy Boys* and *Tom Swift*. After the success of the early *Nancy Drew* books and Stratemeyer's death, his daughter, Harriet Adams, wrote the bulk of the first series using outlines developed together with her father, illustrating in some respects the dream of uniting with a father figure that may have been the fictional character Nancy Drew's own unconscious aspiration.

In contrast, Noshpitz notes that the main purpose of *The Baby-sitters Club* is to provide fictional accounts of how young girls can work together to solve interpersonal problems that they face as developing adolescents. The focus of the books is on the relationships internal to the group rather than on the solutions to an external problem (e.g., a crime or mysteries), and the skills related to female gender roles being portrayed are relational, emotional, and cooperative. Noshpitz notes the similarities between the protagonists of this series and the four sisters in Louisa May Alcott's (2004) *Little Women* where the theme of female gender role is taken up in the context of variations (to a point) of gender presentation among the sisters and where family dynamics, support, and interpersonal struggles and triumphs are at the heart of the narrative. In contrast to Nancy Drew, the girls must cope with an absent father but have the presence of a supportive mother. In *The Baby-sitters Club*, parental figures are largely in the background, but support from adult female role models is occasionally available.

In discussing *Nancy Drew* and *The Baby-sitter's Club* book series, Noshpitz describes two contrasting fictional accounts of female gender roles. Nancy Drew is described as the ego ideal of self-sufficient, high-achieving, and daring women exemplifying the aspirations of an upwardly mobile, mostly White, competitive culture. In contrast, the main characters in *The Baby-sitters Club* focus on friendship, resolution of interpersonal conflicts, cooperative problem solving, and supporting one another. The *Nancy Drew* series originated in the early and mid twentieth-century United States, whereas *The Baby-sitters Club* was conceived in the latter part of that century. When the *Nancy Drew* books were mainly written, women had moved from a primarily domestic identity in the early part of the last century to taking up roles in the previously male-dominated colleges, professions, and work places, and these books illustrate this type of female. What is perhaps surprising is *The Baby-sitters Club* series' return to what some might claim are more traditional female gender roles of relatedness and social concern after the achievements of women in the decades just before these were conceived.

Noshpitz notes that these two fictional accounts may meet different needs of different generations of young female readers. He puts forth the notion that perhaps girls reared in environments where women were relegated primarily to domestic roles took delight in the fantasy of power and external achievement denied to their mothers. In contrast, young girls reared by working mothers with busy careers might long for more interpersonal caring from a small group of friends. While this point is not unreasonable, there may be other considerations. It is noteworthy that the appeal of *Little Women* continued to be great throughout this period, and this is the case despite the predominance of the women portrayed as largely confined domestic creatures. In this sense, the appeal of *Nancy Drew* is more the anomaly. Why, rather out of the blue in the middle of the twentieth century, did this alternative model of femininity gain popularity? The economic demands of World War II and the subsequent consumption culture may have contributed to the idealization of women taking up previously typical male gender roles. It is unclear if *The Baby-sitters Club* is "reactionary" and therefore represents a kind of conservative backlash to women taking up gender roles than had been predominantly male in the past or, instead, if the model of femininity it portrays is in some sense also true to important elements of a woman's gender role. The resourcefulness of the four rather troubled 12-year-olds portrayed in *The Baby-sitters Club* in managing the interpersonal and developmental challenges and difficulties their lives present do not suggest that these girls should be viewed in any way as inferior to the Olympian Nancy Drew. Instead, they represent a reasonable set of gender-role behaviors that can be used for identification by young female readers, quite possibly an essential skill set that women may need to have to manage the complexity of lives that are driven both for achievement and nurturing relationships.

As prescient at these observations are about the changing ways that adolescent girls are depicted in fiction, one wishes that Noshpitz had gone a bit further in this chapter. Where does this contrast in role models, ideals, and interpersonal strategies leave the developing girl? The nostalgia of being able to exist in a purely interpersonal world may hold appeal for some, but the economic and practical demands will not allow this retreat for most young women. Instead, most of them must aspire, to some degree, to the world of work (e.g., becoming Nancy Drew) while also being required to take up key interpersonal relationships and nurturing roles of friend, partner, and mother. Many professional young women run headlong into this contrast and struggle to find an adequate compromise. How these two fictional worlds can come together for a girl of the 21st century is unfortunately not discussed by

Noshpitz. To be fair, there remains no clear resolution of the conflicts that are inherent in the demands of each of the gender roles. Young women are often left to manage both and struggle with the lack of a satisfactory resolution. Much is made of the collaborative and cooperative culture in which children are being raised that may mitigate these processes to a certain extent, but if one turns to look at male gender roles depicted in pictures, film, and fiction, the ideal for male gender roles remains largely traditional. As long as this is the case, it may be difficult for women to find a solution to the problems they face in terms of conflicting expectations about female gender roles. It seems unlikely that a third gender will be the outcome of this conflict, but perhaps a third gender role might be.

References

Alcott, L. M. (2004). *Little women*. London: Penguin.

Bartlett, W. H., Vasey, P. L., & Bukowski, W. A. (2000). Is gender identity disorder a childhood mental disorder? *Sex Roles: A Journal of Research, 43*, 753–85.

Bem, S. L. (1993). *The lenses of gender: Transforming the debate on sexual inequality*. New Haven, CT: Yale University Press.

Grémaux, G. (1993). Woman becomes man in the Balkans. In G. Herdt (Ed.), *Third sex third gender: Beyond sexual dimorphism in culture and history* (pp. 241–284). New York: Zone Books.

Herdt, G. (Ed.). (1993). *Third sex third gender: Beyond sexual dimorphism in culture and history*. New York: Zone Books.

Nanda, S. (1993). Hijras: An alternative sex and gender role in India. In G. Herdt (Ed.), *Third sex third gender: Beyond sexual dimorphism in culture and history* (pp. 373–418). New York: Zone Books.

National Endowment for the Arts. (2004, June). *Reading at risk: A survey of literary reading in America* (Research Division Report No. 46). Washington, DC: Author.

Ringrose, K. M. (1993). Living in the shadows: Eunuchs and gender in Byzantium. In G. Herdt (Ed.), *Third sex third gender: Beyond sexual dimorphism in culture and history* (pp. 85–110). New York: Zone Books.

Roscoe, W. (1996). How to become a Berdache: Toward a unified analysis of gender diversity. In G. Herdt (Ed.), *Third sex third gender: Beyond sexual dimorphism in culture and history* (pp. 329–372). New York: Zone Books.

Zucker, K. J., & Bradley, S. J. (1995). *Gender Identity Disorder and psychosexual problems in children and adolescents*. New York: Guilford Press.

NANCY DREW AND THE BABY-SITTERS CLUB

Joseph D. Noshpitz

One of the greatest joys that life affords certain children is the reading of books. For such youngsters, the availability of their preferred literary items is a source of intense and avid interest, and the youngsters display every evidence of excitement and pleasurable arousal when they can get their hands on these target items. The market has responded to this by producing a veritable sea of literature, and the result has been that some works have floated to the top as prominent and successful titles, whereas others have sunk into an effaced oblivion to be recalled only by the more diligent literary historians. Our business today is to consider two of the most successful such literary creations ever to be offered to children. These two works are in fact in each instance a series of books, each with its own distinct character and each with its own unique message. What is of special interest to us is that the two series came into being over 50 years apart. The central theme of this study then is to compare the style, content, and message of the earlier series with that of the very different recent set. In particular, we will consider the impact of each of these series on the development of their intended population: the grade-school–aged girl.

The earlier of the works selected for this study is the *Nancy Drew* series. This first appeared in 1930 and continued to be issued over the succeeding years; indeed, it is still going strong, with new volumes emerging regularly. The more recent is *The Baby-sitters Club* series, which is currently the most popular such work being read by this cohort (as of the writing of this essay). Although each of these series has a history, the gist of this study is to try to discern axes of observation that would allow for a comparison of the values implicit in each of these series and to consider the way the two approaches sought to capture the interest of and to have some effect on the children in their day.

For several generations Nancy Drew continued to be the beloved and treasured companion of a host of young girls growing up in America. As the female protagonist in a literally endless sequence of novels, Nancy Drew was at once model, guide, inspiration, and object of identification for literally millions of grade-school readers. Indeed, by the middle of the century, it was rare to meet a literate American woman who had not read these books and who did not have fond memories of this sector of her growing-up years. From time to time major studies about Nancy Drew appeared in the media, and she has inspired at least one published poem. Bumiller (1980) described it in this way:

> Millions and millions of little girls would rip frantically through to
> the next page, maneuvering the flashlight under the bedcovers. It was

Nancy Drew ... sleuthing her way through the bloodcurdling screams of mystery No. 12. It was heaven.

In a similar vein, Eileen G. Zuckerman (1986, p. 74) recalls:

At age 11, I was hopelessly addicted to Nancy Drew. At night I reveled in the mysterious and romantic adventures of Nancy and her boyfriend, Ned Nickerson, by flashlight, with the covers pulled tent-like over my head. That is, until my mother caught me and warned that I'd need glasses soon if kept that up. (She was right.)

Let us now turn to the books themselves. Nancy Drew is first introduced in Volume 1 of the series, titled *The Secret of the Old Clock* (Keene, 1930a). She is described as a blond, teenage girl who lives in a small exurban town. She is the only daughter of a respected (in later books, famous), wealthy, successful, influential, upper-class lawyer who dotes on her, and (as the story opens) who has just given her a brand-new blue roadster as an eighteenth birthday gift. Her mother died when she was 3 years old, her father never remarried, and she was raised by a solicitous housekeeper. At the time we meet her, she is neither in school nor employed. Although the text offers no clear sense of her educational background, presumably she is out of high school. Evidently she has no plans for college and elects to spend her time solving mysteries. She is a self-declared sleuth who is turned to by various people in her environment for help with their several problems.

If we pause at this point to take stock of what all this might mean to her readers, several elements emerge. To begin with, any oedipal issues that might otherwise have dogged Nancy's growing up are given definitive resolution by the death of her mother in Nancy's early childhood. In effect, she won the oedipal struggle; her mother left the scene, and Nancy has subsequently had her father all to herself—what Berke (1979) calls the "ultimate Oedipal fantasy" (p. 195) of the adolescent girl. To be sure, her household does not lack a female presence: there is a housekeeper, Hannah Gruen, who is essentially a servant, clearly not a member of the family, and in no sense a rival for father's affections. Hannah is warm, caring, and devoted, but in the way that old family retainers tend to be—supportive but peripheral. Only Nancy has the inner track with father. She sometimes assists him with his cases, and he often shares in her adventures. This fantasy of having father all to oneself is one of the powerful images of female childhood; according to Berke, "Nancy Drew epitomizes almost orgiastically, the enactment of this fantasy" (p. 197).

Moreover, Nancy has little involvement with boys or dates. She is social and has many friends; sometimes she is teased a little about her beau, Ned Nickerson, but, when the chips are down, she is not a very romantic young person. Indeed, Volume 4 of the series, *The Mystery at Lilac Inn* (Keene,

1930d), closes with a particularly relevant exchange. Two of her girlfriends are about to be married and are discussing their forthcoming weddings. They suddenly become aware that Nancy is not involved in all this, and one of them says, "Goodness, Nancy, you must be tired of hearing us talk about steady partners when—" Nancy interrupts and, laughing gaily, she says, "Not at all. For the present, my steady partner is going to be mystery." With this, Volume 4 comes to a close, but the notion of Nancy affianced, as it were, to her career would allow the reader to entertain a deeper meaning, namely, Nancy has no real need for a boyfriend, because she can and, indeed, prefers to retain her link to father and to work in parallel with him. As Zacharias (1976) expresses it, "Nancy's relationship with her father is not incestuous by act, but it does have sexual implications. Here is a man no beau could hope to live up to, and Nancy knows it" (p. 1029).

In any case, not only does the structure of the story allow for oedipal triumph, but it also offers resolution of another possible source of childhood stress. The acquisition of her own blue roadster at the start of her adventures offers a quality of independence, youthful fulfillment, ready achievement, and mastery of separation as additional elements in the heroine's life. Again, at the unconscious level, the reader would see Nancy as having overcome any residual phallic issues. Her father has given her this long powerful, attractive extension of herself with which to make her way in the world. Let others envy her; she needs envy no one.

To be sure, there is another component to the story. Nancy uses the car extensively in the course of pursuing her quarry, and the car is forever going into ditches or suffering some mishap or other, so much so indeed, that by Volume 11 her father has to get her a new and more powerful replacement. Even for Nancy Drew, once you have it, you have to worry about it.

With oedipal and phallic issues thus neatly taken care of, what of the other levels of psychosexual development? Orally, Nancy likes to eat, and the text of the various volumes offers copious details concerning the food, cooking styles, and food combinations she encounters and enjoys; Zacharias (1976) observes that Nancy and her chums remain hungry through 49 stories—and that eventually this becomes incarnate in the form of *The Nancy Drew Cookbook: Clues to Good Cooking* by Carolyn Keene. On the other hand, in the course of these stories, no one nurses a baby, no one vomits, and hardly anyone even drinks too much. Orality is permitted only if food is involved and if proper table manners are observed.

If one moves beyond the oral level, eliminative, menstrual, and sexual functions simply are not mentioned. The word *bathroom* never appears in the text unless one goes to a powder room to change clothes or sees something important through a bathroom window. No diaper ever needs to be changed, no child wets the bed, and no pelvic bodily function is ever referred to by anyone. About the only expression of anal stage derivatives takes the form of people, including Nancy, getting muddy, dirty, grimy, messy, and the like. Showers and other ablutions are then permitted, and all is rapidly set right. As Bumiller (1980) commented upon looking back at 50 years of Nancy Drew: "squeaky clean and still 18."

Nancy gives her all for her mysteries. She is regularly presented with at least two mysteries per volume. Inevitably, these turn out to be derivatives of a single unifying plot, some dastardly scheme for malfeasance that Nancy presently unravels and thwarts. Not enough attention has been paid in the developmental literature to the important role of mysteries during the latency years. All grade-school-aged children are perpetually concerned with a host of mysteries. One of the major issues is, of course, the question of how much magic there is in the world. Grade-school youngsters have only recently abandoned the developmental stages where magic was their primary means of solving problems. Such children have now made the transition from preoperational thinking to the stage of concrete operations. That has entailed the renunciation of one way of thinking (where the rules of magic, dream, and wish determine the nature of reality) to embark on a very different cognitive style (where classification, conservation, the ordering of series, and the rules of logic determine what is real and what is not). In the nature of things, initially the transition is likely to be incomplete. Albeit now ever more oriented to the practical and the empiric, the young readers of these books are still vulnerable to the mysterious and at once fascinated and terrified by the eerie and the otherworldly. They like to tell ghost stories around the campfire, to talk about the spooky doings at the haunted house down the street, and to watch horror films. Mysteries flourish in the fertile soil of their imagination, and the solver of mysteries will be held in high esteem.

Nancy is regularly presented with schemes that depend on the belief in ghosts and spirits to scare people off and to cloak the evil intentions of the villains. Eerie lights in the dark, phantom horsemen, ghostly boats on a lake, strange sounds in the night, all the trappings of the sepulchral, the macabre, and the otherworldly are set forth, and various adults turn away and flee in panic. But Nancy fears none of them. Instead, she plunges in, figures out how the effects were achieved, and unravels the nefarious doings behind them.

But those are only some of the mysteries that beset the child. There are so many other things these youngsters wonder about, so many unknowns, so many complexities that are left unexplained. These mysteries include how the world about them works, how their own bodies work, some of the meanings of parental interactions, an adequate understanding of pregnancy and reproduction, the true nature of sex (what do the parents actually *do* in their bedroom behind closed doors? In some sense the youngsters know, yet it is still a mystery), a grasp of why people treat them the way they do, a conception of illness (what do cancers actually *do* to a person?), a sense of why people act the way they do, and why they sometimes do or say things they did not mean. In short, there are a host of matters that are in them, that surround them, and that they learn about in piecemeal, incomplete, or inchoate form. What a relief to encounter mysteries that are outside their heads, mysteries that are untinged by guilt or jealousy, that are solvable, and that in fact do get solved. Zacharias (1976) regards this as reassuring the 8- to 10-year-old reader "that there is order in chaos, that the seemingly random events of her life and the confusion she perceives in the world do have a pattern" (p. 1027). If only the child could be like the sleuth in the story who is so superbly self-confident and so penetratingly insightful, who gets to the heart of all these complex events and makes sense of them at last. In sum, Nancy Drew offered her young readers an inviting image of how a girl can cope with and master all the mysterious difficulties with which life confronts her. It is worth noting that one kind of mystery Nancy Drew encounters repeatedly is the issue of something missing. Sometimes it is a missing person, but more typically it is a will, or a hidden treasure, or jewelry, or some other item that is vital to someone's well-being and that is either concealed or in some way unattainable. Again and again it is Nancy's mission to find the whereabouts of the missing other or the missing treasure and to restore it to its rightful owner.

Whether the author's underlying theme is to find the lost object attachment of childhood, to undo castration by recovering that vital missing part, to find that ornament or that missing ingredient that would make one ultimately beautiful and desirable, or to do all of these must remain in itself a mystery. To be sure, this symbolic quest is entirely unconscious; nonetheless, it is likely that it contributes to the fascination that this group of works has had for the millions of girls who have read and enjoyed these books.

As noted already, for Nancy investigative mysteries have taken the place of the mysteries of dating, intimacy, and mature femininity. By clinging to the one set of mysteries, she can ward off the pressures of the others. Her response to her boyfriend is that of the latency child. She welcomes his attentions but avoids getting too close. She is a master at solving the problems of latency: she offers concrete responses to concrete stimuli and events (clues, traces left by villains), she knows the good guys from the bad, she can always think of a way out of difficulties, she is literally filled with technical knowledge (everything from horseback riding to medical diagnosis), she is great at distinguishing fantasy from reality, and she is constantly earning praise. She is action oriented, goes from one thrilling experience to another, repeatedly rescues those in trouble, regularly reunites people separated by misfortune, and systematically beats out men at their own game (the evildoers, the police, even her father).

When all is said and done, it is clear that Nancy Drew was designed to be an ideal. She looked good, she dressed well, she drove her own car, she was loved by father to the exclusion of everyone else, she had many friends, she was perpetually doing good for people she met, she was aristocratic in her tastes and was offended by rudeness or impoliteness, and she was bold, adventuresome to the point of fearlessness, and expert at just about everything. She offered ready opinions about arcane matters, and she was almost always right. People were forever turning to her and declaring their admiration for her keenness, perceptiveness, courage, her knack for grasping the import of clues, her skill as a sleuth, and her grit and determination in pursuing the evildoers she regularly brought to book. She was everyone's dream of glory come true. In Berke's (1979) words: "She is pure magic, guaranteed to satisfy all fantasies because the recipe for the series was obviously formulated with this precise end in view: to project a marvelous dream world where good always triumphs and dreams always come true" (p. 200). Her interactions with adults are especially striking. She is always respectful toward the elderly, concerned about the welfare of those with special needs or difficulties, and ready to offer comfort and encouragement to those in distress. Typically these are genteel individuals fallen upon hard times or well-to-do but elderly people who are being bilked or threatened by villains. Often there is a reversal of roles, with the involved adults turning to Nancy to find a way out of their challenging or threatening situations. Not infrequently Nancy rescues some adult being kept drugged or imprisoned by an evildoer; indeed, in one of the early books (Volume 2 of the series), she rescues her father in this way. In one version or another, this theme of the youth as the savior of adults recurs throughout.

There is another aspect of this heroine that bears mention. Nancy is deeply embedded in her culture, an archetypical White Anglo-Saxon Protestant (WASP). Although it sounds strange today, a sinister element in several of the early books is that the malefactor drove a foreign car. Indeed, so profoundly rooted are these themes that in Volume 2 of the series, *The Hidden Staircase* (Keene, 1930b), a curious and apparently irrelevant episode is introduced. In a search for clues, Nancy and some of her girlfriends explore an attic where they find trunks filled with the colonial garments and wigs that had belonged to the family forebears. As a form of entertainment, the young women proceed to dress up in these garments to engage in a proper minuet. (In the same story, the bad guy, evidently a Jew, is depicted as coming from Europe and trying, among other things, to buy, shove, and muscle his way into the American way of life. To that end, he threatens and coerces a fragile old lady into selling him her colonial dwelling, and this becomes one of the many wrongs which Nancy sets out to right.) In many ways Edward Stratemeyer, the originator of Nancy Drew, was representative of his times. The values of the epoch (values that permeated many series books) were decidedly xenophobic and WASPophile (MacDonald, 1974). As Zacharias (1976) notes, "...Allusions to that nebulous body of myths known as the American Dream occur throughout Nancy Drew" (p. 1030). So pronounced were these themes, that in 1973 James P. Jones titled his article about the series: "Nancy Drew, WASP Super Girl of the 1930s." Thus, Nancy Drew is offered to the young girl reader not only as a personal ideal and a source of vicarious mastery experiences but as a model of cultural identification as well.

A final word about gender identity: Nancy is neither very feminine nor very masculine; she occupies a unique middle ground of her own. Somewhere along the line in the early books, she become part of a group and is flanked by her two close girlfriends, Bess and George. Among other missions, the three girls are assembled to provide a rather self-conscious range of the possibilities of femininity. Lean George, with her short hair, boy's name, and active style is a declared tomboy; plump Bess is a somewhat precious, frightened, but romantic example of almost ultrafemininity. Bess will go along on adventures despite her anxiety because she is even more afraid of being left out. George, of course, is always drawn to the possibility of action. Nancy is designedly a member of both camps. She pays a good deal of attention to clothes and appearance, and when she dances the minuet she takes the girl's part; it is one of her girlfriends who puts on the boy's garments and plays that role. Yet Nancy is quick to change a tire without assistance, she plunges unhesitatingly into dark caves or unlit passageways in the pursuit of clues or villains, and, aside from blushing when the matter of her boyfriend comes up, she shows minimal interest in and response to romantic overtures of any kind. Thus, the spectrum of traits she offers allows for ready identification by the large majority of her readers and, indeed, by a wide variety of girls. In particular, she offered a ready role model for the grade-school girl who was not yet very much drawn to boys as objects of romantic possibility and who perceived her male peers either as pests who teased her and who interfered with the activities she pursued with her girlfriends, as possible competitors to outdo at their own games, or as possible beaux to be whispered about to girlfriends sworn to secrecy but never to be addressed directly.

As noted, the first 20 volumes of the series came out during the 1930s and 1940s. By the 1980s, Nancy Drew had been around for 50 years, and new series had begun to emerge that spoke to very different aspects of human adjustment. In 1992, when this is being written, several such series are available. The current favorite of (or at least the current bestseller to) grade-school girls is *The Baby-sitters Club*. Hence, for purposes of comparison, the first 20 books of that cluster will be reviewed in a fashion parallel to that of *Nancy Drew*. The first volume in the series, *Kristy's Great Idea*, was published in 1986. In brief, it tells the story of 12-year-old Kristy who is something of a tomboy, lives in a small Connecticut town not too close to New York City, has a number of close girlfriends, and does a lot of babysitting. Since her friends are often called on to babysit as well, Kristy conceives of a plan to organize a Baby-sitters Club. She arranges for four girls who know one another to come together, have set meeting times, and offer a service to their community. During such a club meeting anyone can call in for a babysitter, and, since there are four of them, one of the girls is sure to have time and be able to take the job. The story then follows the vicissitudes of the interrelationships of the four girls with one another, of their interactions with their own parents, of the issues they confront in the course of their babysitting efforts, of the meaning of the club to other youngsters in their community, and after a while, of the interactions among the adults in the girls' families.

The nature of these accounts thus allows for a good deal of exploration of developmental themes, of interpersonal themes, of group dynamics, of family dynamics, and of certain cross-cultural issues. More than all of these, however, it dwells on some of the complexities of the process of babysitting. The developmental issues take many forms. Thus, although all the girls are the same age (12 years old), at the outset two of them are interested in boys and the other two are not. Inevitably, this affects not only the way they dress and what they think about but also the group dynamics of their meetings and whose side they take when faced with difficult or painful issues. They are designedly different in personality in a way strongly reminiscent of the spread of character types portrayed in Louisa May Alcott's *Little Women* (1868). Albeit written 100 or more years earlier, *Little Women* too is a study of four girls—sisters in that case—during an important developmental moment in their lives. One of them, Jo, is the archetypical tomboy, who, since her portrayal in that novel, has served as the defining model for that word in American literature and folklore. The remaining sisters represent other varieties of femininity, and they are more or less matched by parallel figures in *The Baby-sitters Club*. The depictions of family structure, however, are another matter. In *Little Women*, the mother and father have raised these girls together, but, at the time of the story, the father is off serving in the Union Army during the Civil War. The family structure is thus mother as primary authority and model, with the occasional letters from the father serving as ideal and inspiration. For the babysitters things are very different; indeed, each youngster has a unique family constellation. Thus, Kristy lives with a divorced mother and has minimal contact with her father. One of the issues in the story of Volume 1 is mother's decision to marry again and Kristy's reaction to this news. Another of the girls lost her mother in early childhood and is being raised as an only child by a strict, overprotective, and infantilizing father; this youngster, Mary Anne, is accordingly rather shy, backward, and given to ready tearfulness. A third girl, Claudia, comes from Japanese lineage, and has to cope with an older sister who is a genius—and who is forever correcting her. But Claudia is blessed with a very understanding and empathic grandmother who befriends all the girls. The fourth girl, Stacey, is diabetic; when we meet her, she and her family have fled New York because of her condition and are trying to keep this a secret from her new friends and from the town. One of the issues in the story then becomes how her fear of revealing the nature of her illness affects her behavior and what impact this has on the members of the club.

As a result, rather a rich array of developmental and familial issues is available, and these issues emerge as the various plots and subplots of the stories. It is evident that these stories are radically different in style and message from the *Nancy Drew* books. The babysitters are much closer in age to the intended reader than is Nancy Drew. They are also much less perfect in their performances. They get angry, they get jealous, they get petty; at times they refuse to speak to one another. They quarrel and say mean things to each other, they compete with one another for who will be whose best friend, they eat quantities of junk food—in short, they are prone to many of the vulnerabilities of feeling and interaction their readers will have experienced, and, to put it mildly, display little of Nancy Drew's continuously sterling performance. Hence, the element of idealization, although by no means absent, is far less of a factor.

On the other hand, they offer something the *Nancy Drew* books rarely touch on, namely, a recurrent emphasis on the theme of reconciliation. People move apart and then find a way to come together again. Relationships are sundered—and then mended; what has been shattered is once again made whole; the anger, jealousy, and spitefulness are eventually overcome.

This is a powerful message, and it winds its way within and throughout the series as a kind of leitmotif. It is an ever imminent theme, sometimes emerging in the middle of the story but more often serving as the final triumphant closing of the tale. All tensions are resolved by people coming to understand one another, to accept one another, to admit that they made mistakes, and to apologize. This quality of reconciliation grows during the first several volumes and reaches an initial climax in Volume 4, *Mary Anne Saves the Day* (Martin, 1987a). At the outset, all the babysitters have a battle royal and carry through a series of moves and countermoves within the context of the club as they strive for one-upmanship with one another. One of them, Mary Anne, is so hard pressed by the quarreling, that she turns away from her fellow club members and recruits a new girl who has just arrived in town to be her friend. Ultimately, after many permutations and combinations, these tensions too get resolved, and the new girl is accepted into the club.

In addition to this primary theme, occasionally a different set of issues appears. In particular, from time to time, the child as parent to the adult comes into view as a new and critical message. This special dimension of the story takes its most evident form when Mary Anne finds that a mother is essentially turning over the care of her children as well as the regulation of her household to the 12-year-old babysitter. At the close of the story, Mary Anne confronts this woman and says in effect that she can no longer babysit for her. It is the mother who should be raising these children, not the babysitter. Suitably chastened, the mother promises to do better. Another theme that creeps in and becomes ever more important is the interest these youngsters develop in boys and the vicissitudes of their initial attempts at meeting or talking to the boys to whom they are drawn. Thus, such powerful motifs as the yearning for reconciliation, the reversal of roles with the parent, and the interest in relationships with boys are all woven into these books and offer particularly attractive fare for the young reader. The message here is much less overt than the straightforward offer of an ideal for identification and modeling that Nancy Drew is designed to convey. In the world of the babysitters, ideal figures are rare. At one point or another, most of the principal characters will blunder, be shortsighted, get petulant, and make mistakes. What one can strive for, then, is not perfection, so much as the encounter with and the overcoming of imperfection. Thus, instead of an ideal figure, one is offered the hope of personal and group remediation.

If we consider the historical context within which these works were produced, it is evident that our culture has come a long way in 50 years. As exemplified by Nancy Drew, the earlier notion was that you rear children by holding up before them a model of upright behavior, self-control, independence, self-reliance, enterprise, and courage—and they will then take these traits into themselves and grow up as they should. In some ways, Nancy Drew is a kind of palatable sermon: correct behavior is contrasted with evil action, goodness opposes badness, the whole is coated with an exciting mystery, and the message can then be taken in repeated doses. It goes down easily; indeed, the element of parable is hardly noticed.

Albeit far more realistically drawn than Nancy Drew, the babysitters still have about them a goodly sprinkling of the ideal. Thus, despite the occasional falling out, they can eventually reconcile their differences. Would that things worked out as well in all human relationships. But on the way to achieving their agreements, they fall woefully short of the alabaster figure that Nancy Drew presents. They use the girls' room, they care for children who have toilet accidents or who need diapers changed. They wonder why so-and-so is wearing a bra, and they are, in short, far closer to the everyday realities that their readers live with than was their predecessor. In effect, the current picture of child rearing (as reflected in this kind of pop-culture material) involves not so much the offering of an ideal as it does the empathic reflection of the inner world of the child. Along with that, particular attention is given to a number of sources of pain and tension in youngsters' lives, be they health related, familial, or interpersonal. But it is not only an accurate reflection that this series offers. The major emphasis in the early books falls on techniques for conflict resolution. Again and again the storyline focuses on the themes of how to make up and become friends again after a quarrel, how to patch up differences, how to leap the hurdles of anger, jealousy, and wounded feelings to reestablish frayed relationships.

There is thus a conscious didactic message tucked away in these unfolding stories. Occasionally the text goes further, and the characters offer one another even the concealed interpretations of motives and unverbalized impulses that determine their behaviors. As a result, the sometimes arch little parables become pointed directly at mental health insights. But for the most part, the tales are sufficiently well told that such episodic stepping out of character is not really intrusive and certainly does not disturb the flow of the story.

Among the issues touched on by these books is the question of violence and physical harm. In the earlier books, Nancy Drew is certainly not violent. On the other hand, the confrontation with danger, the threat of violence, and the near miss are often present. Indeed, in 7 of the first 10 books, during the playing out of the story, Nancy is herself rendered unconscious. She is variously chloroformed, has a ceiling fall on her head, is struck from behind, or is otherwise overcome. Her friends sustain snakebites, twisted ankles, and a variety of similar nonlethal and noncrippling assaults. But everyone bounces back with astonishing celerity and is fit for action again within hours. In contrast to this, the babysitters are decidedly nonviolent people, and their adventures are not likely to involve physical action. Anxiety is there aplenty—the threat of the phantom phone call, the threat of strange sounds in the house, the threat of the eerie old lady next door who conveys a quality of being a witch, all sorts of threats and spooky moments—but with happy endings for the most part and the achievement of a measure of mastery. As angry as the babysitters may become with one another, and they have some pretty intense interactions, they never come to blows, and for the most part no one gets physically hurt. Despite Nancy's sterling qualities, she is warned, threatened, or advised to desist, she is forever teetering on the brink of failure, she is repeatedly captured, or chloroformed, or knocked unconscious by a blow to the head; and all in all one never knows where the next crisis is coming from, or, for that matter, where the present clues are leading. It is the encounter with danger, obscurity, and uncertainty, and the mastery of all these vague, inchoate details that some of the pleasure of the story arises.

For the grade-school girl who is very much interested in keeping her nascent, emerging erotic interests at bay, the involvement in action as a diversion is a logical and constructive tactic. She can keep from thinking about the dubious or the embarrassing because, after all, there are a host of activities and skills to master, and she can lose herself in these. To be sure, from time to time the covert inner promptings are not always easily denied, and direct expression of these concealed impulses may well break through. But that is likely to be the exception rather than the rule, or a solitary activity such as masturbation rather than something for all the world to see.

For the most part, things are contained, albeit not without some stress. Then along comes Nancy with her spread of girlfriends (any girl can do it) to demonstrate that there are other exciting possibilities, alternative ways of achieving pleasure, different and allowable kinds of risk-taking. A girl can share interests with her father in ways that the whole world can see, she can substitute the tending of inner fires by attending to outer confla-grations—they provide interest and excitement enough. In brief, Nancy is a compulsive risk-taker who sets the solving of mysteries far above her own social, sexual interests, and her concern with personal safety— and as such she is an object of fascinated adoration by her admiring readers.

The babysitters are not much given to thrills. If the thesis that we are advancing is valid, then the *Nancy Drew* books achieve much of their appeal through addressing the reader's need for diversion from the sensuous and the forbidden by offering acceptable possibilities for thrills and excite-ment in the external world. In brief, Nancy Drew offers at once defense and sublimation, a displacement from internal to external excitement. But the babysitters demonstrate that there are other dimensions of personality that can be addressed and, other means of defense that can be deployed.

The babysitters are essentially social creatures. They are concerned with the rearing of children, with the problems of families, with the stresses of peer-group interaction. They have little in their lives that is thrilling in the sense of encounter with the truly dangerous; no compulsive risk-takers here.

But they do have a major defensive component, and that is humor. Much of the appeal of these books must surely be the way the author employs the elements of comedy as a constant background murmur that accompanies the reader throughout. The humor arises from several sources. The first is the mapping of childish themes onto the adult perspective. When an adult sees a childish misspelling, there is something sadly humorous about it. The incongruity of immature interest—particularly when it is addressing the even more undeveloped concerns of younger children (as babysitters must)—when matched against a fully adult outlook is always funny.

A second source is the language of extremes. The child entering pre-puberty and newly exposed to the riches of language is likely to choose the most ardent and ultimate forms of expression to describe even the more banal elements of emotional life. Thus, if something is pleasing, it is described as awesome. If the cafeteria food is so-so, it is characterized as disgusting. Such a youngster is just discovering a wholly new set of affects and a new range of possibilities for their deployment. It is like being given a computer with a bunch of new programs to play with—for a while every-thing is in a whirl and the adult observer can see all this as transitional, time-bound, and hence funny.

There are many things children take very seriously that adults see in such different ways that the gravity and intensity of the children are at once tender and humorous. The humor lies in the recognition of verities that the children have not yet achieved but that they will presently attain. The adults make allowances, accept the gravity of it all, but there is charm here and whimsy—the adults know it will all pass. The children will see it differently later on.

Yet another source of humor lies in language usage itself. There is a stratum of expression that belongs to childhood. In the preliminary material of Volume 13, the author includes a dedication. The page reads:

> With Love to Peanut Butter
> From Jelly

This is certainly good for a smile. We know the affinity of American children for the peanut butter and jelly sandwich. The very mention of these foods takes us back immediately to the time frame and experiential context of early years. Moreover, the association is likely to be a positive one; after all, it involves the fun of eating sweet-flavored stuff.

But that is only the beginning. There are, in fact, many levels to such a quip. There is the level of orality—the sense that each person is perceived as food carries with it the implication of mutual devouring. There is also the hint of deliciousness; both individuals are presumably comparable to delectable foods beloved by children. A step away from orality brings us to the level of attachment, the analogy to adherence; these two individuals are as close as two spreads on a slice of bread. Moving up to yet a higher developmental level, the personification of these two foods—the implied animism, life in everything, and, more than that, human life, the investing of people with the names of these inspired foods—all of this reminds us of the developmental moment when we were indeed animistic, when there was nothing foreign about the idea that things could feel like people and had a life of their own.

Ultimately, however, and here is where the humor comes in, we know that none of this is true, none of this is real: people are not foods and no one will devour anyone, and no one is as close as two spreads on bread—it is all a game, a playful way of talking—and it is accordingly funny. Moreover, we also know that behind the joke there is something serious here, a way of describing people who evidently take some delight in their mutual relationship, who have some kind of game going, and who use whimsy both to conceal and to communicate the depth of their feelings.

The nature of the humor throughout these books often displays this composite character. Much use is made of the way children emote. When the girls get important news they may wail or shriek or scream. Everything that has to do with feelings is a little excessive, exaggerated, overdone. For the youngsters, the emotions are new; they have not yet been tuned and modulated, they gush out in expressive gouts that would be very uncomfortable if manifested by an adult and that are tolerable in youngsters only by converting the excess into the whimsical. It is this very excess that makes for the quality of the humorous; it is so characteristically childlike.

Then there are the issues to be faced. There are the mock tragedies of childhood and the real challenges that life throws at youngsters. A mock tragedy might be when a boy one of the girls feels is her beau has been seen taking another girl to the library to study. Her friend (and fellow babysitter) tells her about this, and both decide that the boy is a jerk. A real tragedy occurs when one of the girls has to leave the community because her father has been assigned to another city. The first has charm and whimsy; the second brings with it a sense of genuine sadness. The series is laced with both kinds of situations, but the prevailing note is the whimsical one, and the humor acts as the glue tat binds the themes together and binds the readers to the books. In a sense, a *Nancy Drew* novel assembles many fragments of a gestalt; they pour over the reader helter-skelter in rapid succession, and, they set up in the reader's mind a yearning to achieve closure, to complete the gestalt, to see it all come together in satisfying fashion. When all is said and done, however, the thrills are key. They are the nectar that keeps the reader enthralled.

But the lesson of these series goes even further. Indeed, there is something almost paradoxical about the primary nature of their context. Nancy Drew was created during the post-Victorian years of the 1930s. The women's movement did not exist, and, despite the brouhaha of the roaring '20s, a woman's place was still in the home. Then along came Nancy Drew, adventuresome, independent, risk-taking, a woman detective pursuing a male profession, stealing many a march on the police, facing down tough criminal opponents, not a bit interested in homemaking or child rearing yet maintaining her feminine stance throughout. For the little girls reading her adventures, she was definitely a new kind of woman, with high status, lots of freedom, and no reservations about intruding herself where she was not wanted (by the bad guys) in the service of justice and the solving of mysteries.

In contrast to this, 50 years later in the 1980s and 1990s, well after the women's movement had come into being, with most American women working outside the home, the preeminent bestseller to this grade-school age population is *The Baby-sitters Club*. And one of the most notable aspects of the young heroines who provide the action for these stories is the fact that they are indeed babysitters. Much of the drama, the dialogue, the tensions, and the humor of these books arises out of the events connected with child care. There are frightened and anxious children, overimaginative children, spoiled and overgratified children, snobby demanding children, and a host of associated problems to be dealt with. There are also emergencies, crises, tough management problems, minor management problems, pet problems, toilet accidents, and assorted similar challenges to the tact, ingenuity, and creativity of the protagonists. For example, in Volume 6, a wedding is scheduled that will bring a host of friends and relations in town for a week. The guests bring their families along, and the club is called upon to organize itself to care for the 14 visiting children over the course of these festivities. The heart of the story then is the tale of the extraordinary efforts and the valiant adaptations that become necessary to carry out such an undertaking successfully. This gives rise to plenty of action, but the character and the spirit of these events is as remote as it could be from the stalwart derring-do of Nancy Drew. The babysitters are homebodies, nest-building types, fiercely protective of the children for whom they care, and skilled at the management of the many contretemps inherent in child care. The question is, then, why are they so popular in the late twentieth century? This is the time when women are building careers, when they are sharing child care equally with their spouses (and sometimes leaving it primarily in the hands of the man), when women are putting child bearing off to the later portion of their fertile epoch.

At the least it would seem plausible to suggest that there is a certain reaction to the current cultural stance that is expressed by the children of each era. Those youngsters reared within the ambience of women as homebodies devoured *Nancy Drew* with the avid abandon we previously heard about. And their younger sisters today, reared as they are with the model of the ambitious, independent, self-sufficient woman of the late twentieth century, hark back in their choice of reading fare to the adventures of the babysitters. Thus, one basis for reading these series may be to supply something that is missing in children's lives.

References

Adams, H. (1977). Their success is no mystery. *TV Guide, 25*(26), 13–16.

Berke, J. (1979). "Mother, I can do it myself": The self-sufficient heroine in popular girl's fiction. *Women's Studies, 6,* 18–203.

Billman, C. (1986). *The secret of the Stratemeyer syndicate: Nancy Drew, the Hardy Boys, and the million-dollar fiction factory.* New York: Ungar Publishing.

Bumiller, E. (1980, April 17). Squeaky-clean and still 18: Nancy Drew, girl detective, marks half a century. *The Washington Post,* p. H1.

Deane, P. (1990). Violence in children's fiction series. *Journal of Popular Literature, 4*(2), 67–81.

De Witt, K. (1977, July 31). The case of the alter egos. *The Washington Post,* p. H7.

Felder, D. (1986). Nancy Drew: Then and now. *Publisher's Weekly, 229*(22), 30–34.

Fielder, L. A. (1974, June 9). Lord of the absolute everywhere. *New York Times Book Review,* p. 8.

Gates, D. (1984, March 26). Nancy Drew: The eternal teenager. *Newsweek, 103,* p. 12.

Greco, G. (1986). Nancy Drew's new look. *Americana, 14*(4), 56–58.

Jones, J. P. (1973). Nancy Drew: WASP super-girl of the 1930s. *Journal of Popular Culture, 6*(4), 707–717.

Keene, C. (1930a). *The secret of the old clock.* New York: Grosset & Dunlap.

Keene, C. (1930b). *The hidden staircase.* New York: Grosset & Dunlap.

Keene, C. (1930c). *The bungalow mystery.* New York: Grosset & Dunlap.

Keene, C. (1930d). *The mystery at Lilac Inn.* New York: Grosset & Dunlap.

Kensinger, F. R. (1987). As for heroines. In *Children of the series and how they grew, or a century of heroines and heroes: Romantic, comic, moral* (pp. 79–85). Bowling Green, OH: Bowling Green University Popular Press.

Kernan, M. (1972). Hypers! Nancy Drew is 42! *The Washington Post.*

Knox, C. (1980). Nancy Drew. *Poetry, 136*(3), 155.

Lachtman, H. (1982). Lachtman on mysteries: The fate of a preadolescent Nancy Drew fiend.

Lanes, S. (1972). *Down the rabbit hole: Adventures and misadventures in the realm of children's literature.* New York: Atheneum Books.

Lenz, M., & McCombs, G. (1988, April). American notes: The pleasure of reading books of yesteryear. *Wilson Library Bulletin, 63* 15–16.

MacDonald, J. F. (1974). "The foreigner" in juvenile series fiction. *Journal of Popular Culture, 8*(3), 534–548.

Mackey, M. (1990). Filling the gaps: *The Baby-sitters Club,* the series book, and the learning reader. *Language Arts, 67,* 484–489.

Martin, A. M. (1986a). *Kristy's great idea.* New York: Scholastic.

Martin, A. M. (1986b). *Claudia and the phantom phone calls* New York: Scholastic.

Martin, A. M. (1986c). *The truth about Stacey.* New York: Scholastic.

Martin, A. M. (1987a). *Mary Anne saves the day.* New York: Scholastic.

Martin, A. M. (1987b). *Dawn and the impossible three.* New York: Scholastic.

Martin, A. M. (1987c). *Kristy's big day.* New York: Scholastic.

McGrath, A. (1986, October). Eye on publishing: The older she gets, the younger she looks. *Wilson Library Bulletin, 61*(2), 32–33.

Moffitt, M. A. (1987, May). Understanding the appeal of the romance novel for the adolescent girl: A reader-response approach. Paper presented at the meeting of the International Communication Association, Montreal.

Monaghan, C. (1986, August 10). Girl detective at 56. *The Washington Post.*

Monaghan, C. (1987, July 19). The Bobbsy twins. *The Washington Post.*

Moran, B. B., & Steinfirst, S. (1985, March). Why Johnny (and Jane) read whodunits in series. *School Library Journal,* 113–117.

Murphy, C. (1991). Starting over: The same old stories. *The Atlantic, 267*(6), 18–22.

The Nancy Drew sleuth book. (1979). *School Library Journal, 25*(9), 81–82.

Nuhn, M. (1981, March). Nancy Drew: An ageless 50-year-old. *Hobbies, 86,* 104–105.

Radway, J. (1984). *Reading the romance.* Chapel Hill: University of North Carolina Press.

Rouse, J. (1971). In defense of trash. In A. Daegon & R. T. Laconte (Eds.), *Challenge and change in the teaching of English* (pp. 172–174). Boston: Allyn & Bacon.

Shaywitz, S. E., Shaywitz, B. A., Fletcher, J. M., & Escobar, M. D. (1990). Prevalence of reading disability in boys and girls. *Journal of the American Medical Association, 264,* 998–1002.

Sodenbergh, P. A. (1974). The Stratemeyer strain: Educators and the juvenile series book, 1900-1973. *Journal of Popular Culture, 7*(4), 864–872.

Stark, M. K. (1975). Bert and Nan and Flossie and Fred: The Bobbsey twins roll on. *Interracial Books for Children Bulletin, 6*(1), 1, 5.

Stevens, E. (1967, October 28). The two faces of Harriet Adams: The Bobbsey twins and Nancy Drew. *The Evening Star Weekender*.

Wartik, N. (1986). Nancy Drew: Yuppie detective. *Ms.*, *15*(3), 29.

Watson, B. (1991, June). Tom Swift, Nancy Drew and pals all had the same dad. *Smithsonian*, 50–61.

Zacharias, L. (1976). Nancy Drew, ballbuster. *Journal of Popular Culture*, *9*(4), 1027–1038.

Zuckerman, E. G. (1976, September). The great Hardy boys' whodunit: The strange tale of the Stratemeyer syndicate and...Look out! ...Groupies! *Rolling Stone*, 37–40.

Zuckerman, E. G. (1986). Nancy Drew vs. serious fiction. *Publisher's Weekly*.

Chapter 11

Gender development in latency girls

The tomboy phenomenon

INTRODUCTION (TO CHAPTER 11 AND CHAPTER 12)

Susan Coates and Adrienne Harris

Encountering the unpublished papers of Joseph Noshpitz, who conducted these studies in the early 1980s, we are struck that both this chapter and the next offer a rich description of the self-presentation of women self-identifying as tomboys. Joe Noshpitz was far ahead of his times in having been one of the first people to systematically study tomboys using a structured interview. His work was contemporaneous with the first published systematic studies of tomboys by Katherine Williams (Williams, Green, & Goodman, 1979). Those included in Noshpitz's study were adults aged 20 to 40 who simply said that they had gone through a tomboy phase growing up. Most were professionals or support staff, such as secretaries and administrators; that is, they were working women. The interviews bear the imprint of the 1980s rise of feminism, and the new awareness of the complexity of femininity.

Interestingly, there is an indication in Noshpitz's introduction of the interview that after an initial identification as tomboy a number of subjects declined to continue. So this material draws from women comfortable with the term *tomboy* and with gender variance—or comfortable enough. There are many accounts of uncertainty, many potentials for shame and social and personal anxiety, but these women can tell their story. One is left, of course, wondering and worrying about the women then and now who are silenced. Noshpitz does not focus on a clinical population, so girls with some considerable gender or body dysphoria are not in this sample. He reports some girls withdrawing after an initial screening, so it is possible that for some tomboys in this era (as currently) gender variance was a matter of anguish and turmoil (Coates, Friedman, & Wolfe, 1991).

Reading these papers, one admires the easy, measured, interested voice of Noshpitz, his clarity in thinking about developmental processes, and his capacity to hold complexity, noting both different patterns of tomboy presentation and different patterns of stability and of change. This work is, above all, to draw on the anthropologist Clifford Geertz's (1986) apt phrase, "thick description." Noshpitz gives us a wealth of detail: how these girls remember what they wore, how they felt, how their self-presentation conflicted and meshed with the important people in their relational world. He describes the sample as having well-developed self-preservative instincts. They were daring, bold, and competent: always looking for a challenge, and invested in exploring and mastery. They loved the outdoors and nature, climbing trees, riding horses, participating in competitive sports. Some also had female stereotypical interests; others did not.

We can hear in the tomboys' account of sports, and physical life, the great human quest for freedom, the pleasure in activity, aspects of femininity that appear in the writings of early psychoanalytic women (Horney, 1926) and later in feminist psychoanalysts' work (Benjamin, 1988; Chodorow, 1999; Dimen, 2003; Goldner, 1991; Harris, 2005).

Nosphitz recognized that temperament was likely to play a role in tomboys' development. He observed that tomboys differed from their peers in their gender role behavior but not in their gender identification. This observation is echoed in contemporary research (Coates & Wolfe, 1995). One way to understand the role of biology in the development of sex–gender temperament is to study groups of children known to have unusual variations in prenatal exposure to sex hormones. Meyer-Bahlburg has shown that prenatal androgenization of girls with congenital adrenal hyperplasia affects their gender-related behavior in a dose-related manner, but has a modest effect on gender identity (Meyer-Bahlburg, Dolezal, Baker, Ehrhardt, & New, 2006), and has a modest effect on sexual orientation (Meyer-Bahlburg, Dolezal, Baker, & New, 2008).

Noshpitz has some interesting observations on gender differences. He speaks of the wider variation in female behavior than in males over the course of development. He speaks, almost as an aside, of the greater vulnerability in boys and in masculinity. It has taken a long time for clinicians, and in particular for analysts, to develop an appreciation of the difficulties in self-regulation and of the consequences for males of the prohibitions or inhibitions of dependency (Corbett, 2009).

Noshpitz draws some interesting conclusions, many of which seem prescient and very contemporary. There is plenty of developmental variation. It is just this variation that Harris (2005) draws on in thinking about tomboy experiences as manifestations of emergent and nonlinear developmental patterns. Tomboy experiences are continuous for some and discontinuous for others. Patterns beloved at one age become uncertainly held in others, and old lost patterns can come roaring back in new contexts. It is wonderfully the case that there are no monolithic conclusions about tomboy life, only many varying pathways to becoming a tomboy. You must read the specific narratives to locate the phenomena in these women's particular lives.

References

Benjamin, J. (1988). *The bonds of love*. New York: Pantheon.

Chodorow, N. (1999). *The power of feeling: Personal meaning in psychoanalysis, gender and culture*. New Haven, CT: Yale University Press.

Coates, S. W., & Wolfe, S. M. (1995). Gender identity in boys: The interface of constitution and early experience. *Psychoanalytic Inquiry*, *15*, 6–38.

Coates, S. W., Friedman, R. C., & Wolfe, S. M. (1991). The etiology of boyhood gender identity disorder: A model for integrating temperament, development, and psychodynamics. *Psychoanalytic Dialogues*, *1*, 481–523.

Corbett, K. (2009). *Boyhoods*. New Haven, CT: Yale University Press.

Dimen, M. (2003). *Sexuality, intimacy, power*. Hillsdale, NJ: The Analytic Press.

Drummond, K. D., Bradley, S. J., Peterson-Badali, M., & Zucker, K. J. (2008). A follow-up study of girls with gender identity disorder. *Developmental Psychology*, *44*, 34–45.

Geertz, C. (1986). Making experiences, authoring selves. In V. Turner & E. Bruner (Eds.), *The anthropology of experience* (pp. 373–380). Champaign: University of Illinois Press.

Goldner, V. (1991). Towards a critical relational theory of gender. *Psychoanalytic Dialogues*, *1*, 249–272.

Harris, A. (2005). *Gender as soft assembly*. Hillsdale, NJ: The Analytic Press.

Horney, K. (1926). The flight from womanhood. In H. Kelman (Ed.), *Feminine psychology* (pp. 54–70). New York: Columbia University Press.

Meyer-Bahlburg, H. F. L., Dolezal, C., Baker, S. W., Ehrhardt, A. A., & New, M. I. (2006). Gender development in women with congenital adrenal hyperplasia as a function of disorder severity. *Archives of Sexual Behavior*, *35*, 667–684.

Meyer-Bahlburg, H. F. L., Dolezal, C., Baker, S. W., & New, M. I. (2008). Sexual orientation in women with classical and non-classical congenital adrenal hyperplasia as a function of degree of prenatal androgen excess. *Archives of Sexual Behavior*, *37*, 85–99.

Williams, K., Green, R., & Goodman, M. (1979). Patterns of sexual identity development: A preliminary report on the "tomboy." *Research in Community and Mental Health*, *1*, 103–123.

GENDER DEVELOPMENT IN LATENCY GIRLS

Joseph D. Noshpitz

The study of gender issues has traditionally been carried forward largely in the realm of the pathological. In-depth and demographic explorations with populations of homosexuals, psychological and psychoanalytic approaches to transsexuals, and research into men, women, and children with ambiguous genitalia have occupied the primary interest of the several investigators. One must hasten to add that the area has become politicized, so that, for example, homosexuality *per se* has been removed from the *Diagnostic and Statistical Manual of Disorders* of the American Psychiatric Association; whatever else it maybe, it is no longer automatically diagnosable as a pathological state. In any case, it was chiefly in the area of such conditions that the study of gender has been pursued.

In spring 1981, Dr. Lawrence Vitulano and I embarked on a study of the tomboy phenomenon as it occurred in the lives of normal individuals. We were initially interested in describing it more exactly. I had been lecturing about development for years and had frequently spoken of the limited range of gender possibilities open to latency-age boys contrasted to the much wider range of acceptable gender identities available to such girls. Boys of this age may be quiet, but they had better not display effeminate mannerisms, engage in feminine pursuits, wear female clothes, of even cultivate feminine friends during these grade-school years, on pain of being designated a sissy or regarded as freakish by their social surround. Girls, on the other hand, may vary between the most feminine prissy little miss and the most boyish, tough, competitive, daring, aggressive, dress-hating tomboy and by and large will find solid familial and social acceptance. Nor is this discrepancy altogether easy to explain. Part of the reason for the different social responses may of course lie in the outcome of the two conditions. The tomboy state is generally thought to reverse itself in the postpubertal years; as she grows, the former hoyden drops back into the general population of women and becomes indistinguishable from her nontomboy sisters. The sissy boy, on the other hand, tends to persist as such; he continues to be an effeminate young man and will likely be looked at askance by many people for years to come. To the extent that this is true, it perhaps helps make sense of the different quality of social regard and cultural valuation placed on cross-gender behavior in boys and girls. At best, however, it can account for only part of the story. Surely there are important and deeply rooted attitudes toward gender that go back for many years, that express themselves in terms of values, that have meaning for people on a gut level in terms of what is "natural" or "wholesome," "healthy" or "normal" contrasted to gender configurations that are experienced as deviant, unpleasant, dismaying, threatening, or even "disgusting." Ultimately, it all seems to suggest that the acquisition of a sense of gender is a process at which people have to work as they grow up and that they must then act to maintain. More than that, one might derive from this that a masculine orientation is a more fragile, a more vulnerable, and a more demanding posture than is a feminine gender position. Any challenge to boys' masculine stance then is likely to be greeted by a greater emotional reaction, a higher level of rejection, than is a corresponding diversion from the girls' feminine habits. Be that as it may, the truly dramatic shift did seem to be within girls' way of growing up and, in particular, in the tomboy's development. This then became the object of our inquiry.

The methodology we employed was the structured interview. In our view, to conduct a developmental study in anything like an adequate fashion, it was vital to obtain longitudinal data. To achieve ready access to such data, we decided to interview adults who had gone through a tomboy phase during their growing years. We hoped that, despite its retrospective character, much of the detail of grade-school age experience might be recalled and that adequate accounts might thus be forthcoming.

The next issue to be faced was: What questions to ask? Here the answer seemed straightforward enough: start with the conventional dimension of what is culturally current, what is it in fact that distinguishes the tomboy girl from her more conventionally feminine sister? This is no great mystery; one has but to look at some of the Norman Rockwell illustrations, for example, and there she is—dressed in boyish clothes, engaging in boyish sports, contending with a boy in a rivalrous way and, often enough, coming out the winner. So the questions must turn to preferred activities, on rivalry, on clothes preferences, and the like; the questionnaire was thus designed.

Next came the matter of finding subjects. Indeed, there was the difficult—and delicate—point of defining subjects. We decided to start with an easy and straightforward (albeit relatively coarse and noncritical) screening technique. We asked merely whether a woman had gone through a tomboy phase in the course of her growing up. If the answer was affirmative, that was good enough; she was a candidate for the study. We did not try to define the phase; we relied on the conventional and culturally shared sense of what this state involved. It was, after all, an initial effort. We hoped to collect data on about 20 subjects, and we would then be in a better position to winnow out a more precise definition, a more restricted area of the field on which to concentrate.

In the course of all this a small side project also emerged. It sort of appeared; it would be hard to say why or wherefore. The word *tomboy* as such came up for consideration. It is a rather odd word, in particular, an unusual word to apply to a girl. I began to study its origins, and then I got to wondering about whether it existed in foreign languages. Was it a translatable world, and, if so, what was the flavor that accompanied its use elsewhere? After all, in the American culture it's rather a positive, a slightly whimsical, at times even a slightly affectionate term. What form would it take in European languages? Would it appear at all? And if so, how would the word be used—warmly or perhaps in a more neutral fashion? Or would it find place as a chiding confrontation or even as a jeering disparagement? That effort was carried on side by side with the interview work.

As the interviews progressed it became clear that the implications of the early tomboy experience for later development were very considerable. Indeed, toward the end of the original questionnaire, one of the questions had been: Is there any way that tomboy elements have persisted in your life? After the first dozen subjects or so, this became the key question in the study. Gradually, as the ramifications of this early position began to emerge with greater clarity, the interviews began to take longer, and more and more time was spent on the postlatency adjustment of our subjects. It is the material from this mix of data that will here be presented.

Before getting into the case material, some reference must be made to the literature in the field. There is surprisingly little written about the tomboy phenomenon as such. Scarcely anyone has studied this part of the life cycle in depth and detail. Not that the terrain is altogether unexplored; there are, to be sure, some efforts. Thus, in surveying their study population of female homosexuals, Seghir and Robbins report that 60% of their lesbian subjects stated having been committed tomboys during their growing years. In contrast to this, in a population of nonhomosexual controls, only 16% reported themselves to have been tomboys.

Another study, this one a demographic survey, involved investigators standing in the middle of a shopping mall and asking women who went past to fill out a questionnaire. They report that in response to an inquiry similar to our own—when you were young, did you go through a tomboy stage?—some 51% of women answered yes. This seeming difference in prevalence is in fact a function of the screening test used; Saghir and Robins insisted that, to meet their criteria for tomboyishness, a woman must have had a primary preference for things masculine as well as a strong rejection of the feminine. Clearly if one omits the second of these two requirements, one samples quite a different population.

To the extent that the findings of the shopping mall study are valid, it would seem that at least half of all women asked stated that they did indeed go through such a phase. Impressionistically, we would have to say that this is by no means in keeping with the rate of response we got when we raised this as a question among staff groups at various mental health facilities (where the bulk of our subjects were garnered). It was our impression that perhaps one woman in four or five answered yes to our inquiry, which is still a good many more than the proportion found by Saghir and Robins.

In any case, there are a number of psychoanalytic studies of women with such a history; perhaps the most interesting described three varieties of tomboy adjustment and gave case examples of women who had, respectively, each followed such a developmental course: (1) the "daddy's girl" type; (2) the "mommy's girl"; and (3) the woman built upon a more complex borderline personality core to form this character type.

There is a large body of literature on animal experimentation in respect to gender-linked behavior. Thus, there are studies involving changing the endocrine environment of embryonic and fetal animals—and changing their characteristic gender-typical patterns accordingly. For example, rats behave differently in a variety of contest depending on whether they are males or females. However, a female embryo bathed in male hormone will be born anatomically female and behave in a characteristically male fashion. In a similar fashion, many aspects of male behavior can be feminized. Thus, there is at least a possibility that some dimensions of gender mixing in humans may be a function of endocrine imbalances at some critical moment early in development. Studies are currently being carried out with women whose mothers had been given diethylstilbestrol (DES) to help them carry the baby. In any case, the influence on organic factors in development is not to be lightly put aside, and the possible role of temperamental contributions to the formation of gender identity remains an open question.

By and large the subjects were recruited by word-of-mouth expressions of interest. It was striking from the outset that for some of those who agreed to be interviewed the topic had touched some deep wellspring of interest. It was close to the hearts of a number of the participants, and they gave freely of their time and energy to allow the rather heavy demands of the project to be satisfied; they were asked to remember a great many detail from their pasts, to relive what were sometimes rather painful sequences of loss or seduction as we tried to get into some of the important shaping experiences of their gender selves, and to review elements of social and familial interaction, of boy change, of adaptation to growth, of encounter with gender-significant relationship experiences, and other such highly personal and intensely cathected recollections—and they did all this in the presence of a researcher who was writing down most of what they said as they said it. Many of the subjects were professionals; some were support staff such as secretaries or administrative assistants; a few were simply citizens of the community who chanced to be around when one of the researchers made his pitch or who were referred through friends or even neighbors.

The style of the approach to the subjects involved a verbal explanation of the project followed by giving or sending the potential candidate a copy of the structured interview. They were asked to review it, and, if they consented to go ahead, they could contact the researcher to set up an appointment. Or the researcher might call and ask whether they would like to participate.

At this point a number of potential candidates withdrew; having read the protocol, they simply did not choose to be interviewed. For the rest, for the most part they were given 90-minute blocks of time, usually after

5:00 p.m.; they came into the Children's Hospital, and the majority of the interviews were held there. A few came to the researcher's home in the evening. In two cases, the researcher went out to the subject's home to do the interviewing there. In one case only, the entire interview was conducted in a single day and taped as the subject and interviewer spoke. In contrast to the other interviewing, on this occasion few notes were taken. (A rather special complication arose in this instance because for a long time no one at Children's Hospital would type the tape. But the paths of research are never easy.)

Once the basic pattern was set, the researchers considered the possible role of controls. The first possibility was the use of sisters of the subjects whom the subject herself perceived as a nontomboy. Although there would be certain important discrepancies (e.g., the inevitable age difference and the fact that the younger sibling would be growing up in a home with a tomboy present), still there were so many consonant factors present that it seems like an eminently sensible way of going at things. And it probably would have been—except that only 1 sister of the 20 or so we petitioned consented to fill out the form. (We didn't even ask the sisters to come in and be interviewed; we requested only that they write out the answers to the questions—but to no avail.)

Then, after we had started data collections, another type of control suggested itself. Among other queries we posed was one about the kind of people our subjects had disliked during the tomboy period. And quite a few of them said the same thing—they didn't like the prissy kind of girl. They all knew this kind of girl: She never wanted to go play outside, she always worried about getting a spot on her dress, she was forever involved with her dolly or wanting to place house, and the like. And many of them recalled her with distaste; indeed, a few subjects remarked, "And I *still* don't like them!" So I set out to find a group of such former prissy girls—at which point I ran into difficulties. For example, there is no good word for this type of person in the English language. For want of a term I called them *hyperfeminine*, but clearly that is poor usage. Anyway, I have been able to find about four such subjects. Perhaps there will be time later to get into some of those findings.

In any case, with the tomboy subjects it seemed useful to find out what the basis was on which these women thought of themselves as tomboys; that is, why did they volunteer? The answers were interesting. By and large this was a successful population. It included people who felt competent, who had a record of achievement, and who for the most part had a sense of mastery about the important dimensions of their lives. In particular, they had integrated the disparate elements of gender identity in a reasonably comfortable way; in some cases they had a feeling of having been through a difficult and confusing time but now felt like they had overcome the hurdles and had freed themselves from the entanglements. Of particular interest was that the time it took to do this was measured in years—often this state of affairs was not arrived at until the late 20s, or even later. Then the group who had worked this out became the subjects. Many of them were very much intrigued by the substance of the research, nor was this hard to understand since, in fact, it sought to examine an area they may have once experienced as a source of stress and discomfort and now felt they had coped with successfully. Thus, they could tell the story of these events with relative comfort.

At least two subjects began the project and dropped out after the first interview. Even the limited data available suggest that they represented examples of what is probably a large group of women whom we did not interview, people for whom the associated gender and identity issues had not been so comfortably resolved, who had questions and doubts, and who would not have felt comfortable entering into any sort of in-depth exploration of such uncertain and perhaps distressing feelings. This, we feel, is a major conditioning factor that profoundly influenced the selection of subjects and the character of the study population that eventually emerged.

Now to the findings. The initial area for presentation will cover the realm of the phenomenology of this state. What kinds of behavior did our subjects report identifying as tomboyish? Mostly physical and athletic activities, hockey, tennis, baseball, football (although usually the flag or touch variety), swimming, and the like. Many, indeed most, were into dancing as well: ballet, modern, or tap. Whatever spoke for large muscle activity tended to claim them as a major interest. During the latency years (and often enough before as well), their lives often centered around this; they might be good studies at school, but the really top moments came when they could get home and get out onto the playing field. There were of course many who are not particularly able or talented at athletics, but those girls would enjoy participating on any level they could. If there was nothing else available, they liked hiking and camping—the essence was to be active and outdoors.

A favorite sport for a great many subjects was horseback riding. A minority of these women had gone through a stage of absolutely ape over horses—living, breathing, dreaming about horses with a sort of total dedication of the self to the four-legged alter ego. This was, however, not a typical finding. On the other hand, an interest in riding, occasionally a great deal of skill at equitation, or sometimes an unfulfilled wish to ride were not unusual.

For some of the more skilled athletes, there were certain hazards. One of the subjects reported that from early childhood she had been extremely well coordinated and once into latency became a most adroit and effective ballplayer. She literally outplayed every child in her neighborhood, male and female, at a variety of sports. One of her better early memories is the organization of the local little league team. At the time, girls could not join, and as a result she used to look through the fence at the kids playing the game, knowing she could outhit, outrun, and outthrow every single one of them—because in fact she had—and was unable to join in. Being thus barred from the league by her gender, she compensated by coaching her younger brother in how to play, attending all of his games and following his little league career with intense avidity.

Quite a different solution that another child found as she grew older was to turn from the sports arena *per se* to the role of a cheerleader. There her big voice and drive for physical expressiveness found a ready outlet, and she reported with pride that her cheerleading group won the state championship.

One of the subjects recalled that when she was arranging for colleges, she ended up in a school that had no physical education course. She recalled how upset she was at this discovery. "What am I going to do with myself," she wailed to her family, as she contemplated a life without an organized athletic program.

Another youngster, feeling at odds with her world, described the following:

> I developed a curious habit. I got a bicycle from some family members. I'd pack a lunch, take a safety kit, and take long, long bike rides, all-day bike trips. Then I'd sit in a park and commune with nature. I felt terribly courageous, like it was the most daring thing anybody could do. Sometimes it was to places our parents had taken us in the car. [*What was the danger?*] That I would A—get lost, and B—be accosted by someone. There were glorified fairy tales of what monsters you'd meet on the way. [*What kind of monsters?*] I don't know that I thought of any particular monsters. One place had skunk cabbage. I'd been told if you beat them you get a terrible stench. I remember beating them with a stick to see if they did. I felt so secret and courageous; I never told anybody lest I lose the privilege. Looking back, what is unusual to me is that I went alone. I'd have preferred a group but I wasn't wanted by the boys and the girls weren't doing that sort of thing, so if you wanted to go you had to go alone.

In sum, for a great many of these women, the presence of outdoor activities, and especially organized sports, were among the essentials for a happy day, a happy life.

Another characteristic trait that many tomboys shared was a quality of daring. This took several different forms, but in particular it involved taking dares and challenges from people and putting oneself against challenging tasks.

To begin with, the group members I talked to were, for the most part, not accident prone. Some were, of course: one subject reported that all her childhood pictures showed her legs covered with black and blue marks, scratches, bruises, and other testimonials to her special affinity for rough activity. By and large, however, they were a group with well-developed self-preservative instincts; they were daring and did bold things, but these were activities well within their realm of competence. To be sure, some of what happened depended on circumstance. Thus, a woman recalled that once when she was in latency she was much attached to a brother who was older by 4 years. She was, however, all too well aware that he had a sadistic streak. On one occasion, he dared her to climb a ladder to the roof. She goes on to say, "I fear heights. Then I had the terrifying feeling he'd taken the ladder away. And I told myself—I'm not going to be a sissy; I'll climb anyway." And she did.

The need to prove oneself—not to be a sissy, not to be comparable to the scaredy-cat sort of girl—was an urgent and pressing theme for a certain percentage of these youngsters. There was a strong sense of category: one was in this state and not that; one belonged to this group, not to that. The grouping was in no simple sense defined in terms of gender. By and large these youngsters knew well and accepted the fact that they were girls. At issue was the question: what kind of girl? And they were striving to provide an answer to that.

The other form of daring that was important was that related to taking dares. There was a profound and primary need to prove oneself that many of these girls experienced, an inner pressure to show that once could do as well as anyone, accept any challenge that others might offer, not be outdone or outshone by any rival. There was indeed a keen sense of competitiveness that breathed through the accounts of one subject after another. They got a positive delight out of vying with the significant other and besting the rival be sheer application, energy, and whatever measure of skill they could bring to bear on the effort. This could be a human opponent, an animal, or a situation of some kind.

While this pleasure in solitary activity was not quite so typical of this relatively gregarious group, the attitude toward challenge and mastery is quite characteristic. Another subject began her account with the statement, "I was a daredevil on a bicycle—I would go down the highest nearby hills, no hands, as fast as I could." There was a curious avidity for coping that many described, a pleasure in besting challenges that was like a fingerprint of their personalities. A girl who grew up at the edge of a large bay reports, "We'd go out in boats, and I loved it when it got really rough. Sometimes the boys would get scared, and I'd have to take the tiller to keep them calm. I might not want to go back, and they'd have to argue with me."

Among their records is repeated reference to tree climbing. In general, heights seemed to lure them, and the interviews included several accounts of what it was like to get out on a shaky limb high above the ground and feel it bend ominously in response to their movements. Often, however, the emphasis was on the height itself, to get as high up in the tree as possible. There was a social dimension to this: the rivalry with others, the need to accept a dare, the hunger to show one could do difficult and frightening things, the pressing desire to best someone else's achievement or to set a record. But behind that there seemed at times to be a primary pleasure in mounting to the heights that was in itself rewarding. One subject reports, "I liked to climb trees. I'd go to the top of the tallest tree I could find; it was one of the neatest things I would do. I felt like the top of the tree was my domain, and I could see the boys from there." There were a fair number of tree houses described by the several subjects.

> I liked the sound of the wind; it was exciting to climb into a tree, to have something to hold on to and to explore visually. There was a combination of being moved and yet having something solid to sit on. I've always enjoyed the wind. I'd sometimes stand on top of a rock on clear days to see all of the south. A very fresh feeling.

Yet another illustration:

> I was the fastest climber; I'd climb higher than anyone. I used to take dares a lot, big on that. I'd jump out of a tree and grab a grapevine. We had to have had guardian angels to escape some of what we did.

One of the best-documented—indeed one of the defining—aspects in the image that is associated with the word *tomboy* is the special character of the relationships these girls have with boys. In particular, two elements stand out. The first is an attractiveness that things boyish hold for some of them. They explain this in a variety of ways, and sometimes they don't explain it at all; all they can report is that during the growing-up years it just felt that way. The other is the need to prove themselves where boys are concerned: to show—sometimes to the boys, sometimes to some inner judge of these things, sometimes to both—that they can do anything boys can do and indeed, in many cases, that they could best boys, outdo them in the areas where boys felt most able and cost competent. There is, to be sure, a third element in these relationships that appears less regularly. For a sizable minority of these girls, during the grade-school years, they always had some boy who was a target of their love interest, their boyfriend, or at least the object of a crush. Needless to say, at times this mélange could be confusing.

Let us start with the first of these: the affinity for things boyish. In one case, the youngster had attended an academy, and during the fifth and again in the sixth grades there were 20 youngsters in the class: 15 girls and 5 boys. The subject recalled that, at the time, she wanted to be a boy too "because boys were better. They could kick a ball farther, make the home runs." *Better* in this context meant better at sports. Another subject described that at age 7, her mother would take her to the supermarket. A picture was taken on one such occasion showing the child going to market wearing her brother's football helmet and shoulder pads. As she recalls it, "I thought it was so neat." Still another subject reported:

> I identified with my brother, my father, getting wrapped up in the whole male idea. Maleness seemed more fun for some reason. My name is spelled Jo. A lot of teachers would spell it Joe, and there was always that dread that I'd have to say, "No, it's Jo," which meant I'm a girl. I was kind of embarrassed.

Obviously such issues were very much prey to the kinds of social and familial pressures the child was experiencing. Thus, Jo's father was an active and omnipresent influence in her life. She reports:

> When I was 8, my father would come home in the evening, and I would always be sitting, waiting, in my numbered shirt and baseball cap. He'd throw me the ball and teach me how to handle it. He'd say, "You're throwing like a girl"—that meant I wasn't doing it right. I learned—got to be really good.

The same sort of material repeated for a number of subjects: if it was boyish, it was good. Thus, a social work student and now mother of two reported:

> At 9 or 10 I recall a real strong wish that I had been a boy, almost a sadness that I was a girl. I recall really feeling like myself when I was dressed like a boy. I recall trying to get my father to teach me how to tie a necktie. He wouldn't; my mother finally did.

One of my more laconic subjects, a Black woman who had grown up on a farm in a rural part of the South, observed, "I climbed trees, made wagons, played ball. Back there girls didn't play ball much but I liked to. I like to go fishing, make believe. I just liked to play with the boys, games like the boys played." A White woman, the daughter of a minister, recalled, "At some point I found a Boy Scout manual (my father had been a Scout leader), and my aim in life was to be a Boy Scout. Parish members often spoke of me looking like a little boy, and I did find girls a bit of a drag." A bit later in her account, she clarified that her yearning wasn't so much to be a Boy Scout but just a Scout.

This pervasive sense of the attractiveness of the boy's world was not universal among these women. By and large, as a matter of fact, in most cases things were considerably more mixed, and the average tomboy had many areas of conventional feminine interests as well. There might be a powerful and active affinity for boys' team sports among her pursuits, but the girl might also enjoy playing jacks and hopscotch or jumping rope in the company of other girls. However, most of the subjects went through a few years when their interests tilted prominently toward the boyish.

An interesting subgroup denied any special affinity with pursuits or behaviors that were in themselves masculine. They asserted with a certain firmness, even forcefulness, that they were interested in particular classes of experiences, such as athletics, because such pursuits were in themselves rewarding and not because they were felt to be masculine. Indeed, sometimes the strong encouragement would come from a girlfriend (who might also be identified as a tomboy) with whom one shared the play. In any case, however, for these subjects there was no special feel about gender associated with this behavior. A few women in this group recall this latency time as lacking all gender feeling. One of them illustrated this by quoting the German word for girl, *das Mädchen* ("little maid"), where the gender maker *-chen* indicates it is a neuter noun. "And that's the way I felt," she asserted: "neuter." Another said, "I suppose I became conscious of being a female as opposed to a child of neither gender when I was about 13."

In any case, a more common phenomenon was the insistence that one could outdo boys at their own game. A subject recalled that at age 7 "my neighbor would eat red ants so I had to, even more than he did. There was the dare-me game, and the double dare. If I were given a dare I had to match up; it was unthinkable to chicken out. That would have been terrible." Another example: "I was very competitive, very sports oriented. Almost every child on the block was a male child, plus my three brothers. I always played their games, and since I was the smallest and a girl I always had to prove my worth." Still another subject introduced her material by declaring, "I could outrun, outfight, outclimb anybody I played with."

Not infrequently, the tomboyish behavior took the form of fighting. This was rarely the predominant behavior, but it fit in as part of the assertive, competitive style of adoption that was so often present. For example:

I would fight, get into brawls with playmates over who was going to be in charge. I'd fight with my sister because she borrowed my dress or wasn't doing her share of picking up the room. We did it so much that once our mother put us out on the back porch and made us keep fighting. I learned that if I bloodied her nose right away she would let us stop. So I used to do that. There was a boy who was my age. One time we were fighting over who'd be in charge of the cowboy gang. He wanted me to be the cowgirl, Dale Evans, and I refused because she wasn't in charge and I wanted to be the chief of the gang. He clobbered me in the head with a walnut so I quit and didn't speak to him for two days. Then his mother made him apologize so it was a nice victory for me.

Another example:

I had a very belligerent manner of settling arguments—I used to just punch out. Talking was something you did after you fought. I remember at 6 or 7 I wouldn't be allowed to tag along with my big sister; the mothers of her friends wouldn't let me in because I was such a rotten little kid.

A third:

> I was very aggressive and given to physical violence. I'd punch kids, pull their hair, kick their legs. The kids ended up being afraid of me. Either they did what I wanted or got punched. The fights were everyday.

On the whole, however, albeit an actively competitive group and with strong needs to prove themselves, most of these youngsters were not characteristically pugnacious. To be sure, those who chanced to take such a turn could be quite a handful, but they were a distinct minority.

On the other hand, affectional relationships were somewhat more common. Thus, from relatively early in latency there were a number of descriptions of having crushes or selecting some boys as a target for attachment. This took many forms.

Thus, an 8- or 9-year-old girl felt strongly drawn to a boy with whom she shared many interests. Since she was a child much given to fantasy, she dreamed of demonstrating her feelings for him in a direct fashion. This finally led to a plan. After school one day she hid herself behind the door at the exit of the school building, and, as the object of her affections passed in the company of two other boys, she launched herself at him, bore him to the earth, and kissed him. Much chagrined, he turned on her and beat her up. She recalls that she was totally unprepared for that reaction; whatever it was she had dreamed of, it did not include that. A teacher separated them, and she was thereupon hauled before the principal, who reprimanded her severely.

Admittedly this was not the conventional pattern these women described, although not out of keeping with the general style of the tomboy. However, a more typical pattern might be something of this sort: "I was interested in boys from age 5 or 6. Every year there was a different boy I was in love with. In the third grade there was Lee; I tried to impress him with my prowess at kickball."

Another woman, recalling some of the complexity of her childhood experience, reported events in this way:

> From kindergarten on up I had crushes. I don't recall particular ones. But the boys I was interested in were adept, they had status, they had to be cute in some way. I didn't care about their moral character at all. The crush was always a distant crush, and I made a big point of letting go first, getting out of that one and into another one. It would be terrible to be rejected.

Thus, in each instance there is a powerful attempt at mastery, albeit by highly various means.

Sometimes the attachments were directed toward adults; at age 7, a woman recalls she had been sent off to a dude ranch along with her older sister. Both girls thereupon fell head over heels in love with a married staff member who was 34 years older but personable, charming, and a fine cowboy. At 8, there was a different man—this one a friend of her sister. Then at 12, she and several friends all developed a simultaneous crush on a female science teacher. This passion was brought to an abrupt end when the child was playing tennis in a foursome and hit this teacher in the behind. She burst in uproarious laughter, and the crush disappeared. That same year she fell in love with first her riding instructor, for whom she would perform terrifying leaps to win his approval, and then with a fellow student, football hero, and president of his class. Thus, through a long and circuitous route the object attachment began to converge on an appropriate object.

Finally, the most common pattern to emerge was that of a hunger for the company of boys as objects of competition, as a group whose acceptance was valued, and as an in-group where affiliation rather than exclusion was a prime conditioner of one's feeling of personal worth. But these were the criteria rather than romantic interest. The beginning stirrings of erotic responsivity did not usually make their presence felt until late latency at the borderline of puberty.

One curious exception occurred with a small number of subjects. This involved the interposition of a semifantasy as the object of one's affectional life, occasionally as the target of rather intense feelings. Thus, a woman recalls this aspect of her childhood in the following way. She was growing up in a small town in Latin America and apparently had a learning deficit. She reports:

> I was so wild I could never develop closeness to an adult in my younger years. I was never able to feel close to teachers. I had no crushes on boys or girls. Life was so busy, constant motion, always something happening. What I loved between 10 and 14 was to listen to the soap operas. I felt very emotional when something dramatic happened. My mother would say that a bomb could go off next to me and I wouldn't move an inch from the radio. I didn't read much then but loved the radio. There was one character I was very attached to—listened every day. I remember getting very excited about that actor, but I think it was really the plot, the adventure, that captured me.

Another woman recalled that when she was 8 1/2 or 9, she got involved with the *Daniel Boone* television series:

I liked to take long shirts and put a belt around my waist with the shirt-tail out. Daniel Boone had a belt and buckskin top. I thought he looked so handsome in it. I used to dream that Daniel Boone would take me on a trip. I endured all the hardships; I was captured by Indians, and he would rescue me. I guess it was kind of a crush, nothing romantic or intimate. It was just that he would admire me because I could walk 25 miles and endure privations. I wanted to prove to him that I could go the whole distance without giving up.

Of such, then, were the latency aspirations constructed: amorphous yearnings that usually had more about them of identification than object attachment. One would do some extravagant act and prove one's worthiness, one would show that she was company for males by doing male activities as well as or better than the males could themselves. This did not involve a repudiation of femininity; again and again the subjects stated in their several ways: "I could do these unexpected things even though I am a girl; I could do them even though no one expects that a girl could and many question whether a girl should." This is a central theme of the tomboy habitus, and we will return to it again.

Among the many cultural presences that captured the imagination of these youngsters, perhaps none was as ubiquitous as the image of the American Indian. So many elements in the personality makeup of these tomboy children resonated in perfect synchrony with the romanticized notion of the "Red Man" our culture provides our children, that it is not especially surprising to find this threat woven into so many other lives. Nonetheless, I was impressed by the power of this image to fill the fantasy life of one of these girls after another. Nor was this a function of social circumstances. One Black woman growing up on a Southern farm remarked, "I always liked the looks of Indians and wanted to grow up to be an Indian." The woman who recalled being so attached to Daniel Boone during her latency also reported the following:

When I got home from school I'd think of Indian life. Either I'd be a White girl captured by Indians and brought up and Indianized or an Indian girl. I'd think of myself wearing pants and climbing trees and scouting or wearing a skirt. I really admired the Indian people; I loved their way of life, the way they thought about things, the way they lived close to the land. I loved softer clothes, moccasins, unencumbered by all the clothes the Whites wore. Their love and respect for animals, their view of the Great Spirit. I was a little afraid of them because of things I would read. I didn't know any real ones. I think I had an ambition to be able to find a group of Indians and live with them for awhile. I hoped there'd be something of the old style in their life.

It is perhaps no great surprise to find members of this population so intensely interested in nature. They were, on the whole, an outdoor lot, lured strongly by the activities and experiences that pulled youngsters out of the house. While many confined their outside activities to team sports, winning, and the like, a sizable proportion loved nature for itself and would find ways to express this affinity.

One of the interesting dimensions—and I believe another trait that can properly be said to qualify many of these tomboy children—was an interest in exploring. Thus, for the woman who as a little girl was so drawn to Daniel Boone, she remarks,

> We lived out in the country. I loved to go outside, play with my younger brother, explore the woods, find unexplored territories, see how far we could go before we got lost. One thing we loved was to forge paths through the woods. It was exciting to come on a new tract of land, find out what was on the other side of the hill. It had the spirit of adventure.

A Black woman who grew up in the country reported:

> Another thing I liked was exploring. My father had a lot of land. We weren't supposed to leave the yard, but we used to go into the woods. We'd name everything we saw but got lost a couple of times. The explorers were me, my two boy cousins who are 3 and 4 years older than me, and my sister, who is 2 years older; I was between 5 and 7 at the time. I always thought that someday we would discover something really big—I didn't know what—something like great explorers. We made up a bear one day, and each day it got bigger and bigger. It got to the point where I almost did believe there was a bear. They had to convince me pretty hard that there wasn't.

Another woman with several siblings reported, "I'd just go exploring, making bows and arrows, fantasize about being a great White hunter. I would see *Tarzan* and *Jungle Boy* movies. I'd imagine myself in India or Africa with wild beasts around."

Clothing is used regularly as an important gender marker and played its role in the lives of these youngsters as well. Certain dispositions were found in the clothing preferences of this group, but no clear and salient preferences and avoidances that were valid across the board. Thus, alphabetically, the first 10 subjects gave the following pattern of responses. A total of 6 of the 10 didn't like to wear dresses. They usually had attended schools where dresses or uniforms were required garb and they accepted that as a matter of course and also knew that church attendance mandates such attire as well as a number of other such occasions. However, if left to their own devices, they would change immediately, out of dresses and into pants or shorts. This behavior was regular and automatic, part of the daily routine—get home from school, change into pants, and get out of the house to play. A seventh preferred pants for routine wear but enjoyed dressing up in more conventional feminine garb for special events. Two of the subjects reported that they liked tailored simple dresses; one of the two liked pants a lot also. Only 1 of 10 reported that she liked frilly, lacy dresses. However, her account goes as follows:

> I liked to wear frilly dresses; they'd have lace and were gathered at the waist so if you turned they'd spread. There'd be a big bow. I'd tie them tight at the waist and want to look very girly. Half an hour later I was dirty and had ripped my dress. I couldn't keep neat. But for that first minute I liked to try. I liked the look. I think this was in part to attract the boys. The frill was girly, feminine, and would allow me to do girl activities. I'd be available for a crush and to be liked. It kind of solidified my identity. We didn't wear pants—we wore shorts in the summer but never pants. I never wanted pants. I'd go back to the playground after school but always in a dress.

Thus, the drift of preferences is clear even though the spread of preferences is there as well. In attempting to sort out with the various subjects just what they felt as children about this garment or that, it was frequently impossible to get an altogether clear response. On the whole, this is all the more striking, since so many of these subjects were verbal, well-educated, expressive people. But again and again I would get answers like, "I don't know why I preferred pants—it just felt better that way." It were as though the sense of gender is a preverbal experience, an image of self that is concordant with or discordant with some internal template, and this has little or nothing to do with verbal formulations. To be sure, there were a number of explanations advanced for these phenomena. The most common was, of course, the question of sheer practicality; it is trickier to climb trees and fences, to run and play ball in a dress than it is in pants. Then there is the issue of modesty, which a number of subjects mentioned. The boys can look up your dress if they're following you up a tree or if you are going down a slippery slide. Thus, one of the subjects, discussing the question of clothing, expressed herself in this way: "When I came home from school I *had* to wear pants. I didn't throw a fit about wearing a dress to school, but I strongly preferred pants. You couldn't climb a tree in a dress, I didn't want to show my legs, I was sort of self-conscious." A frequent comment was the need for freedom, for informality in dress. However, there are clearly additional factors at work. The same woman went on:

> I wore dungarees, jeans, green army pants, loose-fitting. Dad had army fatigues, so I had to get some. What he had I wanted to have too. I had

a lot of T-shirts, most with numbers so it was like a football jersey. The number I had was 72; it was green and white. I loved that. I always wore girls' undershirts but always white. With those I would maybe be more like boys. I wore girls' white undershorts. I hated frilly stuff; it was so feminine. I didn't want to be that feminine. At the time what was good was to be more like the boys, less feminine. I didn't like that.

That sort of response, while not typical, was by no means uncommon. Something felt wrong or right because it felt more or less feminine—that was the deciding factor. Albeit less informative, it was probably a more precise response at least in terms of how these issues were subjectively experienced. Another subject commented:

I hated undershirts. At 10 or 11 I wouldn't wear them at all. We had plain cotton underwear. I didn't like the lacy underwear because it was scratchy. I still don't like the real ruffly things, I don't know what it is about it.

This feeling she is describing, without being able to quite account for it, stands at the center of the issue of gender identity. There is a gut-level resonance, a matter of looking at something or looking in the mirror and reacting to something, or imagining oneself and feeling good or bad about that image, that goes beyond the rational to some primary sense of what is right, what is proper, what belongs, and what looks good. It does not readily translate into the rational and explicable.

To better grasp the implications of such choice, let us look briefly at some of the intrafamilial affiliations described by these subjects. To some extent, of course, this is a matter of identification. One has an ideal a model a template of some kind, and one strives to attain that. The self becomes a plastic material kneaded and molded and altered to fit the specifications; one sculpts one's identity to conform to the model. The gait is altered, the gesture, the posture, the set of face, the carriage, the whole musculature deployed and transformed in keeping with the desired image. There is a constant reading of the way one thinks one looks and the way one wishes to look; then a point-by-point matching, a detailed comparison is conducted—is one meeting the standard? Does something need to be improved—thrust of jaw, set of shoulder, angle of head on neck, position of limbs, what one does with one's hands, and so on? This concern extends itself to a variety of additional details: clothing, grooming, voice, speech, diction, laughter, interpersonal style. Then there are the more complex possibilities: patterns of aggression and submission, of activity and passivity, of intrusion and reserve. The full range of interactive techniques can be mimicked and absorbed and made part of one's own. Nor can we ignore the negative components of identification. For forming identity, children will be as alive (perhaps more alive) to what they try to avoid as they are to what they hope to arrive at. Thus, we hear not only that a particular element is defined because it feels right but also that another is eschewed because it has about it an aversive quality. The inner template is a model with a message; it can be simply, "Boyish things are pretty keen; seek them out." But it can also have quite a separate element: "Girlish things are pretty undesirable—weak, sissy, vulnerable, helpless—in any case, keep away from them."

In short, gender identity choice can be in response to a variety of instigations, and in no case it is likely to be a simple business. To complicate it further, we have to ponder the role of constitution: Is there not a temperamental factor that inclines children one way or another from the very outset? Not that such an element, or a complex of factors, is likely in and of itself to be decisive. But surely it sets the stage, establishes the framework, and provides the material within and upon which mental forces can then proceed to exert their influence.

In sum, then, gender identity seems to be a function of biological style, child-rearing messages, and identification choice. Together these mutually interactive, mutually shaping forces can induce identity crystallizations in latency that have powerful meaning for subsequent development.

Chapter 12

The tomboy, puberty, and beyond

Joseph D. Noshpitz

The encounter with puberty was often greeted with mixed emotions. For the tomboy, with her sturdy self-assertiveness and her special feeling about things boyish, this was a development that offered very mixed rewards. On one hand, there was the advantage of new growth, height, strength, capability—more to work with. On the other, a series of limitations appeared; those physical changes of puberty particularly associated with womanliness tended to function as and be perceived as problems. Even more troublesome were the social expectations for more decorous ladylike behavior; this was a powerful set of messages and not readily set aside. The lure and excitement of awakening sexuality—this was a powerful voice that did much to ease the transition. The rewards of admiring and responsive attention from boys were by no means trivial. Meanwhile, issues about whether to wear a dress gave way to problems of what dress to wear to look most attractive. And the business of vying with other girls or envying this one or outdoing that one found ready room for growth within these active and competitive youngsters.

It is of some interest that the tomboyish mode of dealing with the world by no means disappeared. Instead, it transformed itself in a variety of ways and had a profound influence on major aspects of future adjustment. This included such items as career choice, pattern of sexual engagement, preferred mode of creating a personal environment, type of social group selected, and other vital dimensions of lifestyle. In short, we are speaking of a pervasive orientation of personality, a mode of adaptation that is characteristic and continuing, and one that in its order of priority is antecedent to most of the determinative events that make any given phase of development. The grown-up who was once a tomboy is likely to be active, to enjoy large muscle activity, to fight back when confronted, and to reach for high goals in facing the everyday business of living. She will stand in marked contrast to the hyperfeminine opposite, who is likely to avoid most sports or muscular enterprises, who is not much of a fighter or who will fight if she must but hates it, whose highest goal is a well-run household, a content husband, and happy children. This is not to imply that health and home are less or more valuable than advanced degrees and executive suites. It merely recognizes that within the province of our culture the one is regarded as less an achievement than the other, rightly or wrongly. Having said this much, now let me proceed to complicate it. For many of the tomboy subjects, but certainly not for all, the tomboy presence was a curiously sequestered portion of the self. They weren't simply this as opposed to that; there were all sorts of mixtures. In some instances, the tomboy stance was consciously a defense—the father was loving and the mother rejecting, so the girl turned to her father and his ways and fled from her mother and her ways. In others, the tomboy moiety was a component of a larger self; it was a compartmentalized part of the girl's inner world that could be invoked at will when the occasion required. Sometimes there was a yearning, a reaching for some kind of bridge to, or integration with a more feminine way of feeling and acting, something that would be achieved as development and maturity went on.

But let us take this unfolding step by step and see how different women of this orientation first encountered puberty. This is a time of profound endocrine changes and radical attention in body contours. Among the earliest and most prominent events is the appearance of breasts. These generally grow out about 1 year or 18 months before the occurrence of menarche. Unlike menarche, however, these are highly visible aspects of femininity. It is conceivable that a youngster could be reared and never hear anything verbal about a penis, bleeding, cycles, napkins, or any other reference to menstruation. But no girl grows up without realizing that breast development is part of what will happen to the body. And if the girl is, in fact, an active, athletic person with an interest in boyish things, what will such a departure mean to her then? Let us survey the observations of a number of subjects.

> I started to develop breasts the year before my father died. My mother took me to buy a bra, and it was an important event. It was called a training bra, but I had enough breast development that I couldn't wear T-shirts. Initially I felt about the changes that they were embarrassing and frightening. After I put on the bra I didn't change my basic behavior patterns; I still climbed trees and all that. As I got toward my thirteenth birthday, my father bought me heels and a lipstick; I used the lipstick only once or twice. I had a girlfriend who was into those things, so I got interested in them too.

Clearly, in this instance, there was reluctance and resistance to the new stage of growth, but the girlfriend relationship was a critical help and catalyst.

> When my breasts began to appear I didn't like it. They hurt if they got hit. That made me more cautious in the ways I'd play. That started at 12.

Several subjects echo this theme, as we shall see. Breasts were sources of vulnerability, and often enough these feelings extended to femininity as a whole.

> Breast development was at 11 or 12. The breast development didn't bother me as much as my menstrual period did; in fact, I don't think I paid it much heed in the beginning. The breast development called for a bra; when you had to stop and waste time putting on additional clothing it was a bother.

A common pattern for the management of this issue was to ignore the whole thing or to peripheralize it. It didn't matter; it was a minor matter.

> In fourth or fifth grade I recall arguing with a boy. He pushed me on the chest, and it hurt; I was surprised it hurt so much. I told my mother; she checked me and told me that I was beginning to develop and that I shouldn't play with boys because they were rough and girls were soft and my body was changing. I really thought I hurt myself. It was a new experience; I was becoming aware that I was growing up. I still had some apprehensions about it but not as much as when I was younger. In sixth grade I began to think of getting a bra and stockings and little high heels—a real change. There was some ambivalence. Between sixth and ninth grade I didn't want to grow up; each year was okay, but I didn't want to go any further. Once I took a bath with my two younger sisters (by 1 and 3 years), and the next younger one reached around and grabbed my breasts and teased, "I've got your mountains." And I recall getting angry and saying, "I'm never going to take a bath with you again." I was 9 1/2 then. I felt I was older than they, growing up.

Here the record speaks for a more mixed kind of emotional response with some positive elements struggling to appear side by side with the sense of vulnerability. Incidentally, one should never underestimate the powerful role of teasing as an important maker of and confirmer of developmental change.

> Junior high school was the worst time of my life. I was so tall, so skinny, so awkward, I had funny glasses and was very flat-chested. That was so painful. I was called Twiggy by the other kids. In seventh grade, changing clothes in school was terrible. I didn't want the other girls to see me. I wanted my period to come.

This shows the effects of the not uncommon experience of the girl whose breasts are small or late to develop. If the girl should happen to be a very competitive person as so many tomboys were, the sense of being left behind by others was painful.

> Overnight I had a mature figure so that where everybody else was flat-chested I was not at all. That was between seventh and eighth grade. I had a mature figure and was wearing undershirts when other girls with nothing were wearing training bras. I bought my first one with my own money; it would have been too embarrassing to talk about this with mother.

Too little has been written about the meaning of a girl's development to her mother. It is unusual for the maternal inhibitions and the stress in the mother–daughter relationship to attain such proportions that even so obvious a step as buying a bra could not be faced together. But in this young woman's life, that was the case.

> Breast development, menarche—those made me feel very much like a girl. Although I still enjoyed playing and being good at games, I found out that getting hit in the chest by a dodge ball really hurt.

Here again is the sideways approach to impending change—the very mixed attitude that was so characteristic of this group. She wanted to continue the tomboy pattern, but femininity meant that she could be hurt, was vulnerable.

> When I was 6 or 7 I noticed pubic hair. [*I remarked that this was rather early.*] Yeah, that's early. Let's say about 10; my breasts developed about 9 or 10. I wasn't interested in that at all. I clung to my undershirts. I pretended that nothing happened until at 11, at the swimming pool, my sister told my mother that I was hanging out and needed a bra. So my mother bought me one.

In this instance mother and daughter appear to have conspired silently to deny developmental reality—until the sister intervened.

> I became heavier over the summer between fifth and sixth grade, my bosom developed, and I felt fat and ugly. I was teased at school and felt very unaccepted by the other kids. My teachers accepted me; one let me correct papers during recess so I could avoid the kids. I didn't want to compete in sports; I felt so ugly I wanted to hide. I blamed myself. My brothers and sisters weren't heavy. They had black hair and dark eyes; I was the only one like that—fat and left-handed with blue eyes and blond hair. So I thought I was adopted; I asked my mom about that. Once I told her I wished I was dead and got a good talking to.

In brief, pubertal change did not come easily to many of these girls.

These examples illustrate quite a range of attitudes. It is noticeable that quite a few of the subjects reacted initially in terms of embarrassment, wished to ignore the whole thing, or attempted to conceal what was happening. Several were impressed chiefly by the new vulnerability they were now exposed to; they could be hurt and needed to avoid this danger or to defend against it. A few were pleased by the new growth, but it was scarcely the prevailing sentiment. A salient factor is that the bosom meant the bra for many girls; this garment as such meant womanhood, with all the complex emotions with which it came.

An even more dramatic event, however, was menarche. So central is this experience to the shift in identity and in gender confirmation that it is sensible to include this within its context of overall pubertal transformation. The following examples will illustrate how these young tomboys reacted to menstruation as an idea and to the actual encounter with their first period. A subsequent set of notations will speak to their general sense of growing up—and becoming fully female.

> I remember twice my mother talking to me about these things. Once when I was 7 or 8 I walked in on her when she was changing a sanitary napkin, and she explained some of it then. Later, she gave me a book made by a feminine product manufacturer. She never talked about it. I asked her later about tampons. She said I couldn't use them because I wasn't married. My aunt asked me if I'd started my periods and that I shouldn't be embarrassed about it. I was, though. I was afraid I'd bleed through my clothes, afraid that it would be visible. It was something you were stuck with, just generally uncomfortable. It felt unfair. I remember telling my mother that men had it better, that my brother was really lucky because he didn't have to worry about any of that. She told me I was right—that we were an unfortunate race.

> My mother didn't prepare me for menstruation. I think she gave me a book, but I knew what it was when it happened. I had learned from street talk, from other girls. It occurred the first time at a fair or carnival. All of a sudden I was bleeding. I left, went home very quickly, and asked my mother, who showed me how to use a napkin. When it happened it felt awkward; there was no pain, but there was blood. It didn't make sense; I didn't see the need for it. I didn't understand why it had to happen, and I didn't know the biology of it all. I was told that it was necessary for growing into a woman and having babies. The idea of doing that didn't occur to me; even now, I have never felt any overwhelming need to procreate. It has seemed like a bother. Some of my friends thought [getting their period] was the best thing that ever happened to them, but that was not my feeling.

The friends referred to here are probably far more inclined to the hyper-feminine frame of mind; one of the most striking observations to emerge from this study were the wildly diverging views of menstruation expressed by these two groups of subjects.

> I must have been about 9 or 10 when the menstrual cycle started. That was a major spoke in the wheel. My mother had prepared me, talked about what to expect. She talked to me and my older sister at about the same time. My attitude was: "I'm too young for that." It sounded like something unpleasant, the idea of your body changing, of not being able to participate in activities: "I can't do this; I can't do that." It's a nuisance, a pain in the neck for this to happen. I accepted it, but not very graciously. When it started, I was riding my bike. I went into the house to go to the bathroom, and that's when I noticed it. I called my mother. She just accepts everything, so she explained again what was happening, told me what to do, and told me I'd be fine. I felt angry. I was between 9 and 10—why now? I didn't climb trees, but I still rode my bike and played ball. I didn't tell anyone about it. I guess one reason I didn't is because I asked my mother, "Does every mother explain this; does everybody know?" She said, "Not necessarily at your age." I wasn't the type to explain anything especially something that I wasn't familiar with. One of the girls I was closest to I didn't tell about it until I was 11 or 12, and then only because she brought it up.

Here was a youngster at the height of her tomboyish pleasures suddenly confronted with the unwelcome news that her femininity was expressing itself—and, again, in a way that felt like limitation, like deprivation of fun and freedom. It is no wonder that she was angry and sufficiently concerned with being different from others that she concealed this for the next 1 to 2 years.

> Somewhere around 10 I became more acutely aware of sexual differences. My sister was 12 and told me a horror story about menstruation, what she knew about intercourse and about having a baby. So I compared this with what other girls had told me and realized it was true. My sister's account of menstruation spoke of bad blood you had to get rid of, a wound, an imperfection, something dirty, a shameful thing. You were supposed to keep it a big secret, especially from the boys; I'd have died if my father ever knew. I was warned that I might be spared another 2 years before I had to deal with it. By 11 I was getting into puberty; at 12 1/2 I looked like I was 16 and got my period. I enjoyed myself and enjoyed the changes. When I got my period I was a cheerleader, I had a lot of friends, I was having a great time. I never went through an awkward age.

Here we see the difference that time can make. Despite an unpromising introduction, the actual reaction is more in keeping with the group developmental timetable, and other activities carried the girl through.

> When my mother talked of menstruation I couldn't picture this egg. Before that I liked my body the way it was, sort of sexual; I wasn't so keen about these changes. I knew of a girl who had her period and was interested, but I didn't want it to happen to me. At about 8 (in third grade) I learned the facts of life from my mother. The year before I'd watched a cat have babies and had run to my mother. She was on the phone so I wrote her a note: "What shall I do?" Later she told me a hole opened up in the top of your leg. I imagined a muscle would split open, and a baby would come down your leg and come out though the hole—that it could hurt. I looked at the top of my thigh and wondered, "Where would it appear, this hole; literally your leg would split open?" Later I found a tampon diagram my sister had. My mother talked about the pamphlets, but I never liked to read them when she was there—only when I was alone. Then I talked with other girls, but I was too embarrassed to let people know how little I knew. I remember when I got my period I got a mirror to see where it was coming from.

Here the chief reaction expressed by this very intelligent woman was interest, curiosity, and an attempt to understand.

> I started my period when I was 12 (in seventh grade). I was anticipating it. In sixth grade they showed the girls movies—all the stuff about babies. I began to think: "You're a girl. Pretty soon you'll have breasts, pubic hair. You're not going to be able to pretend anymore." The actual tomboy period was 8 to 11. By 12 the shift started and then, when the period came, it shifted all at once. When it happened, I noticed blood in my underwear, ran excitedly to my mother (I had been anticipating it since some of my friends had), and told her to give me a pad and a belt and not to tell my father (she did anyway).

For many girls, their boyishness was maintained in a sort of special equilibrium with father. The notion of their father becoming aware of their femininity was very disturbing. The entire equilibrium would have been shaken.

> I began to change physically in sixth grade and didn't menstruate till seventh. The onset was particularly uneventful. I can remember yearning to have my period before it started. I put a pad in my pants and would sit there pretending I was having one. My father had given my sister a little blue book, a manual. This was when she was courting. I read the whole thing, cover to cover, in fifth grade. My mother got a

great many women's magazines, and I made it a point to read all the sexual articles. I was able to answer many questions and correct many misapprehensions, so in sixth grade I became an expert among my friends. When the first among us got her period, she said it was black. Everybody was upset; they came to me. I said knowledgably, "Often it starts in different colors." Then the others started. I wanted to, but I began a lot later than the others.

Here the struggle for mastery of the event took the form of intellectual preoccupation and the development of a pseudo-expertise. Fantasy and play-acting played their roles as well.

My first period was the day I turned 12. I wasn't pleased. It was inconvenient. My mother had given me books and asked if I had any questions. I didn't have any. I was interested, not scared—but it meant I couldn't go swimming, that I had to be careful. It was limitation; it seemed unfair. The sexes were unequal.

The feeling of being cheated, of being treated unfairly, of being up against something where boys were somehow ahead and not to be caught up with this was a not uncommon accompaniment to the tomboy's menarchal experience.

My mother had bought books for my sister put out by Kotex: *Now You Are Nine, Now You Are Ten*. When I was 11 or 12 I was really looking forward to that. I remember checking my underwear all the time. Finally, I was at a *bar mitzvah* party, and I slow-danced with a boy. That's what must have done it. Anyway, I came home, went to the bathroom, saw a red stain, and rushed down to tell my mother. I was very happy; I had been looking forward to it.

The element of being ready for boys, for socialization, for sexual encounter—this was often the anodyne that allowed an otherwise unwelcome presence to be eagerly awaited and highly valued.

All of a sudden one day my mother started talking about what would be happening soon. When about a month later it did happen, at first I reacted with shock and fear. I thought I was dying; I totally forgot. I thought I was really injured. Then I did recall what mother had told me about a month before. We'd seen a film in fifth grade; nobody could figure it out, and the teacher wouldn't answer questions.

Thus, even with good preparation, when the girl is not emotionally ready, it was not easy.

But these menarchal events, important though they were, took place with a context. It is not easy to characterize the rich variety of ecological sets that surrounded puberty of these several subjects. To begin with, they divide most readily into those involving external change of some kind to parallel the inner transformations with the girl experiences and those where the chief site of new appearance was in her body and in her mind. The external changes might include a move the family made, a transfer to a new school, or the death of a parent. Such shifts in family structure or in peer groups were often of fateful importance for the effected youngster and served either to facilitate or to hinder her development (depending on what happened). Let us consider some case examples.

> After my father died I became the strong one at home; I took his place. I'd been fighting with him about lipsticks and clothes and at the time I would think: I wish he would die. Then once, in Texas, we were on a lake. My sister, brother, and I were out with him and the waves rose up. He held them all up till a boat came; the boat clipped him on the head, and he drowned. Mother didn't take us to the burial. I was told that I shouldn't cry because I was the oldest. So I stuffed it back in. We moved from Texas to be near her family. I left my friends, changed schools, and moved in with grandma and my favorite uncle. I was just going through the seventh grade. When father died I became mother's confidante. I was no longer running and jumping; I had responsibilities. That was a sudden transition. Mother was very dependent on him. She knew nothing of family finances. She was a true caregiver; devotion was to be given to your kids and husband and not to yourself at all. She came to me and said, "What should I do about this?" I became my father. I took on a lot of his role. I worked—my mother didn't work—I have worked since I was 14. I had before- and after-school jobs, and in my senior year I worked nights in the hospital as an aide. I'd still dress in a mannish style and pick colors I wouldn't pick now. I wore pants most of the time; I didn't change that until I got away from home. Until my late 20s I didn't buy dresses because I preferred them. Only in the last 5 or 6 years have I moved away from pants or pants suits. The boyish competitive behavior stopped when my father died. Lacy things I didn't start to buy until I was 25 or 26.

Here then is an account of major external changes that took place at the outset of this young girl's pubertal experience. Undoubtedly her prior tomboy habits facilitated her assumption of the paternal role, as did her guilt about her death wishes for her father at the time. She protected herself against the loss. She wasn't really allowed to mourn by entrancing and reinforcing an identification that was already strongly established. Having lost her father, she became her father eventually, working three jobs at once, caring for her younger siblings, and making household decisions. The tomboy orientation seemed to fall away; psychologically, she gave up vying with boys and being "one of the boys" and became the "man of the house."

Her femininity was partially submerged by all this, but gradually, with advancing maturity, the loss of her father was worked through as the need to cling to this paternal identity diminished. With this she began to allow more characteristically feminine aspects of her nature to emerge. These, in fact, had always been present. Recalling her youth, this woman remarked:

> What I wanted was a real frilly bedroom, a canopy bed with real frilly ruffles with eyelets and curtains in layers so they really sit out. What I had were plain curtains, plain bedspread, and a place for dolls. Today the dresses I have tend to be tailored; I don't pick things with lace for outer clothing. My husband bought me a dress with lacy sleeves; I think I've worn it once. But my lingerie and night clothes are frilly.

At this point the investigator remarked, "There seems to be a difference between the outer garments and the private or home or inner garments." The subject replied, "I hold my own better and defend my view better in my professional life; in my married life I took on my mother's role entirely—submissive."

Another subject had grown up in her grandmother's home in a rural Black community in the South. When she began to approach her teens, her mother brought her to the city to live. She described some of her experience as follows:

> As I got a little older, I kind of got interested in—well, when you get into junior high, you see other girls, you feel something within, you want to attract the attention of the opposite sex, you begin to want to look and act a little different. I would hear older girls discussing boyfriends and would wonder how it would feel if I could do these things. I got a feeling that I wasn't a tomboy—that I wanted to grow up, experience different things. I was around 12 when I went to join my mother in the city. I had started to change a little before; when I came to the city people were different; they were dressed different. My mother would tell us different things to wear; it was different from people in the country. I fell in line, began to pick up city ways, to make a change. But I didn't quit playing baseball and basketball, sometimes tennis. I would go to different dances at night and to the recreation center during the day; there was quite a bit of game playing.

Here again the transition in development that comes with puberty parallels the changes in location and lifestyle this girl encountered. A new caretaker, new "city ways," new peers, new school—a host of new possibilities, without understanding at the moment, that she had to cope with the many new emergents within. But through it all she kept a certain basic solidity, one foot firmly placed in each developmental camp—the recreation center during the day and the dances at night.

On the other hand, the environment can produce relatively few changes. There is always the move to junior high; in effect that is a given, at least for the majority. But for many youngsters the transformations of the time come chiefly from within. They come from a sense of many differences, from a series of visible, palpable, sensuous alterations of body contours, from a new meaningful excitement in response to the presence of male peers, from a different mode and manner of response to the new selves, by the social surroundings, from their greater height, and by the sense of competence that heightened intellectual and emotional capacities bring. There are to be many ways to respond to such changes, and much depends on prior experience, characteristic defense modes, and the like. In the following instance the major tactic was denial:

> I don't think I was very aware of the changes. It's not as though I woke up and decided to wear dresses. I never did decide to wear dresses. When I started to menstruate I became aware that there was a definite difference between my brothers and myself and that this was part of being female. But the transition was so gradual that I didn't even realize what was happening. I was still pretty athletic at 12 and 13; I didn't change that much. I still liked pants better than dresses. I started thinking of myself as female as opposed to a person. My body was changing, and I was inundated by talk of being a young lady. The courses at school dealt with cooking, sewing, stuff like that. I didn't think about the changes, only in retrospect. I probably connected with the things I saw in adults. Females were not stronger and were less athletic. I think I thought that I was out of the neuter period and that this was going to happen to me too. In retrospect I probably resented it. But instead of being in an all-male environment I was suddenly in an all-female environment. I was still in a viable competitive plane with females in tennis and basketball. Nobody expected a short girl like me to be able to play ball, and I always got a kick out of the fact that I could do it. I grew 5 inches in 1 year between seventh and eighth grades. Finally, I fit into regular uniforms. I remember feeling pretty good about it. I suppose there are things that aren't considered feminine that I still do, like ride a motorcycle. My wardrobe is more neuter than feminine; I don't know if this has to do with kinds of fashion or what. I still like comfortable things—probably that means loose, not binding. From childhood I remember boys were steered toward and bought certain things. They were expected to be useful, to be daddies and husbands. Girls likewise; I guess I didn't fit the role of the mommy, mother, housewife. I don't

think that if I do have children it will be in the role of mommy, suburbs, parties. I think if I ever do have children they will have a very interesting life. So far I haven't decided if I feel the need to. If I do have a child, I'd like to live on a sailboat again. It would be neat to raise a child on a sailboat. I lived on one from age 21 to 26. They're wonderful. I have five hangers for my wardrobe; it kind of pacifies you spiritually. You get rid of things that are clutter. In sailing, everybody's survival depends on everybody else. Duties are split up equally; gender issues disappear. I don't think of it as a male or female sport.

This is not an unfamiliar theme: to have gender issues disappear. A number of girls, while tomboys, expressed this preference for the neuter. It became and remained a continuing element in this personal value set. They wanted to be neither mannish nor feminine, simply to be human without and striking gender markings. This should not be misconstrued as a simple screen for more complex feelings of one kind or another. There may indeed be defensive components to this position with underlying conflicts about activity and passivity or about castration and penis envy. Indeed, to the psychoanalyst, many such indications are readily discerned. Functionally, however, this sense of the neuter is a working characteriologic position. It is clear, conscious, and comfortable; it is part of the adult's personal sense of self, and it functions as the gender framework from within which one looks out at the world.

It stands in marked contrast to some of the alternative positions adopted by other women as they went through puberty and integrated these anomalous gender positions. In particular, several subjects maintained a sense of dual gender possibility. It were as though the tomboyish stance was set within a larger framework of feminine adaptation and remained as a valued resource during subsequent development. In effect, these women could employ and enjoy both types of experience and use them as they deemed best.

Let us consider a developmental course that pursued such a dual style of adaptation, where the two gender possibilities were valued and cultivated and preserved:

From 6 to 11 I was more tomboyish, more rugged than the other girls. I never felt discriminated against. There were one or two girls who were very feminine, and there was a part of me that wanted that. That was a tough time. I felt like a tomboy in the group. I didn't say so, but there were times when I felt awkward, ill at ease. I wanted to be more feminine than I was. I never felt sad about it. I felt I had enough femininity in me, but there was some envy. They were quieter; I was noisier, always moving around. They were more passive, more sedate, more giggly. I'd envy their comfort in wearing dresses all the time; I'd have to put on jeans to feel totally me. Wearing a dress has a more passive, womanly style to it. Puberty wasn't painful. I began to develop breasts and wear a bra at 11 or 12. I was getting into puberty, into adolescence. The good parts of the tomboyish part, like being active, independent, doing things girls wouldn't do—those remained. But now I wasn't competing with boys anymore; I wanted to enjoy my femininity. Those years—12, 13—were some of the happiest in my life. I didn't have any problem with being a tomboy. I liked it. It didn't bother me, and I didn't feel like it was so extreme that it denied me femininity. I felt as though I knew how to relate to boys by being this way.

What was the difference?

The tree climbing, athletics, swinging on vines, competing with boys. I recall wanting to hit a fly ball in softball. I wanted to be as good as the boys were—to have the power. To be a girl was to be like my mother: dominated. If I could compete with and be like boys then I wasn't dominated. I'd thus gain power, control. It wasn't for popularity; it was to gain control over my life, to not be like my mother. I was very much a girl, yet in certain ways I felt akin to boys. I have always felt very capable and independent and strong emotionally; I hated feeling in any way helpless or dependent on others. I thought of girls as less independent, as sissies, less than what they could be. The passivity, letting someone take charge of your life, not standing up and fighting back, thinking for yourself—I abhorred that. When I got into puberty I was boy crazy. I had lots of boyfriends and their kind of power. I could give up the power of competition for the power of seduction—never toward boys my own age but always toward those two or three grades older. In high school I dated only college boys. I enjoyed the control over boys; I enjoyed the intimacy, the closeness. I had lovely sexual fantasies. Once I got into college—and left home—I was nominated for beauty contests. I said, "I do have the power," and I recall warning myself that if I got too carried away with power I'd never be close to anybody.

Yet another subject spoke of her tomboy proclivities gradually diminishing as she went into puberty, only to "flare up" periodically later in her life.

A lot of it seemed related to where I was in terms of my surroundings. The more I was outdoors—during the summer, in camp settings, or near the woods, which is my love, I had a kind of flare-up. About 11 years ago we purchased a piece of woodland in Pennsylvania, and that's when my active pursuits, my inappropriate activities, flared again.

She went on to relate that she had been living a quiet suburban existence, the wife of a professional, raising two daughters, until they had purchased this woodland lot in the mountains. She was then possessed by a construction demon. She sought out the heaviest possible tasks: dug the foundation, poured concrete, laid pipe, put up walls, did the brick work, put in the electrical system, and on and on—the more massive task the better. She did this with such passion that she would work 10 hours at a stretch without a break until her daughters would literally drag her away and make her eat something. She thus built their country house, largely with her own hands. She then added that in the course of this, and other tasks, she has acquired an extraordinary wardrobe of clothes: all kinds of boots for roofing, for working in water, for indoor painting, for outdoor construction; all kinds of overalls and pants and jackets for wet work, for foundation work, for finishing operations. It is this curious blend of the feminine orientation for wardrobe and the powerful appear of masculine tasks that characterize her way of integrating these elements.

In short, the tomboyish factor is not a passing phase; it is a fundamental element in gender organization, it persists well into adulthood, and it plays a profound role in determining the variety of femininity a particular woman achieves.

Chapter 13

The effects of trauma on the development of self-destructiveness in adolescence

INTRODUCTION

Yari Gvion and Alan Apter

Joseph Noshpitz's theory and his way of conceptualizing the processes involved have evolved over many years, particularly in relation to the treatment of a number of difficult and resistant patients. The type of patient Noshpitz was particularly concerned with in the following chapter is the sort of youngster who appears to be unwilling or unable to recognize an "inner demon," an unconscious critic within, that is manifested by self-destructive behavior. In putting forward his ideas, generated from years of clinical practice and consulting in a drug rehabilitation center for teenagers, Noshpitz uses a developmental perspective that derives from the psychoanalytic writings of Sigmund Freud, Otto Kernberg, Edith Jacobson, and Margaret Mahler.

Noshpitz approaches the well-trodden subject of self-destruction and offers us fresh insights from his long clinical experience with patients suffering from this disorder. In the center of his theory on self-destruction, he emphasizes the term *negative ego ideal*—a presence of "a central self-destructive moiety which acts to shape" and to direct the lives of those people who suffer so much. This element in the character structure of these patients is described in clinical and theoretical developmental terms with special address to its behavioral aspects: "a chronic low-grade sense of inner malaise, a tendency to self-blame for whatever is wrong with family and close friends, feelings of alienation from the larger society around them, behavioral provocativeness in the service of seeking the relief that punishment brings, recurrent gestures of self-mutilation, frequent involvement with cults of devil worship and a record of multiple antisocial acts" (1994).

As therapists working with disturbed adolescents, we can appreciate how the frame of thinking that Noshpitz puts forward helps to understand the origin of their difficulties, to contain transference and countertransference situations, and to enable attenuation of the suffering and destructiveness that those patients put upon themselves. We would like here to elaborate more on the meaning and origin of that negative ideal, which is so vividly explained by Noshpitz.

Idealization and its relation to trauma is seen by Noshpitz as the key factor to explain development of the negative self. But if we look at the formation of early human attachment, we will realize how important idealization is in the enhancement of attachment. Young infants perceive their caregiver as something larger than life; it is typical for mothering persons to idealize infants in a somewhat similar fashion. But basic to it all is the quality of so investing perceptions with positive emotion that the process of perception as such is distorted. Idealization is in effect a misperception. By the same token for babies, this preverbal kind of emotional surge can have an equally powerful sweep in a negative direction, when they experience rejection, rough handling, neglect, or abuse. Also, where the fit of temperament and interaction between infants and their mothering person is a bad one, children will have more frustrating and intensely negative and destructive experiences than gratifying ones. As infants develop, what emerges then are two sets of internalized presence: a positive one allowing self-love; and a negative one mandating self-attack and destruction. On these two, subsequent positive and negative experiences are overlaid. "The positive group becomes the ego ideal, the cluster of idealized internalizations that gives rise to an inner state of self-worth, self-respect, self-confidence, and a sense of feeling good about oneself and about the world." However, "the negative array functions to condemn the self, to criticize blame and threaten to forbid any sense of success or happiness, to lower self esteem in every possible way and to create an internal milieu colored by shame, guilt and to seek at once atonement and punishment in order to obtain relief" (Noshpitz, unpublished paper).

The negative and positive inner images persist as relatively distinct function clusters, which never fuse or unite and remain separate within the dynamic and fluid structural configuration of personality. In time, they come to serve as "two great regulators of inner experience, the nuclei of the superego." On the one hand, we have a vision of our noble motivations, inspiring values; on the other hand, we have awareness of the "dark side of humanity—the evil, wicked and demonic." As such, their power to lead us, motivate us, and modulate our behavior is of considerable proportions. When infants' experiences are more gratifying than overwhelming and destructive, the negative ideal will be present but not dominant. It will make its presence felt as conscience. Alternatively, if there are more negative than positive elements present during the early months (e.g., neglect, immature mother, nonfit of temperament between the mothering caregiver and the infant), then the ideals structures that are laid down will have a predominantly negative cast. The dominant ideal will be negative.

After elaborating on the formation of the two self-ideals, Noshpitz turns to describe the next possible development of the superego—the time of adolescence. As is commonplace observation, adolescence is seen as a great epoch for ideal formation in the human life cycle. Cognitive advances and abstract thinking offer grounds for development and for feelings of grandiosity and uniqueness. Youngsters begin to indulge in fantasies about romantic achievements. But, by the same token, the negative ideal develops and might echo feelings of devaluation, worthlessness, shame, and guilt. The negative self might assault the self, forbidding any sexual temptation with greater tendency toward self-punitive positions, so that teenagers become ascetic or tinged with guilt. Noshpitz describes alternative situations where the positive ideal has had less adequate development and instead the negative ideal holds sway: "The negative ideal might work quietly and indirectly; directly by a steady series of inner messages which tell the youngster that he or she is not worth anything. Indirectly they do things that harm them. Conduct disorder, drug abuse, or losing their job, causing the world to harass and reject them."

Noshpitz's dynamic formulation of self-destructive personality helps us to better understand the effects of trauma on the development of self-destruction in adolescence. The similarity between the thoughts of self-torment that occur after being exposed to a traumatic event and the self-tormented thoughts of self-destructive ideal indulging is an important step for understanding the self-inflicted pain of adolescents who are subject to self-destructive behavior. As Noshpitz writes, "Given the inner turmoil and the immature state of the self regulatory apparatus of the adolescent, it is obvious that for young victims of traumatic circumstance, the coping apparatus that would attempt to abate and contain the intensity of the initial reaction, and the inner assault that might follow, is not yet at its mature adult state. Accordingly, adolescents will be particularly prone to move into self-destructive states."

The negative ideal takes up the pain and the humiliation and the fear associated with the stressful experience and make it part of the negative regulating agency. Any traumatic experience acts to reinforce the negative ideal: "The response to trauma is to swallow it in, whole or in part. It is not the trauma itself that does the damage. It is the inner state of the individual to begin with, the degree of demonification added to the image of the experience."

No doubt, Noshpitz's ideas contribute to the understanding of adolescent problem behaviors such as truancy, substance abuse, high risk or early onset of sexual activity, and delinquency. As therapists working with youth we know how frequently they co-occur. The issues that

Noshpitz addresses will be familiar to most therapists. He offers his readers a way of thinking about the clinical situation in which they are engaged and in which they are often stuck with the possibility of enabling movement and change to take place. Many of the readers will probably think Noshpitz describes our patients so well, and maybe sometimes we will also recognize ourselves in his writings.

References

Noshpitz, J. D. (1994). Self-destructiveness in adolescence. *American Journal of Psychotherapy*, 48, 3.

THE EFFECTS OF TRAUMA ON THE DEVELOPMENT OF SELF-DESTRUCTIVENESS IN ADOLESCENCE

Joseph D. Noshpitz

The nature of trauma is to stamp the perceptual and emotional world of the victim with a sense of helplessness and badness. This impression is powerful and of catastrophic intensity; it is not easily eradicated or abandoned. However, it is metabolized in time along with a variety of different channels.

One of the strange discoveries of those who have studied trauma is that some individuals seem to get over the event and to go back to more or less normal living. They do not recall the particular happenings with equanimity; the sense of the badness of what has happened remains, but the intensity and any distortion of their inner lives or of their interpersonal relationships are simply not evident. They seem merely to have a bad memory that they are able to recall on demand but that does not intrude into the consciousness. In contrast, there are those whose lives are haunted by the traumatic sequence thereafter, who cannot cease dwelling on it, whose lives are changed in critical ways because of it, and who, in effect, "never get over it." What then makes for the difference?

One commonplace observation is that it is precisely those victims of trauma who have been sensitized, as it were, by prior bad experiences who are likely to be more reactive and more vulnerable in the face of subsequent onslaughts. A person with an early history of abandonments, perhaps in the preschool years, might, in adolescence, be the more readily crushed by some later rejection by an important object. When it occurs, that is intuitively understandable; often enough, however, there is no definite history of such early trauma to explain what has happened. Obviously if we seek a more general explanation we have to look elsewhere.

One peculiar aspect of posttraumatic reactions is that they are a form of self-torment. Individuals who have gone through these terrible experiences have somehow managed to internalize it, to carry it away from the time and the place of the event, and to make it part of their psyche. It were as though there was a site in the psychic organization where such things get established and where they remain more or less active thereafter. It is not intuitively self-evident why this should be so. On the face of it, it would seem more likely that such bad experiences would be expelled from these individuals' minds. If they, in fact, survived the awful event, there should be some ridding mechanism to disencumber them of this dreadful experience and to allow them to go forward in their life free and clear. Instead, for the vulnerable, at any rate, the mind seems to pick up on the troublesome reaction—the catastrophic humiliation, the freezing terror, the suffocating helplessness, the agonizing awareness, the overwhelming menace, whatever its character—and to keep it in place, to return to it again and again, to be accosted by it, to have it recur in dreams and flashbacks. What good does it do?

The usual sociobiological explanation is that this can have survival value. If something is that threatening, then one must learn to avoid it; this post-traumatic reaction, then, is a way of driving home the avoidance message.

Let us imagine a scene that takes place some 2 million years ago. A young humanoid is playing with some sticks at the foot of a tree. Although he hears nothing, some tremor in the ground causes him to look up, and there, bounding toward him, is a huge saber-toothed cat. There is time for one second of freezing horror, and then, just as the cat pounces, the arboreal mother swoops up her baby and swarms up the tree, her back racked by claws, but alive—and with her young one intact. What does the baby carry away from the event?

Creatures whose genetic constitution was such that they were deeply impressed by threats to survival would have a more intense reaction that those who did not respond as vigorously. Presumably, after one exposure, the young prehuman would have learned his lesson. That particular threat would never again be allowed to happen. Perhaps it would be endlessly alert, always scanning for danger. Perhaps he would avoid any free-standing trees, or that particular kind of tree, or that part of the savannah in general. In short, the former near-victim would run in a panic from anything that was even a little suggestive of the original source of danger. In the long run, however, uncomfortable and haunted by memories that particular strain of prehuman might be, his particular disposition would make for greater survival efficiency. As a consequence, more of that lineage would survive and reproduce, and, over the millennia, the trait of being very reactive to threats and retaining such impressions for a lifetime would persist.

Indeed, that kind of explanation might account for some of this phenomenology. But the constant revisiting on oneself of the pain of the trauma, the wretched nightmares that can ensue, the recurrent flashbacks that thrust themselves into awareness even when not evoked by a suggestive circumstance, the interference with the smooth functioning of the cognitive apparatus that is sometimes part of the picture—none of these would seem to be functionally useful. Instead, they have the character of a self-punitive mechanism. Individuals assail themselves over and over after they have already been all too maltreated by the course of their life experience. Why do that?

There is an additional possible explanation that seems to me to fit in all too well with certain propensities of the human psyche. In brief, I suggest that what has been an ego problem, a survival issue, has become a superego problem, a matter of conscience. Let me expand on this in greater detail.

We are accustomed to think of the superego as composed of two primary constituents: an ego ideal and conscience. Peculiarly enough, we are not too clear about the nature of the conscience. The ego ideal has had a good deal of attention paid to it and has been studied extensively. The conscience, however, seems to be more or less taken for granted as a sort of special part of the ego (a step in the ego as Sigmund Freud once called it), one that assails the ego when it disobeys its dictates or departs from the model of the ego ideal. This seems to me to be an insufficient explanation for so critical a part of mind. I would therefore suggest that the superego is consistent in its structure; it is composed entirely of ideal entities, and there is therefore both a positive ego ideal and a negative one. Like all ideal structures, both the positive and the negative ego ideals tend to be unrealistic; indeed, it is one of the important goals of development to tame and to shape these ideal structures toward an ever more realistic configuration. When the positive ideal does not become tempered in this way, it remains perfectionist and even grandiose all the lifetime through, and especially so in adolescence. The same holds true for the negative ideal. Its message is just the opposite to that of the positive ideal. Its function is to carp, to criticize, to humiliate, and to injure; to challenge any feeling of confidence, to decry achievement, and to devalue and success the ego might experience. It acts to drive the ego toward a subjective sense of misery and an objective attainment of failure. In its extreme form, it is the essence of self-destructiveness. It seems altogether unnatural to think of such a factor as being present in the organization of the human psyche. Nonetheless, in a great many people, it is demonstrably present.

It is important to recognize that there is something within all of us that does not want to think that we harbor a nucleus of self-destruction. That seems too sick, so foreign to a healthy-minded outlook. Yet even brief reflection informs us that a great many people are their own worst enemy, that it is all too common to find situations where people put their worst foot forward often when they are trying to show themselves at their best, that many people seem to act against their own best interests even while bemoaning the fate that dogs them at every turn, and that everything from girls clinging to abusive boyfriends to those of high IQ who do not live up to their potential to youngsters who assert that their way of life will inevitably lead to an early death all adhere tenaciously to the very source of their pain and destruction.

I submit that these are best accounted for by regarding the superego as containing sort of inner demon, a negative ideal that seeks to achieve just the failure and suffering that so many people put themselves through. One might well ask: If this is such a common presence and touches the lives of so many people, why then is it not evident? Why do we not recognize it as part of what we in mental health deal with? This is indeed an important question, and the answer is twofold.

To begin with, one of the problems with studying this element of mind is that it does not allow itself to become known. It does not welcome exploration. Indeed, asking patients to look at where the negative messages are coming from, where the impulse to do the self-destructive thing arises, turns out to be like asking them to look into the sun without dark glasses. They cannot do it easily; it is simply too uncomfortable. Indeed, some young patients know all too well that they harbor such a presence; they can feel it, they can see it in the way they function. If they try to do the right thing, "something" stops them, something blocks them. They may start out at a job or a school semester and initially do well, but then, "somehow," they start to mess up, to spoil the promise of their initial success. In a vague, amorphous way, they are aware of this negative nucleus within that prevails again and again over their best efforts to achieve a course correction. But it remains forever vague; they cannot get a grip on it—or, for that matter, a glimpse of it. It is there, but it is known by its effects rather than by its structure or content.

That is one part of the twofold answer. The other part is that those who would help them, be they clergy or mental health specialists, cannot bring themselves to think in such terms. An analogy would be the attempt on Freud's part to introduce the death instinct into psychoanalysis. At the time he undertook to do this, psychoanalysis was already quite well developed, and there were many people around Freud who had come to adopt his methods and his theories and to value his thinking. But when it came to this, they could not go along with him. The notion of a self-destructive element within personality just does not get heard of, or, if heard, does not get accepted. It is antithetical to the basic nature of the approaches people within this group of disciplines prefer. It is an inherently dismal notion, and, I venture to predict, it will never be a popular kind of theory.

If, however, despite our native inclinations, we do face this issue, we presently find that it allows us a somewhat different way of accounting for the nature of the effects of trauma. Because once we accept the fact that such a self-destructive ideal is present, then we can readily see that when youngsters are subjected to catastrophic stress, this part of the self takes up the pain and the humiliation and the fear associated with the stressful experience and makes it part of the negative regulating agency. Within the superego, the facts of the traumatic encounter get reinterpreted. Whatever happened is their fault. If they were abandoned, it was because they were such an unlovable child. If they survived when another was killed or injured, it was because they were somehow at fault: The wrong person got hurt; they should have acted to prevent, should have taken a different seat in the car, or called for help earlier, or, in general, whatever it is that went wrong, they should have comported themselves differently. For some youngsters, for example, learning about a previous pregnancy their mother had that resulted in a stillbirth, or in a baby who died in infancy, becomes, in itself, a source of unease. Why did that one die while I lived? Was that fair? Am I getting away with something? Is it something I did wrong? This is sometimes spoken of as survivor guilt, but it is part of a much more fundamental disorder: the dominance of the negative ideal and its absorption of traumatic experience into itself as another means by which to flail away at the self. Only by understanding this component of the experience can we can make any sense of so many of the paradoxical effects of trauma on adolescents.

The peculiar transformations of the superego in adolescence are the next area for exploration. The changes occur in several areas. For the positive ideal, the very addition of the cognitive advances of puberty offers grounds for a special kind of elation. The ability to think abstractly (which opens up at about age 11 and progresses thereafter until the mid-teens) allows youngsters to "see" things that were heretofore hidden, to understand things that were previously inscrutable, and to grasp nuances and distinctions that had never before been registered as such. This is an enormous gift and may contribute to the sense of arrogance and hauteur that some adolescents assume. After all, they have now "caught on" to what is happening around them, they are no longer children, they are fully aware of what goes on, they are "in the know." It is not remarkable that a certain modicum of grandiosity should so often ensue. Moreover, they are all at once biologically potent and fertile, no small addition to their arrays of personal attributes. And all this without even mentioning the increased richness of emotional awareness, the intensity of passionate responsiveness, the increased capabilities to love and to hate that seem so suddenly to be there. Indeed, they have strong grounds for feeling enriched and unique—and grandiose.

At the same time, however, the negative ideal is developing as well. There is a great surge in these youngsters' capacity for gloom and for feeling left out and worthless. There is an awareness of the loss of childhood, a loss of a certain quality of friendship that was for so long their given way of live. They cannot sit on adults' laps, cannot be tucked in at night. There are so many things that they formerly could do that are no longer seemly. Never again can they role-play in quite the same way, never again be a cowboy, a princess, or play house as they did before; life is abruptly more complicated than that. Things are easier, perhaps, for youngsters oriented toward sports activities, be they baseball or gymnastics, or toward music or dance or some other involvement that is continuous between latency and adolescence. But for many children, there is a more or less abrupt cut from the world of childhood and no small sense of loss.

Then there is the reawakening of the set of oedipal preoccupations that are carried upward with the biological changes of puberty. Both sexuality and aggression well up to altogether new levels, never previously experienced as such in the life cycle. The positive ego ideal begins to indulge in fantasies about conquests and romantic achievements; various external personages are turned to as ideal romantic objects. Crushes are rampant, and numerous attempts are made to seek an ideal other among the persons in these youngsters' immediate surroundings. Meanwhile, the negative ideal is also emboldened. Now it has new grounds for assaulting the self. The very hint of incestuous fantasy is fiercely condemned. For youngsters with greater tendencies toward self-punitive, self-denunciatory positions, this is carried to the extreme of rejecting all sexual temptations and turning ascetic. For others, all sexuality, while not rejected, is nonetheless tinged with guilt. Masturbation, with its barely concealed oedipal images, adds to this burden. All sorts of compromise formations ensue, with forms as various as humanity itself.

Even more serious, however, is the emergence of new levels of rage and hostility. Parents are astonished when the heretofore gentle youngsters "blow up"—often for seemingly trivial reasons. They may storm about the house mouthing denunciations of the "I hate everybody" variety. Wild accusations are thrown about, seemingly from nowhere. The ordinarily peaceful tone of everyday living becomes charges and disrupted. And it all makes no sense; there is no evident reason for all the carrying on. Parents comfort themselves by saying that their teens are "going through a stage." This is true enough, but we need to ask ourselves: What is this stage all about, and why does it take the form it takes? Obviously many elements determine this kind of behavior.

Some are, of course well known and frequently described. There is the second individuation stage, as Peter Blos has called it—"the need of the adolescent to seek autonomy and begin to find an identity" (1962). After all, one of the simplest ways of separating from someone is to disagree with him or her. Or, if necessary, take it a step further and challenge the person, prove he or she is wrong. Obviously a more wholesome way of asserting the uniqueness of these adolescents' identity is to find their own way, their own interests, their own form of expression, and, eventually, their own new attachments. The new identity configurations they are trying on are often fragile and tentative. They are all too readily swallowed up by the firmer and more developed adult presences; the youngsters must work overtime to maintain them. They may require brash assertiveness to shore the up when they are so unsure of themselves. Or they may be played out in endless fantasy that is sedulously protected from adult awareness.

In any case, there are strong reasons for a certain amount of grit in the intrafamilial relationships at this time of life. But the matter has deeper roots still. The reawakened oedipal drives are not merely erotic yearnings but are aggressive ones as well. The need to remove the rival is an inherent component of this complex; it is both a love triangle and a hate triangle, and in puberty the hatred is swept toward the surface as surely as is the love. Youngsters are menaced from within both by incestuous wishes and violent destructive impulses toward one parent or the other. These, in turn, act to trigger the superego structures that had been developed in large measure to contain and limit just such a development. To protect the self from the shame and self-loathing that attend such forbidden yearnings, both are displaced away from their original objects. Few adolescent boys, for example, kill their fathers and mate with their mothers, but many such youths seek love interests away from the home and become competitive—and sometimes combative—toward other young men. Many girls seek to be attractive and popular and are jealous if their boyfriends favor other girls. A host of sublimations for rage are always available, such as academic competitions, business rivalries, debates, sports challenges, attachment to a political movement (which pits the youth against existing institutions), even mountain climbing (where the opponent to be subdued is the mountain). In some of the more primitive and antisocial business rivalries such as drug vending, the enactment of murderous impulses is rampant. (Albeit not a very elegant form of sublimation, at least it is not direct parricide.) By and large, where the basic self-love of the ego ideal has been adequately maintained, where that aspect of superego structure is dominant, most of the tension of this work is handled through the sublimations and displacements of the affects, and the home environment is spared much of the sharp edge of these feelings.

There is, however, the alternative situation, the one where the positive ego ideal has had less adequate development and where, instead, the negative ideal holds sway. With this, quite a different family picture emerges. The negative ideal works quietly and is usually not visible as such, but its presence can be discerned by its effects. It works both directly and indirectly: directly by a steady series of inner messages telling the youngsters that they are not worth anything, are soiled, will never amount to anything, deserve to get nothing out of life, and probably will not live very long. Thus, again and again, as researchers study the behavior of antisocial youths, they remark on the ubiquity of "low self-esteem," the characteristic finding that these youngsters often seem to hate themselves or, at best, manifest a radically devalued image of themselves. Indeed, there is much to suggest that one of the vectors driving their antisocial and destructive acts is the wish to get caught and punished, even to get killed. In perpetrating their social malfeasance, these teenagers keep pecking away at society until it strikes back. They expose themselves to various dangers and, often enough, pay the price in the form of arrests and incarcerations. In some of the more severe instances, they act out a pattern of seeking destruction at the hands of others, and all too often they succeed in their search—and pay for it with their lives. For the most part, however, things are not carried to that extreme; what these boys and girls do, however, is, in effect, to mess up their lives. They thrust themselves into every kind of trouble they can get close to. At home they are impossible and are invited to leave—or sometimes physically thrown out. They provoke the school authorities and typically are suspended or dismissed before their education is complete— often before it is well advanced. They get a job, and presently their employers discover they are being angrily confronted or that money is gone from the till—and they lose job after job. They cheat on their lovers, tease their friends, and make their neighbors uncomfortable. They are in a constant state of causing the world to turn on them, harass them, or reject them; they express bitterness, cynicism, and chronic rage and reject the overtures of those who would try to help them. They are, in short, victims of their own self-hatred.

To be sure, this description fits the more severe cases, the small minority of teenagers who are overtly antisocial. The much larger proportion of this cohort does not conduct themselves in a manner that is so flagrantly disruptive. Nonetheless, however, they do betray a good deal of evidence of the presence of the negative ideal. To understand this, it is important to grasp that the ideal formations that comprise the superego are in fact regulating mechanisms. They set the tone for personality, they establish its goals, and they define its limits. They are not coextensive with ego functions, but they tell such functions as the defenses and identity formation agencies of the ego who to be and how to be. It is in the crucible of interaction with these ideals that the functional regulation of the self takes place. Where the positive ideal is preponderant, youngsters feel self-confident, sure of themselves, worthwhile, and tend to expect good from their world. There is an inner core of self-valuation that remains steadfast throughout life's vicissitudes. Under such circumstances, the negative ideal is by no means absent, but it does not set the tone for everyday experience. It may come prominently into view in the face of some temptation or act of violation of their inner standards. In effect, it functions as a normal conscience; it is known about only when something stirs it to activity. In terms of the existing dynamic equilibrium, the positive ideal is the more dominant of the two.

Trauma, however, can change the equilibrium. The traumatic experience acts, in effect, to reinforce the negative ideal. The inner confidence that characterized these individuals' everyday state is shattered. The dynamic equilibrium has shifted, and now the negative ideal predominated. The self feels the burden with exquisite intensity. Self-feeling is regulated now not by the previous overseer; instead, a new landlord has taken over the property, and new rules are in place. The tone of personality is different. There is a morbid, grayish tinge to the sense of self. Unpleasant memories or fantasies thrust themselves unpredictably into consciousness. The trauma is always at hand; it may intrude at any time. The sense of threat, perhaps in the form of an in-thrust of memory, perhaps in more vague and nonspecific terms, hovers perpetually overhead. The inner confidence is gone; the sureness has given way to doubt and uncertainty. The youths feel stained, sinful, at odds with the world. This may or may not become translated into overt action, but their inner lives are now lived out under a cloud.

People notice the change and remark on it. To traumatized youths, such observations feel like accusations, as though they were comments on their wrongdoing. Presently social patterns are likely to change. Many of the familiar relationships are interrupted; these people would not understand. A pervasive sense of wrongness prevails, as though by having undergone the traumatic experience they have sinned in some indefinable way. Indeed, they have had an enormous boost given to the condemning, self-destructive part of the self, and the ensuing feeling smacks very much of malfeasance. For some young people this leads to a series of atonement reactions; they have to be extra good and ascetic and self-sacrificing. For others it expresses itself in terms of punishment seeking, and they have to be extra bad and actively self-destructive. As noted already, the commonest form this takes is to engage in provocative behavior. These youngsters become difficult, oppositional, irritating, argumentative, and impossible to satisfy. Everything is cause for an argument; they seemingly pick at authority. None of it makes any sense, and the adults eventually shrug their shoulders and comfort one another with accounts of the terrible teens.

What commonly gets lost in all this is the purpose of the behavior. The point of it all is to provoke a punitive response. The only peace these youngsters know comes in the wake of some sort of reaction from the authorities, be they parents, teachers, librarians, or group leaders. And, given the density of adult rules that wrap youth around in so complex a society as our own, there is plenty of opportunity to defy and challenge on whatever level they must.

It is commonly assumed that when individuals act against their own best interests, this must be due to masochism, to an attempt to obtain pleasure by experiencing pain. In fact, for the majority of these youngsters, it is not pleasure that drives their behavior; it is, rather, an attempt to relieve pain. This is a very powerful human motive indeed, and when the pain is being generated by inward forces acting on the ego, on the self, then the agony is particularly acute. The hook is in their flesh and cannot be shaken free. It is not an outside issue they can change or from which they can flee. The ego has many resources with which to engage external reality. When the source of the agony is internal, a part of their very own regulatory apparatus, then the problem has quite a different character and takes on a different hue. There is no evading an inner observer, no hiding from an eye that studies their behavior or their motives and, accordingly, every motive, no matter how much they might prefer to deny or dissimulate. In effect, they cannot hide from their own conscience.

The negative superego ideal has a mission: it is intended to hurt, to punish, to destroy. It seizes every possible pretext to do so. The youngsters are buffered against it by the protective function of the positive ego ideal; they can shrug off the accusations and the importuning of the negative inner voice because they have a more forceful sense of their own worth, of feeling worthwhile, of not allowing such brooding thoughts to hold sway. When the positive inner voice is too weak, when it falters, when it can be readily drowned out by the vociferous baying of the other, then they begin to feel the bite of conscience, to get messages that they are unworthy, that they merit suffering, that they do not deserve happiness or success. And in train with that, the promptings come to undo what they may have accomplished, to spoil the good outcome that beckons to them, to abandon the path that takes them forward and go off course onto a destructive byroad.

It is the fact that this is coming from within that so often makes them feel that all is hopeless, that there is no way out. When this mechanism starts into high gear, the young people assail themselves with scathing criticism; they find fault with everything that normally would bring them joy. But as they cast about, some of them do find a way to obtain relief. What they experience is that if they can get the world around them to take up the burden of the assault, to participate in the punishing, to be critical and rejecting, then some of the inner torment relents. They are paying it off. They are able to say, "*You* do not need to torment me; others are doing that. I am suffering; I am in trouble." In that way they can indeed get the inner voice to be still, the pressure to be relieved. Indeed, the more trouble they buy into on the outside, the easier they feel within.

It is here that trauma takes on so major a role in the lives of adolescents. For the traumatized youth is the one who becomes vulnerable to a greatly reinforced sense of inner badness.

References

Blos, P. (1976). *On adolescence: A psychoanalytic interpretation*. New York: Free Press of Glencoe.

Chapter 14

Beyond school

INTRODUCTION

Lawrence Stone

In this chapter, Joseph Noshpitz begins with a brief synopsis of one of our major human concerns regarding the social, emotional, and physical development and well-being of our future generations. He highlights and underscores a "cadre of social problems" related to the plight of the twentieth century: "the child caught up in the throes of poverty." All of the plights he goes on to examine in his outstanding review have true influences and potentially devastating consequences to the future healthy and safe growth of our youth and the security of a meaningful society. Here I must personalize my introduction a little. Noshpitz compares "serious developmental problems with which our society is faced," and he expresses his views as to which of these is the "much graver issue." There are clearly other plights that are and will have important consequential influences on our civilization's development.

Noshpitz was a genuine expert about child development and presented this in his writings, teaching, and practice. He set forth important ideas, views, and opinions that were grounded in comprehensive knowledge about the past, environments of the present, and powerful insights about the future. Rather than enter a debate about his brilliant reflections regarding failing cultures and rather than getting on an intellectual treadmill of hypotheses about their ultimate value toward the improvement and maybe even survival of civilized humans, it seems more rewarding to review all effort being made to synthesize the good from the not good, and productive from nonproductive, the sustainable from those likely to fail.

Societies all over the world are seeing and experiencing human traumas involved in almost every attempt to improve the life in their culture. It seems that almost every societal or group movement toward improving people's quality of life (and even longevity) creates an oppo-site and often more violent or corrupt response.

Noshpitz analyzes and expresses his feelings clearly and expertly about many of the worst human tragedies impacting all human life. In this paper, he presents universal problems of humans trying to thrive in what is becoming a crowded and hostile civilization. Noshpitz, as I knew him, followed a predictable course. He defined failures, elaborated the problems, determined their respective value, generated constructive ideas, gathered information, and reviewed and initiated explorations and investigations. He diligently analyzed all aspects of the processes and the information. Then he put together some far-reaching hypothe-ses about the societal issues of growing up to be healthy and productive in the world today. He promoted grass-roots institutional, intellectual, familial, societal, and individual responsibility, each with a dedication to a response to improve the quality, length, and happiness of people's lives and not to create harm of unhappiness to any. This sounds uto-pian; however, I believe these concepts were the bedrock of his great analytical mind.

When you review this essay, you see that he presents many parts of his vision. You can get a view of other pieces of his genius when you read carefully and completely what he was promoting during his last 50 years. By virtue of his magnificent energy and insights, he played a major part in the journey of child and adolescent psychiatry to join the respected arenas of research and the practice of modern medicine.

While Noshpitz was heavily involved in many pursuits to advance child and adolescent psychiatry, he took on a support and reinforcement role to the academic and practicing child and adolescent psychiatrist. In earlier times those clinicians, researchers, and students were generally looked upon as nonmedical practitioners who were not involved in real medical science. Noshpitz, along with many other distinguished col-leagues, pressed forward a solid foundation for the scientific practice and research of child and adolescent psychiatry. Many of the profound proposals for improvements of our scientific and medical lives had their origins in those early years.

Forthcoming was a period of consolidation for child and adoles-cent psychiatry into the mainstream of institutional medical practice. There followed active evaluations and reviews of institutional, group, and individual dynamics from humanistic and scientific bio–psycho–social perspectives to make serious, far-reaching, and critical decisions to minimize the negatives and accentuate the positives of institutional psychiatric practice. It was the zenith of these years that institutional child and adolescent psychiatry was nationally formalized. With the collaborative efforts of many child and adolescent psychiatrists and institutions, the American Psychiatric Association pulled together and developed and published the *Standards for Psychiatric Facilities Serving Children and Adolescents* in 1971.

Shortly thereafter, an even larger step was taken, and a more significant achievement was accomplished. Comprehensive and applicable standards and survey procedures were developed and implemented by the Joint Commission on Accreditation of Hospitals for Psychiatric Facilitates Serving Children and Adolescents.

It was only a decade later that Noshpitz established a group of his colleagues to collaborate in the development of the gigantic *Basic Handbook of Child and Adolescent Psychiatry* (1979). This was an enormous effort by tireless scholarly colleagues. The focus was on complete encyclopedic descriptions of all psychological, biological, and sociological pathogens, all pathological conditions that affect the lives of any young person, and all known processes of remediation.

During these periods of medical assimilation, another major step was taken to consolidate the science, practice, institutions, and financial aspects of child and adolescent psychiatry. Supported by the determined efforts of Helen Beiser, the American Academy of Child and Adolescent Psychiatry was given a delegates position in the House of Delegates of the American Medical Association in 1985. The academy remains today in the mainstream of medicine.

These are but a few of the historical markers that Noshpitz and colleagues created for the promotion of the total well-being of our young people. After reviewing all of these achievements, I think that he knew that we still have not solved many of our problems with child and adolescent growth and development. He presents in this paper a clear and concise outline for society's consideration. In his "child-rearing center" concept, he elaborates structure, content, and strategies and explains the functions, purposes, and goals of these significant models and ideologies. He is aware of our human tendency to initially oppose and reject most universal recommendations for societal management of young people. It is in fact because of this that his thesis in this paper is so intriguing.

Emilio Dominguez (personal communication), in a thoughtfully constructed critique of Noshpitz's essay, indicated, "My own thought on this very interesting proposal is that it might be a utopia or an impossible dream, but reflecting on today's world, I hope it becomes a reality in this century."

With this hope in mind and Noshpitz's challenging societal reconstruction, I look forward to the demands for improvement created by the knowledge of the traumas of our children and adolescents. In closing I am reminded of an elegant speech delivered by a high school senior after graduation in 1951: "Nor can we live unto ourselves alone. Each person is a part of the larger life stream. No thing that threatens the whole can fail to endanger the part. It is true today, more than ever before" (Butler-Stone, 1951).

References

Accreditation Manual for Psychiatric Facilities. (1972). Accreditation Council for Psychiatric Facilities.

Accreditation Manual for Psychiatric Facilities Serving Children and Adolescents. (1974). Accreditation Council for Psychiatric Facilities. Joint Commission on Accreditation of Hospitals, Chicago: IL.

Butler-Stone, M. (1951). "What Must I Pay for Democracy?" Graduation speech. Robstown High School, Robstown, TX.

Consolidated Standards for Child, Adolescent, and Adult Psychiatric, Alcoholism, and Drug Abuse Programs. (1979). Joint Commission on Accreditation of Hospitals, Chicago, IL.

Standards for Psychiatric Facilities Serving Children and Adolescents. (1971). American Psychiatric Association.

BEYOND SCHOOL

Joseph D. Noshpitz

The problem

One of the great centers of cultural concern in this late part of the twentieth century is the plight of children caught up in the throes of poverty. We know all too well of the stresses that are visited daily on great numbers of such children in the form of parental abuse, sexual exploitation, scenes of family violence, neglect, overstimulation, and a variety of other social ills. Inevitably, as we begin to study the implications of this woeful sequence, compassionate people and social scientists come together to decry the evils of such a systematic destruction of human potential and to report calculations about the enormous expense paid by society for allowing this state of affairs to continue. It is all too evident, and there is an abundance of hard data to demonstrate that this kind of skewed and distorted child rearing will ultimately exact a terrible social price. A host of young people with little capacity for empathy, with blunted human responses, with a totally self-centered outlook, and with profound problems with impulse control, who cannot learn in school, who cannot resist temptations to steal, who lack the ability to put off gratification long enough to take training for a skill of some kind, and whose inner pain is great enough to make addiction a desirable alternative to suffering together form a cadre of social problems that create an atmosphere of danger and degradation for everyone in society.

I do not disagree with this outlook, but I do not agree that this is the most serious developmental problem with which our society is faced. I fear that we have a much graver issue to address. What I perceive to be emerging is a major breakdown in the moral structure of middle-class youth. As a phenomenon, this is quieter, less obvious, and much less dramatic than the dangerous miscreance typical of an inner-city ghetto. Nonetheless, in terms of the average citizen, what this promises is likely to be infinitely more destructive than the worst that the deprived youngsters can bring about.

What we speak of here is the erosion of conscience. Middle-class youths who grow up without an adequate conscience will presently be in a position to deal with far more money and to manipulate far more power than lower-class youngsters are ever likely to get their hands on. Middle-class children can grow up to be a gatekeeper. They are likely to work in a savings and loan institution; they may become stockbrokers; they can become lawyers; conceivably they could enter the employ of accountants or other social guardians. In short, although they may never kill anybody, for society at large, their potential for damage is several orders of magnitude greater than that of lower-class children.

I must confess that I have been appalled by the way our society has responded to the savings and loan crisis. The discussion is always directed toward the amount of money involved, what it will cost the taxpayer, or how the government will handle it. Almost nothing is said about the implications of such a state of affairs for the moral integrity of a whole generation of what should be our best and most trustworthy people. After all, this was not a cabal who acted in a kind of wicked concert; once the controls were off, it was a spontaneous eruption of bad faith by a great many people in responsible positions. Now we hear dark hints that our banks and insurance companies have comported themselves in dubious fashion as well.

Socially speaking this is expensive. Whereas the problems and depredations of the underclass may cost us tens of millions of dollars, the middle-class debacle we now face is costing hundreds of millions and will perhaps cost billions before it is all over. Nor is it just in the financial world that we hear of such events; the fate of so many of our marriages, the litigiousness of our business interactions, and the nature of what is happening to so many of our children from every walk of life bear mute but radical testimony to the state of our interpersonal affiliations and commitments. It may seem to be a considerable leap to translate that into child-rearing issues, but I think there is much to suggest that, in very significant degree, this is what it comes down to.

In short, I see us as having not only a problem with underclass children and families; I see us as having a national problem involving all our children. Indeed, I wonder sometimes whether the very emphasis we place on poverty-stricken children and deprived families does not serve to help us avoid looking at the much more widespread and potentially more serious difficulties of our middle-class youth. To translate that into our parochial terms, what I speak of here is the emergence of severe personality disorder as a major social issue of our times. This kind of emergent is formed in the crucible of development as surely as is the personality of the dangerous mugger. Hence, if we are to begin to think of solutions, we had best consider how to address the children of the country at large rather than to focus on only one group.

I must confess that I say this with fear and trembling. I would do nothing to diminish the effort and enthusiasm of so many dedicated and self-sacrificing people in their magnificent efforts to bring help to those impoverished children in such great distress. I would not wish that my observations be used as an excuse to deny funds or support of any kind to the many inner-city sites where it is so desperately needed. I would hope instead that more widespread and vigorous efforts be made on behalf of all children, for, as I perceive it, the need is even more general (if not as overt) than it is usually considered to be. In brief, most of our children are in trouble.

Of course, the problem with personality disorder is that it has none of the self-evident quality of the more obvious disturbances of conduct. A child's development must be followed closely to become aware of what is happening. But at this epoch of our history, it is the most common form of psychiatric disturbance, and we have no choice I believe but to seek to forge instrumentalities that can come to grips with it—or, more efficient still, to find ways to deal with these conditions while they are still unformed and just coming into being and to head them off before they can burgeon and take their full form. It is with that in mind that these suggestions are offered.

The family

Thus far, little has been said about the family. It is not an easy area to work in. One of our most treasured cultural myths is the notion of the happy family that functions well and supportively for its members and that is solicitous and devoted to its children. Such families do indeed exist, but they comprise probably not more than a fifth of our demographic reality. On the other end of the spectrum, another fifth is so grossly pathological as scarcely to be recognizable as a family at all. In between are a great mass of divorced families, single-parent households, reconstituted families, gay families, people just living together and incidentally having children, where the involved adults are more or less neurotic, more or less troubled, more or less effective as parents. In short, given the nature of late twentieth century Western society, the average family can raise children who will not need institutionalization, but it cannot protect them from a high rate of drug and alcohol abuse, troubled work careers, broken marriages, discomfort in interpersonal interactions, and the ravages of all too much personal unhappiness. Little by little we are learning that the family as child rearer is an unpredictable factor and that too many children are coming away from their stressed homes with patterns of inner discomfort and interpersonal unreadiness and are then unable to cope with the demands of the larger society that awaits them. Many, perhaps most, of these children need far more help than the average family seems able to offer them. The youngsters have trouble learning, relating themselves to others, and, in all too many instances, finding even that minimum modicum of inner peace that would allow for health and even for survival.

Nor is all this inevitable. We live in a time when child development is better understood than ever before and when the promise of the neurosciences is gradually coming to be realized in remarkable ways. The problem becomes one of getting this knowledge delivered to the families and children, not merely made available to them but actually brought to bear on their lives in systematic, functional, and efficient fashion. No ready mechanism is available for doing this.

Meanwhile, a devil's brew of social dislocations has been making it harder and harder for many parents to rear their children. Family fragmentation, family moves, loss of the extended family network, new social expectations, grandparents who live longer and who sometimes become major burdens, chronic economic stress requiring that both parents work, changes in cultural values in areas as fundamental as abortion, sexuality, religion, sexually transmitted diseases, feminism, and on and on all have combined to pose many families confusing, unexpected, and often enough unresolvable problems. Not unexpectedly, people turned to their children's school for help with the children's difficulties. But the current school system was never designed for many of these roles and has proved a weak reed on which to rely for their fulfillment. Something different is necessary. In brief, would suggest that a new institution arise, one that for the moment, I call a child-rearing center. For, as I see it, this is the great need of our time.

As I envisage it, such a center implies what this essay began with: a whole new quality of relationship between society and the family. As it now stands, the existing relationship between the family and the state is to say the least ambiguous. Theoretically, a man's home is his castle, and the state should keep out. That, however, is rather a hollow bit of theory. In fact, with respect to children, it has become incumbent upon the state to be more and more cognizant of what goes on in the individualist home and to develop means for dealing with the problems that arise. This is true at every level of childhood. For the fetus, we are concerned about maternal nutrition, about sexually transmitted diseases, about drugs, alcohol and tobacco, and about care for maternal health problems that impact the growing baby. The grim statistics about infant mortality and morbidity make this everybody's business.

The issue goes deeper than that, however. Attention must be given to what it means to a society to have a new baby arrive. The ethic that protected families from invasion by the state was conceived during an epoch when families did indeed raise their own children. There was a continuous presence of a parent (or an extended familial member), there was a continuing regard for the children, and there was a more or less automatic transmission of values between the generations. The business of the family was to raise good children, with the self-esteem of the parents dependent in large part on their success in accomplishing that mission. Today much of this has changed. In probably the majority of instances, the extended family is no more; for a goodly number, the move to the suburbs broke that up, and, for many others, the repeated moves across the country have fragmented that cluster of ties. More and more children are born out of wedlock to younger and younger mothers. There is in addition an increasing tendency for families to break up via divorce, and single-parent families are commonplace—with all the economic stresses and vicissitudes that are implicit in such a pattern and with children out in someone's care while their caretaking parent works. On the other hand, where both father and mother are present and the couple is together, the majority of parents of small children are both working, and the child is cared for by others for many hours of the day. Often enough, people have two jobs, or they are simultaneously working and going to school. Reconstituted families are becoming commonplace with the many stresses inherent in such arrangements. All in all, the society of today is not the society for which the current educational system was designed, and the children are suffering accordingly.

The state

The nature of the state has changed as well. Social legislation has moved the state into the home in a variety of ways. In many jurisdictions, the state now requires that children be vaccinated; to fail to do so is to violate the law. In almost all the country children must attend school between certain set ages (usually between 5 or 6 and 16). To withhold children from school is, again, to violate the law. Within the home, children may not be brutally beaten or sexually used by adults; to do so is, again, a violation of law. Thus, bit by bit, the state has come to play ever more of a role in the management of children in the home. In special ways this has become extended to additional dimensions. Thus, the once sacred province of sex education has gradually been transferred from a sole responsibility of parents to a shared responsibility between parents and school. Much of the thinking that has gone into these determinations has reflected the gradually increasing awareness that parents are simply unable to do many of the things that we have come to recognize that children need—or, if parents are able to do them after a fashion, they are unable to do them well. Parents cannot teach children to read, write, and cipher in an adequate fashion. Parents are demonstrably inadequate as instructors or guides for their children in the area of human sexuality. Some parents are unable to control their sexual and aggressive passions in connection with their children. Idyllic images of home and sturdy visions of protected castles notwithstanding, these are some of the sobering realizations that underlie many of our current cultural practices. I would propose that we carry all this one step further—that we undertake to redefine the relationship between families and the state in a new and different way.

The school

Since we speak of a restructuring of the relationship of the state and the family, we must first recognize that this significant interface exists on many levels. Currently, for most families, the prime site where the family meets the state is certainly the school. School attendance is enforced by law; the schools (the public schools at any rate) are provided at public expense and staffed by people who are paid from the public treasury, and the governance of the school is ultimately in the hands of voters who elect the school board. Unfortunately, there is much to suggest that the established school system in our society is in trouble. I say this clinically rather than critically; the ideal of free public education has been well realized in this country and in certain ways has achieved monumental success. By and large, we are a literate and informed people who can point to the educational level of the average citizen as a major cultural achievement. But, however meritorious it has been in mission and original conception, the current system emerged roughly 100 years ago and was intended for a different culture from what we now have created. I suggest that our society has moved well beyond the point of needing the system we have. New problems have arisen that demand far more than the inculcation of learning, and new knowledge has developed that the current generation of educators are not prepared to implement.

In its original design, the target of the school was the average child growing up during the era of the first industrial revolution, and its mission was to teach some variant of the three R's. Many of the parents of that day were newly arrived immigrants, and there was a certain basic nucleus of knowledge that had to be acquired quickly for the family to "make it" in the new world. With the passage of time, however, the value system of the culture has evolved (or, perhaps, eroded, depending on one's point of view), the character of work has changed, the character of the home has changed, the nature of the family has been transformed (and in many ways fragmented), and the population has altered in respect to both where it lives and how it lives there. Accordingly, schools have been asked to take on a variety of additional functions. Among these are babysitting, mental health counseling, vocational training, social rehabilitation, parental counseling, eliminating racism, detecting cases of child abuse, preventing drug abuse, dealing with the handicapped, assimilating students with AIDS, and dealing with early childhood education. In fact, the school system is trying to do all of these plus some additional chores and, in all too many instances, doing none of them well. Moreover, these many demands have acted to prevent or impede the school from carrying out its intended primary mission: to teach.

If, for the moment, we confine ourselves merely to the dimension of transferring and inculcating knowledge, even there things do not seem to work well. The current school system often does not meet the needs of either upper-level students who are bored and insufficiently engaged or lower-level youngsters who characteristically need far more remediation than they are likely to get. Nor does the middle group fare well. Failing test scores, public disenchantment, high dropout rates, low rankings in international competitions, and a generation of students who are famous for their inability to read comfortably, write coherently, or express themselves in appropriately constructed language—all these and more testify to the extent of the difficulties.

Beyond the school system as such, throughout our society there is a pervasive and oppressive sense that our children are not doing well. A variety of social indicators testify to this: the need for additional prisons, soaring rates of drug use, ever more pregnancies among ever younger teens, a relatively high level of suicidal behavior, and chronic underachievement all send the same message.

The proposition offered here is that the basic notion of school as a place for teaching and learning is no longer a viable social concept. There must be a whole new kind of agency created: one that is more in keeping with the needs of the times and that fulfills the necessary social functions with which the existing system so ineffectually struggles.

Principles

Since we speak here of redefining the relationship of family and state, let me suggest some principles that I believe should dominate such an approach.

First, every pregnancy that mothers plan to carry to term is a major societal event. As immensely important it may be to the persons immediately involved, it also concerns all of society and has profound implications for the future of the body politic. Like a marriage, it is at once a private and a public event, and its mere presence demands very active response by society. In fact, it merits at least as much societal involvement as a crime. A crime disrupts the homeostasis of society, and we expend huge amounts of public resources to record, evaluate, and act on such crimes as come to public attention. A pregnancy too disrupts societal balance—and merits a very rich response. It is the skewed reaction that expends so much energy on the one and so little on the other that leads in part to a sense of social unease and a feeling of wrongness about what we do.

Second, children need support the full length of their development; the notion of school starting at age 5 or 6 misses primary opportunities for help and support to children and their families during immensely impressionable and formative years, including the period *in utero*. What was once offered uniquely by the family in the home is now absent; unattended pregnancy and catch-as-catch-can daycare are worse than no solution; they are a dangerous and often enough destructive form of address to such problems.

Third, our children need more than they are getting. Our times demand more. Much of this is due to what we have learned. We simply know too much about child development today to allow so many of our children to grow up without the benefit of this knowledge. For the first time in human history, we are approaching a day when we will know how to rear a child. Throughout the entire column of human records, this has never before been true. People raised children all the time, but they did it by guess and by gosh, by hook and by crook; they did it as well as they could. They did it as once they practiced medicine: groping in the dark and using a mixture of common sense, a host of maxims from the past, tradition, superstition, old wives' tales, and instinct alongside the products of some empirical trial and error. There was little or no understanding of why these methods did or did not prove effective in a given instance. That is how we have reared children for all these many generations, until today. Now for the first time we know something about temperament and something about fit. We are getting a grasp on what are the developmental needs of children and how to meet those needs. We are beginning to understand what makes for vulnerability in children and what hampers development. In short, we are approaching a moment when we will know how to rear a child. This is a monumental breakthrough. A good deal of the necessary work has been done, and the rest is clearly on its way.

These are the principles that define the role of the child-rearing center. It starts with pregnancy and offers services to families right on through until high school. It is government run and funded, just as the public school has been; presumably it would be paralleled by private agencies that people could elect and make use of just as they may choose private schools today. Its mission is to support parenting work and the development of all children in the country regardless of their socioeconomic background and to see to it that the best child development knowledge is communicated to families and brought to bear on all individuals it serves. It would seek to accomplish this mission by collaborative work with all families who care for children. This agency would have the force and sanction of law, but it is conceived in the spirit of giving backup and support to families rather than acting as a police officer. Nonetheless, the legal sanction would be there, and child attendance would be as necessary and as much the focus of the truant officer's work as is true for schools in general—only now with the added element that family participation is also required. On the other hand, family involvement would also be rewarded from the outset.

As noted, the services of such a center would start with the fetus. For the purposes of this agency, its initial target population is the pregnant woman who plans to bring her pregnancy to term. Wherever and whenever that kind of pregnancy happens, it will be responded to as an event with significant public implications. Society will be profoundly affected by the outcome of this process; it is correspondingly interested in the quality of the gestation, and it will seek actively to help bring it to a successful conclusion. One could approach this in a variety of ways. For example, attending and participating in a recognized program for prenatal care will earn women a series of rewards—perhaps a certain amount of money (a given sum for each prenatal visit she attends), perhaps 2 weeks of vacation during their pregnancy at a well-run government-sponsored camp, certainly a certificate of special recognition. Meanwhile, the center would offer services both in the home and in the center proper. A series of home visits and social work studies will evaluate the safety and integrity of the environment that will care for the newborns and will marshal services to optimize conditions when that is necessary. Following delivery, children's birth and the associated adaptive issues would be reviewed and evaluated. The true beginnings of both cognitive and personality development are present well before birth, and it seems reasonable as a point of departure to start at the beginning and to become familiar with the many influences within the immediate environment that affect how these children will grow. Training pregnant women and caretakers of newborns in appropriate child-care and child-rearing methods might be the single most effective intervention such a center can offer; this element of its functioning might well serve to head off a host of later problems including those associated with failures or distortions in cognitive growth. Thus, from a purely cognitive point of view, this approach is in a sense a logical extension of the tendency already strongly in evidence to push back the beginnings of formal education to ever younger periods.

In sum, a concern with all fetuses destined to be planfully carried to term and a site to which mothers would bring all newborns on a regular basis, along with a pattern of home visiting for the taking of observations and offering training at home, would be central to one component of the functioning of the child-rearing center. In effect, the same kind of legal approach that originally mandated school attendance would now be extended to require all caretakers of newborns to become trained in principles and practices of child care and child rearing.

Day care

Then, as the children grew old enough, the center would be the primary site for day care. Given the socioeconomic pressure on many families, this should become available sometime during the first half of the first year of life; required attendance (in the sense in which school attendance is required) for a certain number of hours each week would not begin until 18 months of age. Again, there would certainly be a variety of private day-care services that could be used if the parent chose to do so, but the basic service has too much implication for the welfare of the public at large to leave it to the chance and haphazard arrangements that currently characterize what is happening to children the country over. Inadequate day care can be a bruising and traumatic thing for a child and can leave deep emotional wounds in terms of capacity for attachment, self-regulation, and other vital social presences. To the extent that the state takes on a measure of responsibility for the mental health and personality development of its citizens, this is an essential service.

There would then be a toddler and preschool division where the principles of child rearing as they are currently understood would be applied and where the parents would be expected to take active part in their children's care and progress, to attend seminars, to spend a certain amount of time participating in the work of the center, and to meet periodically with staff members to review the current developmental status of the children as well as to assess the nature of any existing problems.

In general, such centers would be organized along three major axes. Each of these would represent a mission, an attempt to reach a specified goal within the framework of a particular realm. Each merits individual discussion.

The first axis

The first of these three axes is personality growth. This would be a major mission of the center. It would certainly be fully as important as cognitive development, and it would be given as much time in the curriculum. It would involve a variety of strategies designed to help children work on social techniques, interpersonal skills, values and the rules of social exchange, the learning of traditions and cultural or subcultural usages, communication and assertiveness, as well as self-restraint and fairness in interaction—in short, within the framework of the child-rearing center philosophy, from the very beginnings of life, getting along with others in a complex society would be considered a primary focus for formal training efforts. This kind of program would seek to head off the emergence of both the excessively socialized and proudly ignorant jock on one hand and the isolated, weirdo, oddball brainy nerd on the other. Socialization should no longer be left up to chance, such as the hazards of recess and the playing field. We know something of what can be done to help children at every age; these methods should play a legitimate and formal part in the services offered to every child during the full span of the developmental years.

To illustrate this axis, let us consider the techniques that have been developed to help with one area: the moral or ethical growth of the child. We select this because there is no realm that has been more intimately connected with the duty of the family and the values inherent in family life than this. In fact, families do not do very well with moral training, for the most part because they do not know how to do it. By and large, in the home, morality is either not taught at all, it is taught in conjunction with politeness (which is a very different thing), or it is addressed through hectoring, lecturing, or attempting to evoke guilt. Sometimes it is relegated to the realm of religion, and it is expected that church, bible class, and the minister will take care of moral training. There is no doubt but that appropriate religious training has much to do with conveying values and traditions, but whether this subserves the end of moral training is yet to be demonstrated.

There is, however, a body of research-based knowledge that has arisen in this realm. Investigators have found that children can be brought to concentrate on moral issues by offering them a number of carefully thought out dilemmas, situations where they have to make a judgment about right and wrong. The discussions and work on these ethical problems can be demonstrated to raise the moral level of youngsters in testable ways. Curiously enough, the most successful design for conveying such values as fairness and justice is to pair together children who differ only slightly in level of moral development. Higher-level children can better convey the requirements for a higher level of ethical thinking than if children are paired together whose levels are too far apart. Let us suppose we deal with a child who thinks quite concretely that the reason you should act right is to avoid punishment. This is by no means an unusual attitude, but ethically it is rather a primitive stance. If you match such a child with another who understands that if people act well they are happier and all of society gets along better and ask the two of them to work together to figure out an ethical dilemma, they will each come up with a characteristic solution in keeping with their levels. If, then, you ask them to discuss why and how they arrived at their conclusions, the more concrete child can learn from the other, get the idea, and presently catch on to an important concept: one acts well not only to avoid getting punished but also to make the world a better place for everybody. If, however, you match the concrete child against a youngster who thinks in truly abstract terms, then the abstract child will try to convey that one should act well because there are broad general principles of ethics that should govern one's behavior and that virtue lies in living in keeping with such principles. This will predictably leave the more concrete child behind, who will not understand what the other is talking about.

There is a gradually emerging body of practices used in various remedial settings that I would suggest as appropriate, indeed necessary, for the training and preparation of *any* child growing up in so complex and crowded a culture as our own. This includes training in a wide variety of skills that in turn lead to the competencies necessary for attaining good human relations and achieving a decent measure of personal happiness. They are considerably more important than are the cognitive attainments—the reading, writing, and arithmetic—with which we are all familiar. Indeed, the attainment of adequate interpersonal skills creates the context within which such cognitive abilities may best be acquired. Without these elementary relationship competencies, individuals would be radically hampered in their striving to reach some degree of cognitive accomplishment.

I would submit that today there are a great many things individuals need that are not readily conveyed by the existing instrumentalities of the culture. A brief list of topics will serve to illustrate some of the areas to be covered. For example, instruction can be given in:

- How to play
- How to cooperate
- How to be a friend
- What to do if you feel shy
- What to do if you feel you have made a mistake
- How to start a conversation
- How to cope if you feel that you are being laughed at
- How to manage your temper

- What to do if you feel upset
- How to meet a new group
- How to fit into a group
- Why people tease
- How to handle teasing
- What to do when a bad thing happens to someone
- How it feels if you see another child hurt
- What to do if someone picks on you
- What to do if someone takes something of yours
- What to do if someone takes your seat or your place on line

Children at different ages would of course have to learn the material appropriate to their level of development, but the notion of teachable inter-personal skills would prevail throughout. The preschoolers have their tasks, the grade-school children a different set of issues to address, and the teen-agers their own unique array of problems. This list would be items in the roster of group topics for the younger children. But a host of stresses arise for adolescents that our society leaves entirely to chance, or to the vagaries, of local events. If in a given school, for example, two youngsters become pregnant or a youth commits suicide, there are likely to be a set of *ad hoc* seminars or group meetings initiated in the course of which some attempt is made to address the associated issues; more often than not, though, nothing gets built in. After a while, it all dies away until some other disaster strikes, in the wake of which another brief flurry ensues. Perhaps that is overstated; certainly there has been a meaningful movement in the direction of intro-ducing course material on human sexuality into at least senior high school. But the resultant sex education courses have been uncertain and poorly integrated into the curriculum; they are a far cry from the advice given by every responsible professional, which is that sex education has to be offered at every level of development from preschool onward, albeit couched in language and concept appropriate to each age level. The most serious deficit with most sex education is that there is no context within the curriculum for such a course to fit into; there is no other site within the academic frame-work where personality and adjustment issues, ethical and moral problems, interpersonal and social relationship difficulties, and internal emotional control troubles are naturally and regularly addressed. Without attention to such matters, it is not surprising that merely informing youngsters of sexual realities does not necessarily change their behavior.

Moreover, there is not even the attempt to consider courses in the other great dimension of adolescent need, what to do with rage, with resent-ment of authority, with reaction to frustration, with response to a feeling of having been unjustly treated, with offensive remarks by a peer, with provocation, with teasing by the group, with, in short, some of the every-day, garden variety challenges that arouse anger and hurt and a desire for retaliation—often enough with accompanying feelings of helplessness and inability to respond in any kind of meaningful way and with a resultant sense of total devaluation. Such feelings might be worked out with a friend—maybe. They might be worked out with a family member, a parent or a sibling—maybe. They might be brought to a teacher—sometimes. But more often than not, they are metabolized somewhere within as best youths are capable: they smile bravely and go on, and the hurt may rankle inside for a lifetime, or a lifetime can be abruptly abbreviated when the hurt seems too great to bear. Often enough, adolescents' rage continues in series with a deeply felt rancor from earlier years, only now they are bigger and stronger and can strike back—and we have to deal with the phenomenon of delinquency. There is probably no area in our culture that has been so frustrating to those who would serve society as the many attempts to come to grips with this abrasive and persistent social ill. If some of the theoreticians are correct, then what we have here is a deficiency disease, a deprivation of necessary human warmth and caring in early, vulnerable years, and if we would address this condition then the course we perforce must follow is to seek through such means as have outlined here to prevent such deprivation to begin with, and, where it has already become established, to provide the constant supervisory caring for a prolonged period to end with. The community-based supportive living arrangement may well be the means of the future for all but the most dangerous youngsters. But the better road for the future is to seek by every means to prevent such deprivation from occurring—and to do this we must contact every child in the culture and guarantee these little ones their necessary and essential care.

The point is that children need an enormous amount of help in the process of human socialization. Theoretically they are supposed to get this routinely and automatically in the course of their child rearing at home; in fact, in all too many instances, they are not getting it at all, and, in a much larger percentage of the cases, they are getting some truncated or even troubled version of social experience that stands them in poor stead when they go out into the larger social world. Perhaps one child in five is given the full roster of support he or she needs; the rest must make do as best they may. Since it is demonstrably possible to teach a great many interpersonal skills, to teach children how to handle feelings and how to be better related to other children, it is in my view only a matter of time before awareness of the existence of this body of knowledge will create its own demand.

In addition to what can be offered to children as such, there is much that can be made available to parents. A body of practices is emerging that bids fair to have a considerable effect on the methods of child rearing. There are new ideas in discipline, in communicating with children, in understanding children's developmental needs, and in coming to grips with the effects of the parents' own childhood experiences on the way that they conduct themselves as parents. Heretofore, as a culture, we have taken education seriously and made it a matter of statute and requirement. By implication we have said that most parents cannot be adequate educators of their own children, that this is a matter for people with special skills and training, and that this is also a matter of sufficient cultural importance as to be wrapped about by the force of law. I would now propose that we take child rearing just as seriously, that we make sure that all children are given the best that the culture has to offer by way of supporting and informing the parents in their child-rearing efforts and supplementing what they do with a careful program of instruction and interaction for all children precisely in the realms of interpersonal competence, personality development, and character formation.

The second axis

The second major axis is children's cognitive unfolding. Cognitive development is a critical component of personality growth and is in some ways coextensive with what has traditionally been regarded as school work. But it is subtly and powerfully different. To begin with, if one would seriously attempt to address cognitive needs, there would have to be a minimum emphasis on the content of what must be conveyed within the time frame of a given period. Instead, the individual learning style of all students would become a focus of study, and both the particular competencies and specific difficulties would have to be teased out, classified, and then used as the basis for program building. The cognitive assessment would be basic to the construction of an individualized training program: one designed to engage children's identifiable interests, to address their areas of native endowment, as well as to offer remedial and compensatory programming for the detected areas of failed development or inherent deficiency.

Some recent work is opening up all sorts of novel styles of cognitive support. One suggested approach uses the role of continuing relationship as part of the learning matrix within which individual students must be embedded. Specifically, instead of having a change of teachers every year, there would be a pattern of continuing with the same teacher for far longer periods of time. A 3- or 4-year sequence would be the norm, with the opportunity offered for teachers and students to get to know each other over time and to develop an enduring relationship. Thus, the human aspect of education would take on a subtly but powerfully different tone, there would be a far more intense quality to the interplay between students and teacher, and the opportunity would be open for significant reparative and adaptive milieu shaping as the teacher would gradually come to know the nuances of each child's learning profile.

Parallel with this, the use of computers in the classroom is emerging as another dimension of educational advance. A variety of interactional programs is being developed that allows both for interesting approaches to teaching and for built-in remediation where learning problems appear. For example, a child may sit before a view screen and enter his pretaught code. The screen lights up and the image of a teacher says, "Good morning, Johnny. Which would you like to start with today, arithmetic or spelling? Press green for arithmetic, and red for spelling." The child presses red, and the lesson starts. The teacher writes on the blackboard and says, "Cat. C-A-T, cat. Now you look at your keyboard and see if you can pick out these letters." The child proceeds to insert: C-T-A. The computer automatically initiates a program designed to help with problems of reversal, and the "teacher" proceeds on that trajectory. Children who do not display a tendency to reverse get a different program. The computer gradually builds up a picture of all children and the particular learning problems they display. Special drills are included automatically as the children proceed.

A major area of advance in our time is the gradually accumulating knowledge of cognitive testing. This is an as yet unfinished effort, but it is becoming clear that within a relatively few years we will be able to describe with some certainty the nature of a given child's cognitive capacities, style, and needs. Along with this better ability to diagnose will come improved styles of fostering the growth of different individuals in these several realms.

In another area, some research suggests that cognitive growth is fostered by specialized small group participation in projects with cognitive dimensions. That is to say, if children with highly diverse cognitive capacities, children who are brilliant, children who are average, and children who are limited are all brought together to solve a problem or to carry out a project, then the mutual support and the permission to employ a variety of cognitive styles seem to enhance the intellectual growth of each participant. They all learn. These and other novel methods of working with children go far beyond the question of "instruction." All these methods drive children to become active agents in their own education and allow them to progress in highly individualized ways. As these techniques advance and refine, they bid fair to revolutionize the methodology of fostering cognitive growth.

What is happening in our day is that trained, cognitively oriented professionals are devoting themselves to the youngsters who need remedial work. What *should* be happening is that all children get the benefit of such methods throughout the academic environment, especially during the preschool and early grade school years.

The third axis

The third major axis of planful intervention is the intrapersonal one. Here the more clinical types of assessment would be used. Particular attention would be paid to children's genetic loading; tests would be made regularly to see whether a specific inclination (e.g., a familial tendency toward depression) was being realized. The role and impact of parental circumstances and special problems of any sort would be constantly weighed against children's temperamental proclivities. The emerging character structures, affective styles, and coping mechanisms would be recorded from early on and addressed regularly in ways that would give some glimpse of the child's inner adjustment. An effort would be made to track children's responses to any major stresses they might encounter and various interventional methods employed as seemed necessary. While the work in this realm would not be given the same time allotment the other two axes would share, when a problem arose in this area, the ameliorative efforts would take precedence over the time commitments to courses, meetings, and techniques subserving the goals of those first two axes.

The child at risk

In the nature of things, it is inevitable that such a closer look at children and their families will turn up a number of instances where social conditions will indicate that a child, often a newborn, is at risk of becoming the target of major stresses. This happens all too commonly today, but it is largely a matter of chance whether society will step in and attempt to do something about a catastrophic situation. It depends on whether neighbors or relatives decide to call; if they do not, a serious situation may go unrecognized—or at least unresponded to—for a long time. Since the basic proposal is already calling into question the existing balance between family and children on one hand and the force of social requirement on the other, it would seem not inappropriate at least to ponder the implications of such discoveries on the proposed child-rearing center. One possible solution would be to create two classes of children at the centers. There would be the regular attenders, and there would be a group of children designated as *at risk*. The determination of *at-risk* status would be a formal matter conducted with scrupulous regard to due process. Once infants or children were found to be *at risk*, this would allow for a considerably greater measure of social observation and control; in particular, it would require attendance on the part of caretakers at various supportive and ameliorative arrangements designed to improve their parental competence.

In short, I am suggesting that a new context be created. Within it, child rearing would be perceived as a function actively shared between family and society, and all the families in the land would, by the nature of the process, be significantly involved. However, the degree of involvement would be determined to some extent by the question of *at-risk* status. For children not so designated, the family would be the primary caretaker, and the center would seek to support the family by means of teaching, enriching, and optimizing child-rearing practices. For children who fell into the *at-risk* category, the community would take over some of the functions of the family and act as participant observer with the family to help rear the child.

There would have to be an appropriate administrative arrangement for determining *at-risk* status. This would establish a means for deciding when children should be considered *at risk*, would create a suitable mechanism for making such determinations, would hold the appropriate hearings, and would take the necessary action. As is true for any other regulatory agency, its decisions could be appealed in court.

Implementation

One might well ask: If such an idea were to be tried, how would society go about it? Surely one does not go overboard for an untested idea, and no serious person would give credence to so radical a change in our values and practices without a considerable degree of trial and testing. One must explore to see if the underlying concepts are realistic, or if they are merely another in the long series of ideas that have been tried only to be found wanting.

I can only hope that the approach to this kind of agency would be undertaken by evolution, by a preliminary testing at the hands of private agencies that would try to offer such cradle to college services, that would try to build in the three tracks I speak of here. One could interest a group of parents who would take a chance on a new concept and work with the system to get the help I believe that 80% of parents need in rearing their children. An alternative way that this could come about would be by means of a gradual transformation of the existing school system (i.e., by the addition of new services, new courses, new arrangements with parents, by altering the training of teachers in gradual and progressive ways), until they became more and more the clinicians that society in fact needs. I would then hope that as the teaching profession drew closer to social work and psychology, more and more of the determinations of child placement and child care would move into the arena of school (for which read child-rearing center) involvement. One way or another I see this kind of change as the road to the future; our children are simply too precious to allow the creaky, jury-rigged apparatus that currently manages and shapes their lives to go on indefinitely. The only question I see is how and at what pace the changes will come about.

Summary

It is critical that the nature of child rearing within our culture undergo a radical transformation. It is long past due that the school system be discarded in its present form and replaced by a more realistic enterprise. A key factor in all future thinking must be to devise some means to bring about the implementation of known child-rearing principles. The ideas offered here are one means of moving toward that set of changes. Regardless of whether they are considered in themselves feasible, it is hoped that they will provoke the kind of thinking that will move us closer to the necessary reconstruction of the way we rear our children.

A final note: Some months after completing a first draft of this paper, I was intrigued by an article I encountered in the October issue of the *American Journal of Orthopsychiatry*. Dr. Ed Ziegler, one of the great figures in American child development, had the lead article in that issue of the journal, and he spoke with the kind of forceful passion and scientific rigor that are his unique characteristic of the need for an American system of day care. He proposed that such a day-care system be centered in the existing school system, that it begin in the third trimester of pregnancy, that it offer outreach home care during the years of infancy, and that it move the child on to beginning school attendance at age 3. Thus, he would graft the pattern of child care for working mothers onto the existing school system and use the current child educational facilities as the nidus for a system of out-of-home care. It seemed to me that his views and mine converged in the area of length of care (i.e., from the end of pregnancy on up), although we diverge from one another in terms of the universality of need (I see the system as needed by *all* families; he saw need chiefly by families with working mothers). A final area of difference is that I would replace our current educational arrangement with a total child-rearing apparatus, whereas he would build upon the existing pattern of schools. But the sense of a major national effort directed toward meeting the requirements of families with children is central to both proposals—and I offer it to you as one of the major goals for America in the twenty-first century.

References

Ziegler, E. (1989). Addressing the nation's child care crisis: The school of the 21st century. *American Journal of Orthopsychiatry*, 59, 4, 484–497.

Chapter 15

The ethics of rage

INTRODUCTION
Bernard Spilka

I knew Joe Noshpitz for 42 years, and it is still hard to realize that he died 13 years ago. He had, however, what we might call a *haimisch* warmth and sensitivity that endeared him to all. It was appropriate for him to have written on religion for he was a true landsman who knew a lot about Judaism plus some Yiddish. When he would come to our home 54 years ago, he conducted the Kiddush welcoming the Sabbath. This did not mean that he was traditionally observant; he was not, yet he thought much about it, as this chapter will show. Exposed to religion early in life in his home and in school, particularly during adolescence, Joe once said that he was interested in becoming a rabbi. Still, when we talked about religion, it was not in any institutional sense or even with an attachment to spirituality. He wondered about religious origins and expressions in an open, free-ranging manner. At that time, his orientation was primarily philosophical and traditionally psychoanalytic. A half-century ago, these views dominated educated thinking. Today, evolution and genetics have entered the picture, yet room still exists for alternative perspectives. This paper represents an original Noshpitz interpretation. An argument might also be advanced that these ideas border on theology. The image of humanity offered contains elements one might expect of Calvinistic Christianity and Orthodox Judaism.

I am convinced that this essay is an inspirational exercise by someone who loved playing with ideas. When a notion struck, he usually wrote it down, saw where it led; above all, he would not let it be stillborn. To explore and even glorify rage as he does here, allowing it a significant place in and potential for religion is a creative venture. A major feature to keep in mind is that rage is often equivalent to energy and motivation, the expression of which can be positive in addition to negative.

Obviously, recognizing the universality of religion across societies and cultures meant searching for either a biological source or an inevitable universal experience. This led Noshpitz to the initial helpless state when humans enter the world. Powerlessness may be the ultimate source of frustration, and the extremely limited response repertoire of the newborn implies a primary need to develop mechanisms for control. An extensive psychological literature going back at least 70 years further notes that the dominant response to frustration is aggression or, here, rage. This is regarded as the omnipresent basis for religion. Taking rage as a foundational natural reaction, survival needs eventuate in the crying and thrashing that infants manifest. None of this invokes higher mental processes. Agitation from physiological dissatisfaction clearly results in responses to counter whatever frustrations the new offspring senses. Simple respondent and operant learning experiences in the presence of caretakers will, courtesy of the awareness from a rapidly developing nervous system, personify outside gratifying power. In a surprisingly short time, infants recognize such power in beings whose presence is variable. Commonly, their attention brings pleasure and the reduction of frustration. Rage is satiated. That very basic biopsychological process of primary stimulus generalization is embodied; care giving is symbolized, concretized, and reified. Superhuman agents are conceptualized into gods and their associates.

We grow and increasingly realize that those who love and esteem us are few in number. Inwardly, we continue to rage at our shortcomings, and we look to the gods for reassurance and love—the highest and most powerful being of all directs love toward us. We seek and join with others who, possessing our delusions, support us with theirs. A security of social and cultural structure assuages our rage. Our shared systems define us versus them, and rage is directed outwardly leading to the hostile excesses that institutionalized faith often sponsors in its compact with government. Indeed, "God is on our side." The energy of rage creates systems rich in fantasy and illusions of love and special consideration. We are the selected, the chosen ones. The deity knows and values us. Religion becomes a paean to our narcissism, which is allied with a rage that may break forth with violence if realistic controls are not achieved. This individual potential finds its parallel in governments that "act(ed) on the basis of rage or narcissism."

Though established religions are commonly in league with governments, they provide the means of restraint for all societal levels. Ethical systems are created and legitimated by god-reference. Rage is thus tentatively mastered. The hoped-for outcome must be a "religion of respect." The beauty of Noshpitz's language carries the field as his aspired respect is variously specified. This socialization of rage is a continuing struggle he feels makes us "worthy of respect." To the extent we are successful we attain value, achieve truth, and deserve honor. Given his evident idealistic yearning, he lets us know that this is not the religion he has known. Caught between experience and dream, we read of "self-recrimination ... [and] the inner voice of ridicule and torment." This is truly Noshpitz's personal revelation of pain and struggle, of desire, shortcoming, and self-delusion. He clearly states his plea: "I need faith." Opposing the "religion of rage," he finds the solution in respect, a fully social phenomenon. Internal integration and social connection are his religious goals.

Having stated his high objective, he is immediately called back to a distressing reality that includes conflict and war, historically and contemporaneously. The scene shifts to an ever present awareness of aggression he attempts to analyze. There is a break here as he returns us to infantile needs for nurturance that when not gratified seek fulfillment in imagery. This leads again toward religion, the desire to avoid loneliness and isolation. Such motivation creates great works and social order. Once affirmed, we are again called back to a distressing reality of human deficiencies, fantasies, hostilities, and their temporary solutions. Always, Noshpitz expresses hope, which he then dashes through awareness of human inadequacy, weaknesses, and rage. Traditional faith was not an answer for him.

One cannot be criticized for seeing in these efforts to reach high a harsh countering by a human reality that is aptly described in the words of cartoonist William Steig. In *The Lonely Ones* (1970), he opines that "people are no damn good" (p. 78). This premise lurks in the background ready to spring forward when the clouds let a little sun in. The potential for good is a tenuous aspiration that Noshpitz will not allow to escape.

Rage as negative energy is ever present, yet some of it is siphoned off to exalt the good. Placing this within a religious framework suggests to me that despite his unhappiness with traditional faith he always felt religion, broadly defined, offered something better.

This is not an optimistic statement; it does, however, offer a glimmer of hope. I am convinced that this essay is an inspirational exercise by someone who would not let the good, even if derived from what we regard as negative, be suppressed.

Reference

Steig, W. (1970). *The lonely ones.* New York: Duell, Sloan, & Pearce.

242	The journey of child development

THE ETHICS OF RAGE

Joseph D. Noshpitz

January 19, 1987

The proper basis, perhaps the only basis on which a religion can be founded, is rage. We are a desolate species, abandoned by our maker, yearning for it and unable ever to attain its presence or its interest. Our rage is deep and unforgiving, valid in its origins and maintained by the conditions of existence. It is the only rational foundations on which to found our ethic.

Once, long ago, some entity created the conditions that eventually led to the emergence of our species. It may be said to have created us in its own gradual, evolutionary way, very much as we grow a colony of bacteria in a Petri dish. It may be that someday it will return to make use of the preparation thus brought into being, much as we return to the incubator after 24 or 48 hours to look to our culture. We can have no more awareness of what its purpose is than can the bacteria thus growing in our experiment can discern our motivation; the maker has a different time scale and its own purposes. What we can know is that we are created and abandoned, left with the yearnings for care and nurturance and love that characterize our kind, and all too aware that none of this is forthcoming from a world with physical laws and functions but without ethical principles.

In our bones we know this, and our rage knows no bounds. We are brought into being with enormous needs, and the need gratifier is not interested. We are designed to long, and the object of our longing is not available; to yearn and the presence for which we yearn has forgotten us, or at best has put us aside until later. We know our condition, and it is in our nature to strive to cope. We like to think that we are rather good at that, but in fact we are not; the quality of our coping tends toward the self-deluding and the self-congratulatory. To recognize our abandoned status is painful, so we say that god is omnipresent and all-attentive. Then we stand on our heads to rationalize his obvious lack of involvement. To realize our own lack of importance hurts our pride, so we build systems that assure us that god loves us and has a plan for us. That affirmation of the "fact" that we are loved also helps with the stress of being angry all the time—that's hard work, and it is much easier to assure ourselves that god loves us. From that it follows that we don't need to be, indeed shouldn't be, angry because it's really such a nice world, full of sweetness, light, and affection. All we have to do, we tell one another, is bask in the light of god's affection—in the course of which we are choked with spleen, despoiled by our fellow lovers, and twisted by aging until we die. But our monumental capacity for self-delusion rides over all that, and we use our good capacities for reason to construct the weird and tortured logic that will allow us to maintain our illusions.

Let us forego such satisfying and self-deceptive formulations and consider the matter on its merits. We have no one but ourselves to turn to, and the system that ensues must be of our own devising. To attribute this to a deity does not help; we need to consult our needs directly, to consider our capacities, to face our nature, and to set our own course. If we would live together in communities, if we would survive with a minimum of pain, then an angry species like our own must set up a great many rules and establish radical systems of enforcement. The basic question always is whether we wish to allow for that change. If we opt to do so, then we are caught up in the nature of what we call "freedom." If we choose not to encourage or to allow much change, then freedom is the enemy, and we must strive with every fiber to maintain sameness. The choice is an arbitrary one, and in a very real sense it is the only choice we have. Human beings can be relatively happy under either system, with their rage abated to some degree by the implications of each. It is better controlled under a system of sameness; everything is prescribed, everyone knows his place. There is no need for overmuch ambition or effort; the very structure of society tells us where we will be tomorrow, what we will be doing, and, pretty much, what will happen. In particular, there is no point in getting mad; it is all cut and dried. It works best when it enables people to take care of themselves and of one another according to ritual and formula. Using that approach, the Australian aborigines seem to have maintained a more or less stable social order for 40,000 years. Of course, that sort of system does not do too well in the face of natural disasters or external invasion or even when confronted by technological novelty. It is not designed for change; it is created to avoid alterations in the status quo and usually does not have the resilience to adapt.

The alternative approach can adapt all right but lacks the satisfying system of controls that the static style carries with it; it—the "free" kind of culture— tends to have lots of turmoil, violations of its rules, challenges to its governance, and all sorts of complications arising out of its relatively unstructured character. For certain kinds of people it is immensely satisfying; for many others it breeds stress, dread, and feelings of failure and exclusion. It does have the immense virtue of allowing for more direct expression of the religious rage proper to mankind, but it plays the price for unbridled anger in that its citizens assault one another all too readily either by means of direct violation of the rules or by dint of using the rules as a technique of attack.

January 21, 1987

This matter of rage is hard to consider. We ward it off instinctively; we know how dangerous it can be. Yet we are a savage species; our very highest level of development is maintained by a balance of terror that more or less keeps the peace between two rather idealistic societies. We have no way to get at our maker, so we take it out on one another. It hurts to be abandoned, but only by facing that can we even begin to build. Otherwise we are forever caught up in sham and delusion, eternally hypocrites. We lie to ourselves and to one another, and we protest at the human condition; even those who seek to come in out of the snowstorm of pious rationalization can do so only in unfortunate ways—by becoming cruel or selfish or destructive. In a way, all that is understandable, just as all delinquent behavior bred by deprivation is understandable, but it most certainly is not endurable. There has to be a better way than that. And there is.

An honest reading of the nature of things will give us a point of departure from which we can arrive at some usable propositions. In essence, it comes down to the understanding that the matter of regulation of the human condition is entirely up to us. That may sound self-evident, but in fact very few of us have ever accepted such a position. The point is that we create reality; it is really our own, our fabrication, our responsibility. When things go wrong, they do so because we did not construct the current edition of reality very well; we have to face the task of redoing it. That has to stop being evolutionary (in the sense that it sort of happens to you as life goes on because of the overall rules which seem to run things), and instead it must become consciously practices and artfully studied. And in the midst of it all we can never forget our rage, never relent in respect to the maker, but keep what belongs to that entity directed there and not displaced to our own group. It is hard enough without that.

January 25, 1987

The notion of rage as the basis for religion is resisted on at least two grounds. The first is the sense that it arises out of our unimportance, a notion with is *a priori* unendurable. When we recognize that god has deserted us it fills us with humiliation; it hurts. We shrink to a kind of insignificance that is hard to tolerate. We are all too well aware of the nature of our universe, that we are a dust mote and less than a dust mote in an enormous cosmos. There are more galaxies than grains of sand on our greatest beaches; and each one is filled with myriad stars without number; and each of those may well have planets. The aggregate numbers are stupefying, beyond comprehension. How rewarding then to reassure ourselves that, nonetheless, there is a deity out there that takes special cognizance of us, concerns itself with watching over us, interferes occasionally—or constantly—depending on one's belief system in our affairs, indulges in an occasional miracle to make sure some plan is carried out as it wishes, and ends up by punishing or rewarding us for what has happened. What about all the other entities in the cosmos? Well, we'll address that one when we have to.

The issue is not an easy one. It is far more difficult to allow ourselves to think that we are alone in all this immensity, that we can sink or swim as it happens to turn out, and that nobody cared about us. To say the least, that is a stressful position for our kind of beast to endure. We are willing to stretch the borders of the possible to a very considerable degree indeed to avoid that one. The very invention of religion is one of the ways we have coped with that kind of cosmic loneliness. If that kind of religion does its job, then we are never alone; we are always watched over and accompanied by some one of the elementals posited by our faith. There is always something to which to turn.

More than that, there is the personal sense of our unimportance that such a point of view confronts us with. It is humiliating not to be special. It hurts our pride. And that is never something to underestimate. This has been called the Age of Narcissism; probably it is only slightly more today: it has always been the Age of Narcissism. We are simply constituted that way; as a species we are self-centered, and self-aggrandizing, and demanding, and feeling entitled, and expecting a lot from those around us, and somewhat grandiose (or more than somewhat), and full of inward calculations we do not reveal since they will show us up for the inappropriate people we are, and so on. No great discovery there, but of considerable import when we put that together with the notion of faith and religiosity; in a curious sort of way all these elements are at once denied by and satisfied by religion. God satisfies so many of our yearnings, listens when we speak to it, concerns itself with our status as though we were someone important, loves us no matter what, watches over us in a sort of personal if not exclusive way—narcissistically it is all very rewarding. At the same time, most religions teach that these pretensions to importance must go. They are the enemies of true belief and religious success that following its tenets can achieve; there is the attainment of enlightenment, or the arrival in paradise, or happiness here on Earth, or conquest over our enemies—there is always a lure and a payoff. But surely the most potent achievement that religion opens up to us is the guarantee that we are each important. This narcissistic reward is of immense meaning to people and in its own way binds them to whatever faith they select. If for some reason this function fails, then the quest is on for some other attachment that will serve the multiple needs: for attention, for companionship, for approval, for personal concern, and the like. Cults have flourished by attending to these needs.

That, however, is only one reason for resisting the idea of abandonment and rage as the primary bases for religion. The other aspect of resistance to such a notion is the feeling that this sort of idea is a destructive force, one that, if allowed free play in society, will inevitably cause no end of trouble. After all, rage is the source of violence, and so much of ethics is devoted to ways and means of avoiding this element in human affairs. It is not hard to see why men would prefer love or brotherhood or comradeship (all true socialists, for example, address each other as "comrade") as the core element on which to build a system or a society, yet there are some notable exceptions.

The founding fathers of the American government looked at the patterns of governance that they had known and recognized that most of them were based on some sort of false or deceptive view of the human condition. Thus, the theocracies eventually became tyrannies, the divine right of kings led ultimately to madmen wastrels at the helms of governments, and oppression was the rule rather than the exception in human history. Most governments most of the time acted on the basis of rage or narcissism; they dominated, humiliated, exploited, enslaved, deprived, or arrogantly lorded subjects, took the result of their toil for the selfish ends of the governors, misused their daughters or sons in bed or in battle, and maintained a state of terror and domination often enough for generation after generation. When a ruler was wise and merciful or concerned about the welfare of his subjects, this was so exceptional that he was likely to be remembered. For the most part, rulers acted in this destructive and altogether human way and were accordingly forgotten. So those who contemplated this history set about establishing a method of governance that would attempt to take into account the nature of people as they knew them and accordingly created a system of checks and balances. This implied that no one would be too honest, that everyone was going to be out for himself, that eternal vigilance was the only guarantor of safety from oppression or exploitation, and that the nature of the system had to be such as to protect the people from its governors. Now, to be sure, all this was done in the name of god, with many calls on deity for its attention and protection—but the actual running of things was taken most explicitly our of the hands of the religious, and any hint of connection with governance with religion was categorically proscribed. The success of this system depends on its recognition of the pernicious in human motivation, and the inherent bulwarks are built in to protect against the dominance of those meanest of human passions or emotions. In a sense this is implicit instead of explicit; the founding fathers did not say that since men were all evil that we have to be protected from ourselves. They simply designed and crafted a method to do that—in the name of god.

It would seem more desirable still to have a religion that would face the realities of the human character rather than deny them and that would set forth an ethic based on these realities. Here psychoanalysis can help. It is not very good as a science; its methods do not lend themselves to control or to replication, and it tends to overgeneralize from insufficient data. But it does make observations that are not otherwise attainable, and it does have an ethic that is absolutely fundamental to religious progress: it insists that we face the uncomfortable and the painful; in our interior worlds, that we address the actual about the human condition, that we take an unvarnished view of what we think and feel and are, and that we build our lives upon the basis of such strict honesty in our internal recognition. Nowhere else in history has such a radical devotion to the truth found overt expression, and this has given psychoanalysis a merited preeminence among the psychological sciences. At the same time, the lack of rigor in its methodology has led to a devaluation of much that it has found.

January 28, 1987

Any religion worthy of its name must have some form of worship. It need not be excessively reverential, but there must be some kind of value that prevails and to which the members of that faith give special heed. Clearly, where the deity itself has failed, one does not worship there—it would be a mockery. What then is left?

The word *worship* has no place in our lives, except as we would give ourselves up to the primitive and the infantile. But there is left the sense of respect, and I offer this as a religion of respect. We can, and indeed must, value many things, and our valuation takes the form of extending to them our deep respect. Let me give this a personal character and list some of the things I see in this light.

I respect the suffering and the rage engendered by our abandonment.

I respect the coping and the struggle to contain this anger, all the inner effort entailed by the sense of unfairness that dogs the footsteps of the species.

I respect maimed man. A poorly made and evidently unfinished creature whose vermiform appendix parallels his incapacity to control his passions, he will no doubt be replaced eventually as he replaced his simian forbears. He is the victim of a typical bit of slippage in an indifferent universe. His facile maker is off elsewhere. It would be gratifying to think that the entity was at least working on an improved model, but that is not very likely. If it considers man at all, it is probably relying on the system it originally brought into being to get there eventually with a better product. Meanwhile, man has no choice but to dog-paddle as best he may with the equipment at hand, to hurt, to be angry, and to make do.

I respect man's travail, and the emergence of that greatest of human virtues, compassion. For it is compassion that we can find the only anodyne to the hurt and the only answer to the rage; without it, we would destroy one another and destroy ourselves. Angry creatures do that, and that is not hard to understand. Indeed, given the strictures of our natures with the recurrent confrontation with incomplete mastery, it is a kind of rationality. We perceive ourselves as struggling against the hopeless.

Yet it is exactly here that we become worthy of respect, the fact that we do struggle, and that we do sometimes prevail. We build something that stands; we organize something that works. No matter that for every success there are so many, many failures; as imperfect, incomplete beings it must be that way. But we do strive and we make breakthroughs—and thereby become objects of value, objects of respect.

We need hymns, and our poets are the pathfinders for us in this trackless waste. To be sure, some have been lost to their time and culture and devoted themselves to various kinds of unreal worship. But for the most part they have celebrated the efforts of our tormented species to rise from its Wahoo state and find its way to truth and to respect. We have to learn to listen to their songs.

I would like to write such a hymn, but I fear the outcome. I have no true poesy within me, only the yearning for expression, and that is not enough. My gift is rather to look with the eye of the imagination and within the framework of science to speculate as to the possible. And the impossible.

I find the path of religion as I have known it to be among the chief impossibilities that have confronted me. But never before have I attempted to find an alternative. I am at the moment of bitter self-recrimination, unable to free myself from the inner voice of ridicule and torment. I fight the battles endlessly over and have now developed a sequence I am fond of replaying. I imagine myself to have done things well, to have answered my enemies, to have confronted my accusers, to have responded to my critics, and to have routed them utterly. Then I recall that it was I who was humiliated and routed utterly, I who failed and was laughed at, I who bear the onus and the memory. I tell myself that that is the only version of which I will henceforth think, but then I catch myself at it again, imagining a victory instead of defeat, mastery instead of devastating failure. And it all replays.

Were I of my own-created faith, I would have some buffer against that. I would know that the rage that fills me and that turns now against me is the eternal rage of my kind; I would know how to respect that presence within me and to value the efforts I am making so unsuccessfully to cope with it. I would learn respect for myself as the creature I am, and I would be freer to struggle with perfectibility and with imperfection. I need faith.

January 29, 1987

Is respect enough? Does not a faith need passion, total commitment, absolute dedication? The answer to all of these is yes. Respect is enough if it is experienced not passionately but profoundly. There is a difference, one measured by emotional style and degree of maturity, but of even greater importance, one measured by intensity and the sense of validity that only the truth can command. Revelation required that we transcend truth (presumably to get to a "higher" truth); the religion of rage accepts no heights or depths; there is only truth, and it cannot be transcended.

Thus, respect is enough and more than enough, and it always has been. In any case, it is the glue that holds society together—respect for law, respect for authority—the sober value we put on our social arrangements to make life endurable. Respect is what allows such angry entities as the members of our species to live together in some variety of communal style. It is the antidote to the more toxic aspects of the condition of rage—for surely the spleen with which we are filled could turn upon us and on those we value and destroy everyone. We are saved from this all too likely outcome not by love but by respect. We may name the target of our respect by different titles—the law, one's fellow man, human feeling, duty—there are no end of formulations. But it is that which has kept society functioning during the normal everyday fair wear and tear of humdrum existence. Surely there have been impassioned moments in history: times of revolution, of nationalism, of religious revival, of simple mass psychosis. These come and go; they are a part of our thrashing around as we sort out our abandoned condition and find yet some other way of belonging to a greater entity, or of punishing one to which we had belonged and which had let us down yet again. Occasionally such eruptions break up some particularly impacted and sluggish organization; for the most part, they accomplish little and are merely the slow heavings of history as we writhe and turn about in our seeking.

It is the assumption of respect for the condition of man that holds out the best hope of bettering things. For on that basis an ethic can be built that has some relevance to the realities of our existence. We start with rage and hurt, we know these have to be channeled and adjusted to, and we seek for the best way to do this. Implicitly, every legal system is just that; the amount of superannuated complicating rubbish tends to be excessive, however, and it would advance things just to look at what is and to build on that.

It comes down to having respect for mankind's imperfect state and faith that it is worth striving for perfectibility, or at least for optimizing what we are and what we have.

January 31, 1987

The history of mankind is the history of aggression. A number of figures are bruited about (there origins are unknown) to the effect of there being 90-plus years in all recorded history when there was no war to document somewhere and there being about 40 armed conflicts going on at the same time in a current review of the interactions among the countries of the world (or within given states). That is probably more true than otherwise; we are an aggressive and dangerous species. Nor has civilization as we currently construe it altered that to any great extent; we have already noted that the most advances technological states are locked in a balance of terror, and the Moslem fundamentalists who are probably the most religious part of our civilization are also the most warlike. All in all we must reckon with the fact that we have been and are a very violent species.

Let us therefore consider the nature of aggression. It is used variously to indicate a normal press to action that may be entirely constructive and a tendency to deconstructive attack. This fluctuating meaning makes it difficult to discuss without specifying what one intends. We will confine the meaning we apply to it here to the realm of attack. Within this framework there appear to be two kinds of aggression: the explosive kind, which follows a threat or a sudden frustration; and the predatory kind, which requires planning and considered forethought. The explosive kind is usually reactive and without anticipation; the predatory kind involves stalking behavior and long-range intentionality. It is a bit like the difference between first- and second-degree murder: the one with malice aforethought; and the other unplanned and unexpected (if not altogether unintended).

In any case, what we here concern ourselves with is the predatory kind of aggression, the wished-for, planned-for injury to another. We have much of that, in thought certainly, and in act all too frequently. And we are always surprised at the fact that it happens. But there is no reason to be surprised; we are an understandably angry and reactive species. We have the biologic mechanism for it and then come the realization of our bereftness and abandonment, and we have the psychological trigger as well.

Many years ago, Sigmund Freud tried to explain some psychological phenomena by asserting that the infant, the very young infant, dealt with the experience of unfulfilled need for nurturance by hallucinating the breast. The baby would imagine the source of gratification with enormous intensity; at best so young an entity would not have developed good ways of discriminating between inside and outside stimuli, and when the yearned-for source of relief of hunger and oral pleasure was not forthcoming, the baby coped initially by picturing the breast, perhaps making sucking movements with his mouth, feeling in fantasy the good, warm milk coursing down his throat, and holding the full thrust of hunger at bay in this manner for a little while at least.

To be sure, this model has been rejected by subsequent investigators, who have determined that the capacity to form and manipulate inner images does not become established until much later; nonetheless, there is a sense in which something like that may well happen. In any case, once the ability to form images has developed, this kind of thing probably does happen, at least with some babies.

The suggestion I would advance here is that this is the mechanism that underlies most religious thinking. To be alone in so great a universe without companion, guide, or caretaker is to be deprived indeed, to the point of unendurability. And so the species has hallucinated a breast, a caring deity of some kind, an accompanying presence that knows all and gives all. Often enough this role has been delegated to some concrete person who was a god-appointed ruler, or prophet, or messenger. Cults of emperor worship have been documented for at least 5,000 years, from the time of the ancient Egyptians up to the current Shinto faith of modern Japan. Indeed, one of the great commonalities of the species has been the predictable presence of some religion within its social organization, so much so that when exploring the remains of possible precursors of man we say that this is a modern species because there are evidences of ceremonial practices, religious observations of some sort. Our species cannot stand to be alone, at any age. So we hallucinate what we yearn for and then lend our formidable intellectual capacities to justify our particular hallucinations. Some magnificent structures have been thus erected in the form of holy books and commentaries on holy books, some of the most extraordinary of all human creations. One need not diminish the richness and value of such great works by recognizing the basic need that brought the original idea into being, and the infinite irrationality of that idea. To satisfy a need and ease a yearning a hallucination is understandable, but scarcely reasonable. It is certainly not realistic, and the religions that have been created to bring peace and order have failed signally at that mission. Their messages are not in question; it is merely that by failing to recognize the basic core of human deprivation and by offering only fantasy solutions presently they are overridden by the very aggressions they so often seek to curtail, and human violence breaks out once again. The hallucination will hold the baby's hunger in check only so long, and then it erupts once more.

Some other basis must be found, some nonhallucinatory schema, some pattern that reflects the reality of the human condition more correctly, more realistically—something that gives at least the hope of finding an ethic that can work. Here the ethic of rage holds promise.

In brief, man's sense of abandonment and his endless fury in the fact of this perception are key. They mandate that man has nowhere else to turn but to himself, and they press him to make that effort in a manner and to a degree that heretofore he has been able to evade. So long as God and God's emissaries were there, man could get out from under; it was someone else's problem. Now there is no recourse; man's rage is man's problem and one at which he will either succeed or fail, entirely on his own, no miracles, no divine intervention, no battle between good and evil—in fact, no one cares. If he sinks, he sinks, and it makes no difference. Perhaps there will be further biological trials within the framework of evolutionary process; perhaps a new and better arrangement of proteins and lipids will be devised with better staying powers. Maybe a species will emerge that will at once be more intelligent and have better impulse control. Once it realizes what has happened, perhaps it will set as its goal to find the maker and demand an explanation.

That would be an end worth striving for: to find God and hold him accountable. Not that it is likely to do much good—the answer is likely to be, "Oops, sorry"—and then what does one have? But it would still be better than make-believe, than not knowing. And who knows what might come out of it after all?

Meanwhile, we do not at the moment appear to be the species that will accomplish that end. We have the problem of predatory aggression arising from we know not where (or, more precisely, we will not let ourselves know) and of the resultant threat to our existence. We also have the need for religion, for faith, for a belief system. Let us then tie the two together; let us set as our faith the resolve to worship certain aspects of man, to worship that which strived, to stand in awe of those things with us that create and contrive and discern. Let us be what we are—emperor worshippers—but choose for once an emperor who is part of every man, not a single figure, a particular embodiment, but as aspect of humanity itself. Let us begin with human rage, for that is the root force that drives us. Let us fear it, for like any great force it can escape its bounds and ravage and destroy—that we can never forget. But with all the awe and respect which we tender the mighty, let us give ourselves to the worship and the mastery of rage.

Human rage is like atomic fire, like toxic chemicals, like superheated steam. Each of these has infinitely useful potentials; each can and has been a great destroyer of our kind. Unlike us, they are insensate forces without self-knowledge; they merit a measure of respect but not true religious valuation. Only man, so far as we know, can be aware of meaning, and only man can contain within himself at once the elements of great destruction and the mechanism for their redirection and control. Hence, it is in the management of predatory aggression that the true greatness of the species lies, and to that we must give true and ceremonious respect.

February 1, 1987

There are four axes along which we worship human rage. They have to do with the meaning and functions of that rage in our lived. They are these:

1. We worship rage that drives us to build, to earn, to create a civilization.
2. We worship rage that drives us to seek one another in love and companionship.
3. We worship rage that drives us toward the beautiful, rage that drives us to imagine and to depict the unutterable and the hidden that can find form only as sound and image and movement.
4. We worship rage that drives us to defend, to protect, to maintain those whom we care for and what we have built.

Many of those who have written about aggression have recognized that the positive side of aggression is the force behind all our greatest efforts to make the world go forward. We battle with nature to wrest for it the secrets it holds; we struggle with the forces of storm and flood, weather and gravity, and an opulent but altogether grudging Earth to retrieve the materials and to fashion the artifacts we need to give ourselves shelter and convenience. We drive to pursue and press forward in the face of infinite difficulties to prepare a foundation, rear a wall, build a highway, advance our technology to where we can have hope and see a better life for ourselves and for those who matter to us. It is always a battle, a joyous one for some and a bitter one for others, but always a battle.

Whatever we build, it is through our capacity to attack. Perhaps first of all we must build the inner discipline to attack with skill and with wisdom, but that is only a question of method. We do best when our rage knows its channels, but we must have the rage to pour into them.

Long ago, Freud and his followers knew about the ubiquity of ambivalence. They knew that rare indeed was a state of love worthy of the name "pure," that the usual and indeed the normal human condition was one of mixed emotions, a pastiche of love and hate and jealousy and territoriality and revenge and awe and tenderness and recrimination and regret and many other emotions, all bound together in a knotted skein of connectedness with its ensuing ups and downs, its distancing and arguments, its reconciliations and tendernesses, its unexpected components and its overt declarations. Sometimes one affect or another would predominate, but for the most part in such instances there was a considerable defensive element present, with elaborate patterns of undoing or reaction–formation driving the behavior. Again, it is always a matter of dealing adequately with rage. Rage is the centerpiece, the significant component of human interaction. Properly contained and diverted, it becomes protective tenderness and support. Allowed too free an expression, it can turn into sadism and abandonment as we live out with others what we know so well ourselves. But in all human love relationships, so-called rage is at the center. Only by knowing it and giving it the respect and the worship it merits can we relate well and truly to one another.

Then there is beauty. Here, if anywhere, the validity of rage as core experience becomes manifest. Always within every work of art, the mastery of rage is at the center.

Finally, there is little need to emphasize the profound vitality of rage to energize defensiveness. We protect because we fear, and the fear can drive us to the ultimate excesses of anger and violence. For this we must fear our fear and work with utmost diligence and with the greatest awe and reverence at the mission of mastery. Here is where we are in greatest danger, the peril of losing control of rage. That makes a mockery of religion; that is the ultimate violation. We have here the essence of evil: to allow the magnificence of inner destructiveness an insufficient form within which to be contained and expressed, to allow that which is great to become that which destroys greatness, to allow ourselves the self-indulgence of failing to control the most godlike of our inner qualities. We venerate rage because it is the builder and the creator, but to fail to know its capacity for sweeping away all we compose—which indeed it allows and enables us to compose—ah, there lies the truth of sin.

Afterword: The life and work of Joseph Noshpitz

Robert S. Wallerstein

When I accepted the invitation, as a very long-time friend, to write the Afterword for this posthumous volume of unpublished papers by Joseph Noshpitz, I found myself in a very singular position. All the other contributors in the volume had been involved as colleagues, friends, and students of Joe over the years of his productive professional lifetime in Washington, D.C. (with interludes in Israel), where he was such an iconic figure in child and adolescent psychiatry and psychoanalytic child therapy and served as editor-in-chief of the magisterial seven-volume *Handbook of Child and Adolescent Psychiatry*. I knew Joe best before any of this, at the very beginning of his psychiatric career, when we were residents together in the Menninger School of Psychiatry in Topeka, Kansas.

I came to Topeka in 1949, and there I found Joe, who had arrived a year earlier. Joe was a bachelor member of a group of close friends that Judy, my wife, and I quickly became part of. We were indeed mutually attracted. Joe was an impressive intellectual with a wide range of knowledge and interests. He loved ideas and to talk about them, and he also loved food, as has been mentioned in at least one of the commentaries in this volume. As an example of the latter, we once invited Joe for a Thanksgiving Day midday dinner at our home, a goose dinner. Joe accepted happily but asked if we would put the time off by an hour, since he had an earlier turkey luncheon at another home and a roast beef dinner afterward at a third, and ours could then be nicely sandwiched in between. Joe partook of all three Thanksgiving feasts, and, at least at our home, also eagerly accepted seconds.

Joe's romances were also multiple. And they also shared in one particular feature—they invariably died out after about 9 months. At one point Judy invited Joe for a luncheon at our home to meet a new prospect. Judy said that she was a charming, quite beautiful, and very intelligent newcomer to Topeka who also was French and had earned the *Croix de Guerre* for her wartime exploits in the underground resistance, including an encounter in which she had participated in killing German soldiers. And, almost best of all, her training period in art therapy would be only for 9 months. This was Charlotte. Joe met her happily, and when Charlotte's leaving time came up in 9 months, Joe couldn't stand it and had become involved in what turned into his lifelong happy marriage. For Judy, it was the only successful *shit-tach* (matchmaking) of her life.

We never knew about the early death (at 47) of Joe's father when Joe was 10 1/2—a father who in Russia, before he came to America, had been a rabbi and who impressed in Joe his intense Jewishness, nationally and culturally (and gustatory), and his fierce yearning for scholarship. But we did know Joe's mother, who periodically visited from Chicago, with her suitcase bursting with chopped liver, gefilte fish, lox, bagels, and other proper goodies Joe then shared with his cluster of friends over the following week. A highlighted trip for his mother was the occasion when Joe had just been appointed director of the children's ward at the Menninger-affiliated Topeka State Hospital. When his mother arrived at the airport, she saw a copy of the *Topeka Daily Capital* on the newsstand, prominently displaying Joe's picture and the story on the front page. It proudly confirmed his mother's convictions about Joe's proper place in the world of psychiatry.

Joe shared a rental apartment with a fellow resident, Ed Knight, later a psychoanalyst in his native New Orleans, a many-generations blue-blooded southerner, on the face of it, an unlikely pairing. But both were truly intellectuals, deeply interested in psychiatry and committed to fusing their psychological interests with a strong identification with issues of social justice and doing good in the world. Years later, when Ed was a practicing psychoanalyst back in New Orleans and also an elected member of the school board in the throes of dealing with the ever-turbulent desegregation of the school system, Ed, unlike so many of the educated class, insisted on being true to his principles and kept his own multiple children in the public school system.

And Joe started his psychoanalytic involvement in Topeka, going into analysis with a young Texan, Al Owers, trained at the Topeka Institute. Again, a seemingly unlikely twosome: Joe, who had once thought of the rabbinate as a career, and Al, from the conventional WASPish southland. But Joe liked it and loved to repeat a favored remark from his analysis. Once he had interrupted an unduly prolonged silence by bemoaning the fact that here he was, killing the hours (Owers). He was acutely aware of the deadliness within the humor of the remark. And when Joe left Topeka to work on Fritz Redl's inpatient unit for unruly adolescents at the National Institute of Mental Health in the Washington area and sought to go on in his psychoanalytic training, he was strongly urged by Len Duhl, another ex-Topeka psychiatric resident, to take advantage of the perk of government employment—that the Federal Employees Health Benefits Program would cover his entire psychoanalytic treatment costs. Joe was shocked. Personal analysis was so important; one should work hard for it and at it, and it should always represent a substantial personal sacrifice. How could it be worthwhile if it had no cost? The two friends, Joe and Len, found it hard to understand each other.

This was Joe Noshpitz, our close Topeka friend in the early 1950s, a deeply intellectual colleague with a boundless curiosity about the world that he was exploring, and a profoundly ethical man, committed to trying to make the world a better place by his work in it. We very much regretted our loss when he left our Topeka world and we stayed. We maintained only desultory contact after that, by mail, occasionally by phone, and rarely being able to meet on some occasions that would bring us together. And over all those years, we also had occasion to meet Joe's and Charlotte's son, Claude, during a San Francisco visit. But mostly I was aware of Joe's career from a distance and once, in a working context, when Joe, as the then editor of the massive *Handbook of Child and Adolescent Psychiatry*, involved my wife in contributing a chapter on the impact of parental divorce on children across their developmental trajectory.

So now, as someone who felt like I knew Joe so well and so appreciatively during our psychiatric training years in the 1940s and '50s, I have the opportunity, occasioned by this posthumous publication of much of Joe's lifetime unpublished writings, to help, along with so many distinguished colleagues, to reassess what Joe Noshpitz stood for and what he accomplished over what clearly became an iconic lifetime in child and adolescent psychiatry in the Washington, D.C., area where he resided, and nationally in his long involvement in the American Academy of Child and Adolescent Psychiatry, with his special role as editor of the *Handbook* and even extending internationally to his participation in the fashioning of child psychiatric training and treatment in the early days of the State of Israel.

It is amazing that Joe, for whatever reasons, sought not to offer for publication so much of what he wrote during his lifetime. In his part of the Introduction, Carl Feinstein tried to offer an explanation for this. I have known from the beginning that Joe had an acquisitive and very articulate understanding of the intellectual world he was dealing with but conveyed less of this in publishing than he could have. Not that he could not write: Joe, in the old-fashioned sense, was always a real wordsmith. His writing style has always been fluid and graceful—and quite distinctive. The readers of this volume I am confident could recognize it as his, even if offered in anonymous form. And in his editorship of his *Handbook*, Joe, in his turn, complimented my wife by indicating that her contribution was almost the only one that he had not felt it necessary to largely personally rewrite.

Nor did he lack for ideas. This volume has been properly named a journey (a theory) of child development. Joe's essays extended the findings and writings of Daniel Stern and with periodic references to the contributions of Spitz, Mahler, Jacobson, Kohut, Kernberg, and occasionally various others. Joe's essays create a coherent, seamless developmental account, centrally built around the emergence of infantile experience, happenstance, and trauma, of positive and negative ego ideals, each linked to approving or condemnatory superego structures and in their fluctuating interplay account for all the many vicissitudes of individuals' growing up process and their mark on the world.

The subject matter of the chapters is varied but constantly circles around the unifying theme of the interplay of positive and negative ego ideals as they pertain to different phenomena. As with any singular vision of development, the fit between theory and the phenomena at hand varies, being quite compelling in some contexts and more speculative in others. All the subjects dealt with in this collection are strongly developmental and quite engaging, with the particular Noshpitz spin of language and ideas.

The first chapter focuses on what Joe calls the ethics (or the ethical problems) posed by the developmental process—more specifically, the tension between the privacy rights of the family unit and society's growing right and responsibility to intervene when there is evidence that parental guidance is lacking, misguided, or detrimental to the child. He finds the first arena for public intervention to be the public schools, enlarged in his purview to provide emotional and physical safety to endangered children by cultivating the formation and maintenance of appropriately positive and negative ego ideals. He moves on to the relationship between the formation of these ideals and society's obligation to promote healthy development by fostering, and participating in, music, the visual arts, prose and poetry, mime and dance. And he goes on to describe aspects of pop culture, such as the Teenage Mutant Ninja Turtles, with their appeal to growing boys, and Nancy Drew and *Baby-sitter's Club* novels, with their appeal to girls of different eras with their different concerns in relation to the formation of ideals. Several papers address Joe's concerns with the development of healthy narcissism across the childhood years, whereas others reflect his fascination with the tomboy phenomenon in growing girls and the challenge of the tomboy's subsequent transition to more typical adolescent issues and preoccupations. It is noteworthy, he believes, that there is no socially acceptable counterpart to tomboyism in growing boys. In all these papers, Joe is acutely aware of concomitant traumata that actuate or intensify the developmental processes in question.

The two penultimate chapters concern the Beyond School and Joe's optimistic, perhaps even utopian, vision of the future establishment of child-rearing centers that will provide prenatal observation and counseling and then will assume a monitoring function in the growing child's life, literally from cradle to college. The final chapter on religion is Joe's provocative meditation on the creation of religion as humankind's way of coping with the universal infantile rage engendered by the inevitable deficiencies and frustrations that arise from the infant's helpless dependency.

These many topics are woven together into a consistent narrative of development. Needless to say, Joe's perspective represents one narrative account among many. But it is, I believe, an important account, always propounded engagingly and elegantly, and enlivened from time to time by clinical vignettes that strikingly illuminate Joe's gifts as a clinician, such as the story of the 9-year-old boy struggling to master his upset and confusion in the wake of his parents' divorce. Throughout the volume, we are edified by Joe's intriguing linguistic creations, such as his distinction between what he calls categorical affects and vitality affects, his construal of salience and intensity experiences in terms of crescendo and diminuendo, and his characterization of emotional experience in terms of shifting and swelling and ebbing and weaving. There is little doubt that clinicians and theorists, neophyte and experienced alike, will extract valuable insights from this body of work, which comes to us belatedly, a decade and a half after Joe's death. Of course, it is for individual readers to decide in what manner to employ these insights, how to frame them, draw on them, and integrate them with other developmental perspectives and emphases.

Having read this collection, I ask myself what it adds to the Joe Noshpitz I met and admired at the outset of our careers, the Joe Noshpitz who was my one-time colleague and lifelong close friend. In these pages, Joe emerges in all clarity as that rarity in life—an extremely ethical man, a good man in every sense of the word, a man who believed wholeheartedly in the goodness to which humankind should aspire and of which it should be capable. Then and now, I appreciate Joe as a life-affirming idealist who found it difficult to acknowledge the deforming existence of evil, despite the many references throughout this collection to the detrimental pressures of negative ego ideals. It was his idealism, no doubt, that fueled his proposal for child-rearing centers and his belief that the political powers-that-be could be made to understand the necessity of such centers and—at some point in the future—make them a matter of public tax-based support.

And, of course, being a good man, Joe's goodness embraced the world, which meant he was powerfully committed to issues of social justice, of doing his best for all people, especially our children, no matter what the cost. Joe would have understood this commitment as his own participation in the Jewish tradition of *Tikkun Olam*, of the individual's obligation to do what little he can to repair the world. And with it all, Joe remained a warm and sentimental man, a regular guy, a *Mensch*. Readers will readily discern these qualities as the underpinning of Joe's vision of the journey that all children and adolescents undertake and that our society, he believed, should be willing to safeguard for each succeeding generation.

Index

Vitality affects, 56, 60–61
    as acceleration components of
        emotional life, 100
    experience of, 68–69
    and music, 62
    in sound, 64
Vulnerability of technical systems, 10

W

Waltz and intersubjective awareness,
    95
White Anglo-Saxon Protestant (WASP)
    in *Nancy Drew*, 155–156
Worship forms, 247–248